DIG OR DIE,
BROTHER HYDE

DIG OR DIE, BROTHER HYDE

By *William J. Hyde*

As told to Harriet Harmon Dexter

ILLUSTRATED BY SUSANNE SUBA

HARPER & BROTHERS, PUBLISHERS, NEW YORK

Library of Congress catalog card number: 54-6902

Contents

DIG OR DIE,
BROTHER HYDE

1

"Terms Accepted"

THAT early June morning I looked proudly at the Smith
Company wagon with which I was about to start out for
another season. It had been packed with an eye for effect—
common hardware far in, iron pots and kettles toward the center
where they could be reached by turning up a flap of the side
curtains; in the back the dishes, silverware, glassware; and just
under them the pins, needles and a variety of trinkets.

It was good stock and the wagon was newly painted. This
summer of 1885 was the third season that I had worked the Bay
of Quinte area in Ontario and since it was the end of my junior
year in college it would be my last summer with the Smith
Company. By next summer I would be graduated and getting
into my lifework.

My chief joy this season was my horse. Mr. Curlew who assigned the outfits to their routes each year had told me once that
my horse always came in in good condition at the end of a
season and "mebbe thet should count fer sumthen." So this
summer he had given me Lad, the manager's horse of the previous summer. He was a sleek bay, neatly proportioned, alive
but not impatient. This was a most desirable quality in a huckster's horse. A horse that drooped while it waited for housewives
to examine all of Smith's Superb Specialties made the wares
look like last summer's leftovers, while a horse that twitched
with impatience made prospective buyers of pins and pepperpots
feel hurried and uncertain. It is odd how much a horse had to
do with making a successful salesman.

"Which road are you going to start on, Willie?" I knew what
was in my brother Albert's mind. He was fourteen, eight years

9

younger than I, and sometimes would ride the ten miles in to Belleville when I went that way.

"Might take the Back Road, but might start out on the Front Road toward Shenandoah. I don't collect so many trade-ins on that road and there isn't much space in the wagon for them when it is fresh loaded."

"Is that the only reason?" This was a nip from Lizzie, my pretty snappy-eyed younger sister of eighteen who understood that sometimes the best reasons are the concealed ones.

"It's six o'clock," Father said coming up from the barn. "Let's sit down to breakfast and you boys can finish the chores after Willie gets started."

We followed him into the house. Father walked erect; if he had been two inches taller he would have been perfectly proportioned. Father never pushed people unnecessarily, but he always gave the impression of knowing what he was doing. Now he knew it was breakfast time.

Mother had a pile of buckwheat cakes waiting on the back of the stove. "I brought up some of our best maple syrup for you, Willie." Mother moved about the house quickly. She was just a shade above medium height with a trim figure, and she always dressed neatly. I guess I was the son of both parents; not very tall like my father and not very heavy like my mother.

We sat down to the table, not as big as a few years ago when nine children had crowded around it. Now my oldest brother, Dan, had a farm near by; Sarah, who had been like a second mother to us younger children, was married; and so were Jane and Mary Ann. James was the adventurer of the family and was often gone two or three years at a time; he had been in different parts of Canada and to the States. Elizabeth, whom we called Lizzie, and Harry and Albert were all that were left at home now.

We always had good family talk during mealtimes. "Save your troubles till they won't hurt your digestion," Father used to say. During this last breakfast the family ribbed me a little with good advice.

"Don't give away everything you have to the Robertses," Harry cautioned, reminding me of my first year out with the Smith Company when I would feel so sorry for people who wanted things they could not afford that I gave away quite a share of my stock and had to pay for it myself.

"Don't forget to give the recipes to Mrs. Fletcher," Mother reminded me. I always delivered a variety of things and messages to people along my route. I was the borrower or returner of everything from butchering kettles to baby cribs.

Breakfast was about over and Father wiped his moustache, so we knew it was time to be quiet.

"The Bible, Harry." Father always led the family devotions before we left the breakfast table. This morning he read from the first Psalm:

> Blessed is the man
> That walketh not in the counsel of the ungodly,
> Nor standeth in the way of sinners. . . .
> But his delight is in the law of the Lord. . . .
> For the Lord knoweth the way of the righteous:
> But the way of the ungodly shall perish.

As I listened to the familiar words I recalled that he had read this same passage the morning that I started back to college last fall. "The Lord knoweth. . . ." That was Father's special message for me, I was sure. He prayed briefly. His prayers always said something; he prayed for our specific needs and he thanked God for our blessings, and he always named the blessings. In England Father had preached at times for the Salvation Army and he believed that God worked right along with people, and for people, but a person had to be on personal terms with Him to get His richest blessings.

Father pushed back his chair, rose from the table and the rest of us did the same.

"Well, Willie, you better get under way."

The family trooped out to watch me start. Albert, in true young brother importance, looked over the horse to be sure I

had him harnessed properly. Harry suggested he might take over
the route next year; Lizzie gave me messages for the girls at several farms—I think I detected that she sent messages to the girls
who had good-looking brothers. Mother came running out of the
house with a box of lunch.

"You don't know where you will be when noon comes. I de-
clare, Willie, you hardly give a thought to your own needs.
You're like your Grandpa Hyde that way."

"Thanks, Ma." I took the box of lunch, kissed Mother,
climbed up onto the seat of my huckster's wagon and picked up
the lines. Father gave Lad an admiring pat as he said to me,
"Where do you think you'll be for Wednesday night service?
We'll miss you here, but you can be home for Sunday?" That
was like Father—all schedules tied into the church.

I started down the road toward Shenandoah. It was true that
this road had more prosperous farms along the way than any of
the others. It was true that fewer women would have handmade
rugs to trade in and fewer men would have furs to sell, but it was
also true that Minnie lived down this way. Minnie Grills' father
had the best farm in all these parts. He was especially proud of
his horses; he bred them well and he cared for them well. I
knew he would be glad to see me traveling with Lad this season.
And Minnie liked horses, too. In addition, Mrs. Grills was a very
good customer; it might be a good idea to give her the first
choice of Smith's selection while the stock was complete. I
could get to their place about noon.

"Gid-dap, Lad."

But on second thought, maybe it would be better to take the
turn onto the side road and visit the Fletchers and Skroggs first,
then I could reach the Grills place in the late afternoon. The
almanac indicated a new moon that night. There is something
about a new moon in June—

I had forgotten how easily a person takes a horse into his
confidence until I found myself once again on the road with Lad
for a summer companion. When we passed the little Wesleyan
church on the road toward Trenton I must have pulled up on

the lines a little because Lad slowed down and with a flick of the
ear seemed to demand an explanation.

"Yep, that's an important place to me, Lad, but we better
keep moving."

We jogged on, but my mind stayed behind. It was in that
little church that I had first heard my father "exhort." Our
family always worshiped together in this roadside church. In the
Canadian Wesleyan Methodist churches it was the custom for
the minister to preach the regular sermon and then turn the
service over to someone who had the special gift of pressing
home the message and calling sinners to repentance. It was a
rare gift to be a good exhorter. Brother Vickers, our preacher,
was very emotional, letting his voice rise to a high pitch and
boom out with terrific strength; but we always said, "That's just
Brother Vickers' way." After listening to his tirade against sin
and the devil it was a great relief when he wiped the perspira-
tion from his brow and announced, "Brother Hyde will please
take over for the exhorting."

Then my father would walk to the front of the church rather
quietly and deliberately and begin to talk in a natural voice. I
liked to listen to him.

"Brothers, Sisters, I think we all know we're sinners and we
stray far from the path God would have us follow. Sometimes we
get so far away from Him that we find it hard to come back—
we feel lost. But even in our darkest hours we have all felt the
grace of God work both on us and within us." Then he would
recite his own experiences with God's love and earnestly be-
seech any of the friends sitting there that night to come and beg
forgiveness and claim their share of the Father's love. A hymn
of invitation would follow the exhorting and by one's, or two's
or three's, "sinners, friends and neighbors" came to the front of
the room to kneel with the preacher, confess their sins, and start
a new life in the sight of God and the community.

I grew up with a great desire to exhort like my father. Sometimes I felt as if I just had to speak out and many times as a
youngster I would sit on the rail fence and exhort the trees,

the cows and the horses. By the time I entered high school I knew whole pages of the Bible by heart as well as most of the hymns in the old Methodist hymnal and many a time the plowing in the back field was slowed down because I had to take time out to practice a Psalm with varying effects and all the gestures!

Before I was out of high school I had achieved one of my ambitions and was a regular exhorter in our small rural churches. By the time I was well into college I knew that I wanted to go into the ministry. Now I was at the end of my junior year at Albert College, in Belleville.

"One more year, Lad, and I hope to be preaching." The horse nodded his head, whether in agreement or from the sheer joy of being on the open road I didn't know.

After a winter of study on the campus it was good to be out in the country again. June is a fresh season; the air is clear, the colors are intense, details stand out in high relief. Patches of green moss by the roadside were beds of emeralds sprinkled with dust of garnets and pearls. Chipmunks scurried across the road, chattering gleefully with Lad and me. A deer stood statue-still in the middle of our road then bounded noiselessly over a fallen tree and we watched its white flag wave in the air till it was lost in the brush.

My first stop was at the Fletcher homestead.

"How's everything going?" I inquired.

"We've had our ups and downs, but I guess mostly ups," reported little Mrs. Fletcher. "Sammy here broke his arm. He's an awkward child, aren't you, Sammy?" But she tousled his shock of brown hair lovingly.

"Maple syrup did all right," added Mr. Fletcher, "D'you think you could sell fifty gallons for us?" I promised to make inquiries when I got back into town. The Fletchers bought very little from my wagon but I had not expected to sell them much; they were still getting started and cash was scarce.

"I almost forgot Ma's recipes!" So I delivered them and was on my way to the Skrogg place. As I pulled into their yard I

knew from the clothesline that I would be greeted at the door
with the cry of the fifth little Skrogg—all in a tiny two-room-
with-a-lean-to house.

I made three more short stops before I arrived at the Grills
farm about five o'clock. This was the best farm for miles around.
To the original one hundred sixty acre homestead Mr. Grills
had added another quarter section. He farmed well and gave his
stock good care. Their house was kept painted and the yard was
always clean. It would have been the show place of our region
if there had been tourists in Ontario in 1885.

As I pulled into the yard Mrs. Grills came out to greet
me.

"Welcome, Willie. Climb down and come in. The men are
at the barn but the girls—" Before she could finish the sentence,
Margaret, Minnie's older sister, and Mattie, who was still in high
school, were out by the wagon.

"It's about time you came, Willie."

"Our hair crimpers are broken and we never ran so low on
pins—"

"To say nothing of three kettles that have been soldered till
they look like they had chicken pox."

On they rattled. But where was Minnie? I tried to keep my
eyes off the door of the house.

"Maybe Willie will spend the night with us," said Mrs. Grills.
"It's too late in the day now to go on. That'll give you girls time
to look at everything. He'll love that!"

"Thanks. I'd sure love stopping here."

"What a beautiful horse, Willie." The voice I had been waiting for spoke from behind me. I turned around and there stood
Minnie. She was almost as tall as I and she had dark hair and
brown eyes that did a lot of talking even when her voice said
nothing. She had even features and a clear complexion, and she
was very good to look at. I had not seen her since Easter vacation and of all the million things I might have said to her all I
could think of was, "So you're more interested in my horse than
in my wares?"

"Or in the driver?" And with that parting shot Margaret ran into the house and the others vanished, too.

"Willie, come on down to the barn and see Lady's colt. Father thinks it's the best one we ever had on the place. Weren't you lucky to get Lad for the summer? How did it happen?"

I had not remembered that Minnie talked so easily. I always thought I carried the conversation! She seemed changed in other ways, too. Can three months make such a difference in a person or was I seeing her in a new light? The first few minutes were confusing.

At the barn Mr. Grills and Will, the only son in the family, were doing the evening chores. I offered to help but they said they would be through before I could find old overalls and get ready. Minnie went up to the house to help with supper and before long we men washed up on the back porch. By the time we sat down to the table I was feeling entirely at home again. Mr. Grills told about the new cheese factory that was collecting milk from the farms in the area now; Mattie had stories of the spring's activities and Margaret had hilarious stories to tell on Minnie. Minnie's name was really Mary, but she was never called Mary. This was her first year out of high school so she was taking over more of the household work and was learning to sew.

"You should have seen the pants she made Will!"

"Yep, she had both legs going in the same direction," he complained.

"But I noticed I got them good enough so that you wore them when you took Sally skating," Minnie retorted.

Underneath all the fun they poked at each other ran a deep affection. One sensed it not so much by anything that was said as by the way everything was done.

That evening Minnie and I sat on the porch steps. The almanac produced the new moon as promised and as it sank the stars began to pierce the northern sky. I wished it had been winter and we were on a sleigh ride. Holding hands was an accepted part of sleigh rides, but young folks didn't do it just sitting on the porch—not in 1885. Well, not too often.

So the summer began and so it rapidly passed. Financially it was a good season. The Smith Company paid me twenty-five dollars a month and furnished the horse and wagon. Board and room didn't cost much because I was usually a guest in the home where I stopped at noon or at the end of a day. Families in the more remote areas were glad to have the company to break the monotony of life and since I slept anywhere from the hayloft to a pad on the floor I was not much extra work. "Anyway, it's worth a little trouble," Mrs. Cook said one day, "because the only prayer our children ever hear is when you say grace at the table."

I learned a lot about business that summer, too, and the most important thing I learned was the value of a good reputation. From childhood I had heard all the familiar quotations about honesty's being the best policy and "doing unto others" but having been reared in a good Christian home I had had little experience with people who did not practice this philosophy. My first summer with the Smith Specialties wagon I was surprised when people examined the merchandise to be sure I was delivering what they had ordered. On my first visit to the Skrogg farm Mrs. Skrogg reported, "One year I bought from the Waller Company man and when I unpacked the six tumblers he had stuck full of straw to fool me I found the bottom three all broke to smithereens. And he'd pulled out and gone before I got to the bottom of the box. He never came back."

So this third summer with the Smith Company when the Wilburs—they were the farthest from town of any family on my circuit—gave me their winter furs to market, knowing I would not be back their way for a month at best with their money, I realized that people trusted me. And I was glad.

It was a summer of happy associations, too. Not infrequently the young folks had a party, or went berrying, or took a day for a barn raising. As the summer wore on I found myself figuring that the Front Road was always better than a side road and landed at the Grillses more frequently than my merchandising really warranted. On occasion Minnie's mother let us sit up alone as late as twelve o'clock! We learned to know each other's ideas and ambitions; we both liked music, poetry, the woods, children, and even hard work; and by the time fall came we knew that we wanted to build our lives together.

It was in the latter part of this summer that a group of us organized the Hallelujah Band that worked together all through my senior year at college. During the school year I lived in Belleville, about ten miles from our home farm and somewhat farther from Minnie's home. She was one of the ten or twelve young people who helped form the Band but she lived so far out in the country that much of the time she couldn't go with us. We went into any of the churches that invited us if they were within driving distance of Belleville.

Mr. Asa Vermilyea, a man in the boot business in Belleville, was the organizer of our Band. I had met him when I was still in high school and doing some of my first exhorting. He offered to help finance my college education if I wanted to go into Christian service, so for four years he assisted me while I was in Albert College. The tenor soloist in our Band was Willie Finkle. Enos Farnsworth did the preaching and I was the exhorter. During that winter of my senior year we covered the whole area bordering on the Bay of Quinte. When Minnie could be with us her fine voice was a great help when no instrument was available.

One Sunday our Hallelujah Band went to a remote schoolhouse to hold a service. On the way out I was trying to explain to Minnie why I liked mathematics; geometry, for example. I told her there was great satisfaction in standing before a class and proving to them by a reasonable and logical procedure the eternal truth of a mathematical theorem. I must have become a little over eloquent as I was lost in the "beauty of eternal truth" because Minnie giggled and remarked, "When you become a preacher I hope you don't slap all your prospective converts in the face with the horses' reins."

That evening after Enos Farnsworth had preached about fifteen minutes he asked me to lead the exhortation. I knew that

the audience in this little schoolhouse was made up of families—
families who had to work together and live together, often
isolated from other people for long periods. I recalled our family
home and what my mother and father had meant to me. That
memory was so beautiful that I felt an urge to tell these people
about our church on the road to Trenton and about the night
when I was "converted." I was sitting there with the other
members of my family and our neighbors when they all started
singing and a wonderful feeling came over me.

> Just as I am,
> Without one plea
> But that Thy blood
> Was shed for me.

I walked down the aisle to the altar. My father came and
knelt on one side and my oldest sister, Sarah, on the other side
as was frequently the custom for members of a family to do. My
father put his arm around my shoulder. I felt a wave of happiness
sweep over me. My only testimony was, "Jesus said, 'Come unto
me,' and here I am. I accept His promises." That was all there
was to it, no shouting or excitement, but in my heart a great
sense of peace that came with surrender.

I told these people this simple story of my conversion and
added, "God can do more with your life than you can, and you
can do more with God's help than you can without it. Maybe
tonight some father can kneel with his son as my father knelt
with me. Or maybe a child can lead a parent even as Jesus said,
'A little child shall lead them.' "

There was a creak of the door at the back of the room, the
sound of shuffling feet, and even before the congregation started
to sing,

> Why not now? Why not now?
> Why not come to Jesus now?

old Archie Lynn came stumbling down to the altar. No one
knew why Archie happened to be at the church door; supposedly

he was waiting in the wagon at the hitching rail, as was his custom, while his wife and two girls were in church. How long had he been listening to the service? Had he ever before crept up to listen? I never knew the answers to these questions.

All I knew was that Archie was a mean man; he had never said a kind word for years; his face was set in hard lines and his voice was a snarl. But this night he stumbled down the aisle and with twisted and calloused hands he grasped the back of a bench.

"It's the child that done it. She brung me to Jesus. It's Rose. She died and I hated God." His shoulders shook with a sob. "I hated everybody—my other children because Rose was gone; my wife, because Rose had died; my neighbors, because they didn't save her. But as she was dyin' she said, 'Pa, won't you come to Jesus with me?' I ain't never said His name since then except to curse Him. But now Rose done it. She brung me to Jesus, too."

The bench seemed frail as it shook under the impact of his sobs. Mrs. Lynn came up and knelt on one side of old Archie and his daughter Pansy on the other side while everyone bowed in prayer.

The experience of that evening helped me decide the exact kind of work I wanted to do. I wanted to work with people who were on the frontiers of life, both geographic and spiritual; people who worked with basic elements of life, rain, wind, sun and soil and for whom religion would be something basic and elemental, not a fringe around the edge of a multitude of other interests. I wanted to be a missionary preacher.

It could be called coincidence or it might be called the hand of the Lord, but very soon after I reached this decision I was called into the office of the president of the college. President Jacques took a personal interest in every student on his campus and always interviewed the seniors during their last semester to discuss their prospects for work after graduation.

"Sit down, Mr. Hyde, and we might talk things over for a few minutes." The president held a sheaf of papers in one hand and as we passed a few remarks about how fast a college year goes by and how my folks were getting along on the farm he was glancing over the papers. Then he tapped one sheet.

"You've been doing good work, Hyde. Philosophy, mathematics, rhetoric—good grades. Did you ever think of teaching?"

"Not very seriously, Dr. Jacques."

"I have some good positions open along that line and I thought if you were interested I would suggest your name. You still thinking of the ministry?"

"That's what I have decided on, Dr. Jacques."

He picked up my transcript of grades again.

"Well, I think we ought to be able to place you pretty well. Some of our eastern churches would start you at five to eight hundred dollars a year. I've got a good letter here from one church," and he fingered through his sheaf of papers, "but they want a married man."

He looked over his glasses at me with a twinkle in his eye.

"I think that might be arranged," I answered with mock solemnity.

"I wondered about that, but I didn't like to be so bold as to ask the question point blank."

"What kind of a church is it, Dr. Jacques?"

"Oh, it's a good one; been established about twenty years, prosperous community, people with a little reserve laid up, good educational facilities, good social life. Frankly, we will have to send a promising candidate to them. I wouldn't want to compliment you too highly but I would be glad to submit your name, with my recommendations."

In the matter of thirty seconds I could see it all—Minnie and I would be married this summer, we would have a good home and a place to start a family without too much financial worry. Minnie could have the advantage of fine friends with music and all the things that make a good life. Why didn't I snap up this offer?

Dr. Jacques glanced through several other letters in the sheaf he was holding, and made running comments as he glanced at each.

"This church wants an older man . . . not good feeling in this church . . . here they want someone who speaks French . . . H'm, how would you like to be an assistant in a large Toronto church? Fine experience." He looked up at me.

"I am sure it would be, Dr. Jacques, but I think I would rather start with a smaller church and work up."

"You've a point there, of course. Sometimes learning the hard way is the surest way."

The president came to the last paper in his hand. He looked at it at some length then tapped it with his letter opener as he commented, "I have a letter from Dr. A. D. Traveller." He smiled a little as if with happy recollections. "Traveller was a former student here and he knows what kind of men Albert College turns out, sometimes. He's now Presiding Elder in charge of the Methodist Churches in Dakota Territory in the States. He wants a young man out there—but let me read you part of his letter: 'The church must keep pace with the government in opening up this new territory. This would be a job down at the very grass roots of society—' "

I must have shown some eagerness because Dr. Jacques turned to the second page of the letter and said, "Wait a minute, Hyde, till I read you the qualifications of the man he wants." He found the paragraph and read on: " 'I need a man, a young man, who can face the impossible and conquer it even if it takes a life time.' "

The president folded the letter and slipped it into an envelope. "Take this with you and read it over again. It has Dr. Traveller's address in it if you want to write to him. I'll hold open these other appointments for a few days too." His face relaxed and out came that strong, friendly hand that had helped so many students at Albert College. "And Godspeed to you, Brother Hyde."

I knew right there that I wanted to offer my services for this work in Dakota. The pull toward the job was strong, but I knew also that it meant I would have to leave Minnie behind for a year or two. From Dr. Traveller's letter I realized that this work would be attended with no luxuries. Life seemed to lose its spark when I thought of two years without Minnie. Even if I steeled myself for the separation, was it fair to her? On the other hand, think of working in a church where everything was in its beginning stage! The next day I wrote to Dr. Traveller.

I couldn't get away from school long enough to make the trip from Belleville clear out to the Grills farm so I also wrote a letter to Minnie. I told her about the job and asked her, if possible, to come to town with her father the next time he came to market so we could talk things over. I felt I knew Minnie well, but this was a sudden and a severe proposition. And what would her parents say? Would they ever be willing for me to take their daughter into the pioneer unknown? I could scarcely wait for a chance to talk to her.

I had read a great deal about the States. My brother James had been there and I had also heard stories from the runaway slaves who had escaped into Canada and had found refuge in the homes of some of our friends and then settled down in the community. I think I was unconsciously identified with the United States, but always in some remote future. Minnie and I had frequently talked of the possibility of going to the States—sometime.

College work now took on new interest. I was on the verge of being tried out in a real job—in Dakota or some other place and every experience held increased significance. It got around the campus that I was considering the wilds of Dakota and I became the butt of a good many jokes connected with Indian scalpings. The doleful neighbors counted the miles to Dakota and sympathized with my mother over what would happen if Willie was ever needed back home in a hurry. "With a family as big as yours you just never know!"

But my family shared my point of view. They were a pioneering family. My parents had migrated from England because Canada held more possibilities for their children. They had taken up a wild tract of government land, had hacked out a little garden plot and that first year had lived off vegetables and wild game. Gradually they cleared the land and got a few acres into wheat. Twice a month my father would put a sack of grain over each shoulder and walk into Millbridge to have the wheat ground, then carry the flour home again. In the early days he had to carry a rifle with him, whether plowing in the field or walking into town or working in the sugar bush. Mother had the same pioneer fortitude. Of the eleven children in our family eight of them were born in a small Canadian farmhouse without the assistance of a doctor. My parents knew both the hardships and the rewards of pioneer living and they did not discourage me. Nor did they push me into the undertaking. This had to be my decision.

An almost immediate reply came from Dr. Traveller. He set forth the conditions under which I would be considered for the work. I was to pay my own railroad fare to Aberdeen, Dakota Territory—fifteen hundred miles. He promised plenty of hard work. He promised not one cent of financial support; none was available from any source, not even missionary money. There was one further stipulation: if I turned out to be the wrong man they would pay my expenses back home!

I wrote a brief note to Dr. Traveller, as much to the point as his had been. "Terms accepted. I'll be there. Wm. J. Hyde."

A few days later Minnie came to town with her father. She and I walked along the shore of the Bay of Quinte, one of our best-loved walks. It was wonderful to be with her; her very presence filled me with an odd combination of calm and excitement.

"I've heard from Dr. Traveller since I wrote to you."

"So soon? What does he say?"

I gave her the letter to read and wondered how it would sound to the one who would be left behind to wait.

"Have you answered it?"

She looked across the Bay, not at me.

"Yes, Minnie. I wrote him, 'Terms accepted.' I told him I would be there."

"That's doing business in a hurry, isn't it?"

"I guess it is, but this is the kind of opportunity that you take in a hurry. It's the church out on the frontier like we've talked about."

She let me flounder for a brief moment before she looked full at me and the smile in her eyes was braver than the one on her lips.

"Of course, Will, I knew what your answer was. That's the right way to look at it."

I looked hungrily at Minnie and at that moment I think her courage was stronger than mine.

"What about you, Minnie?"

" 'Where thou goest, I will go' "; she quoted as she put her hand confidently in mine. "But I'll wait for you to come back and get me."

The night before I left home there was a big party attended by the people from the whole countryside. The Brick Street Church and the West Belleville Church took the initiative. It was a gay evening. There were five Grillses, ten or twelve Hydes, and neighbor families in about the same numbers from Belleville and the outlying country. As the evening passed a serious mood settled over the room. Mrs. Burt pulled out the stops on the reed organ and began to play. After a few strains Willie Finkle took his place beside the instrument; his clear tenor voice led the whole group in "What a Friend We Have in Jesus" and we sang the three verses with warmth and conviction. The minister of the West Belleville Church gave a short talk expressing the appreciation of all the churches for the work I had done for them, and then presented me with a gift. Sixty dollars! In 1886 sixty dollars was a lot of money. I knew from long experience how many gallons of maple syrup, how many eggs, how much cheese or butter, how many days of work it took to make sixty dollars.

I tried to tell the people how much their friendship and encouragement had meant to me through high school and later through college. I told them that their gift would go with me to represent the Belleville Methodists in opening up that great nation, the United States of America. Railroads, industries, towns—all were pushing into the vast new territory and the church would move along with them to carry the Gospel message. I didn't need to use their money for travel expenses because I had saved some and my parents had supplied the remainder needed to buy my ticket. Everyone seemed happy to think that this money would represent them in pioneer missionary work.

The next day I said the final good-byes. Minnie's last words to me as she stood on the depot platform that June day were, "I am proud of you." Simple words, but just like her. The brakeman signaled to the engineer, the engine gave its first slow chug-chugs as the Belleville friends waved me off to Toronto—and points west.

2

"As One Sent"

AFTER Toronto, the next important stop was Detroit where we entered the United States. As we approached the border the woman across the aisle from me was very nervous. She stopped the conductor several times to ask if the inspectors would open all her luggage. Would they take everything out, and why didn't they trust people instead of insulting them that way? Some of the men in the back of the coach joked in loud voices about swallowing their diamonds, putting on three suits and sitting on their furs. There seemed to be a general air of suspicion on the part of the passengers.

My luggage consisted of one large metal suitcase, sometimes called a hand trunk. I had it open on the seat and while we waited for the customs officials I noted the contents: a dozen schoolbooks, one Bible, one old Methodist hymnal; an extra suit of clothes, some underwear, socks and handkerchiefs, and a few miscellaneous articles. No wonder I was not worried about inspection!

The train ground to a stop and the door of the coach opened, letting in cinders and smoke and stirring up the stale air, heavy with the smell of orange peel and ham sandwiches. The customs officer worked his way down the aisle and stopped at my side.

"Where are you headed, young man?" he asked pleasantly.

"Dakota Territory, sir."

"Hope to fight the Indians?"

"No, sir, I'm fighting something worse than Indians."

He looked over the rims of his glasses at the contents of my trunk. He picked up the hymnal. "This your fightin' gear?"

"Part of it," I answered.

"You can't be a preacher?" He seemed incredulous.

"That's what I'm hoping I am," I answered.

"Well, boy, close your trunk and good luck to you."

I was disconcerted. What made it so unbelievable that I was going to be a preacher? I took stock. One sound body, five feet seven inches tall, weighing one hundred twenty-five pounds. Nothing imposing there, certainly. Personal possessions, meager. Financial assets, well under fifty dollars. By that time I was serious with myself. What else did I have?

Gratefully I remembered Mrs. Peal's words to me one night, "Willie, God can use your voice. It prays right along with the words." One voice, one asset. But that voice could not sing. Therein was a liability. I thought some more. In my pocket was the first letter I had received from Dr. Traveller. "We want someone who can face the impossible and conquer it even if it takes a lifetime." Here I was on my way—maybe the determination that had started me on this journey would be my greatest asset.

A burst of noise from the engine, the jerk of the coaches down the line as the train got under way, and I realized I was about to enter the United States of America. Already I had complete devotion to this country. I had read volumes of her history. I had poured over maps of the States; I knew that westward I would cross Michigan, Indiana, Illinois, Wisconsin, Minnesota and enter Dakota. They were names only. Involuntarily I looked back to Canada. To some people Ontario, too, was only a name on the map, but to me it was the blue water of the Bay of Quinte in the summer or its frozen glare of ice in the winter; it was woods with meandering deer paths; it was soft snow piling higher as the winter wore on; it was towns, families, homes. Would I soon have the same personal feeling toward the States? I began to feel the excitement of adventuring in new places.

The train ferried across the Detroit River, ran through southern Michigan and across the line into Indiana. Forest land and grassland; the country was becoming flatter, but not monotonous. Little towns, straggling, struggling affairs. We rounded the southern curve of Lake Michigan. This water with its peculiar translucent blue was part of the great chain of lakes that linked Chicago with my Belleville! Finally we pulled into Chicago, railroad center of the West. The first rails had been laid in the early 50's; now there was an amazing crisscross of tracks all going someplace important to someone. The train jerked to a stop.

"Everybody out!"

It was night. I took my hand trunk, boarded a horse car and went straight to the Young Men's Christian Association where I got a bed. In the morning I reversed the trip and boarded the train for Minneapolis.

We headed west again and north. Wisconsin was a beautiful state. Rolling green hills not yet faded by the summer sun. Great wooded tracts, oak, maple, pines. Talking with some men on the train I heard stories of virgin forests to the north. Westward through the afternoon. Many names recalled the early French days—Juneau, La Crosse, Eau Claire. The conductor sat down beside me and answered questions.

By dark we were on the banks of the Mississippi which were crowded with boats even though the railroads were transplanting river navigation. We had only a few minutes in St. Paul but at least I could say I had been in the capital of Minnesota. Then across the river to Minneapolis. Here I spent my second night. The next morning I saw the elevators and flour mills rising angularly against the sky. Doubtless some of the wheat from my Dakota would be shipped here.

Westward again. Always headed into the sunset but never overtaking it. The deep cliffs cut by the Mississippi gradually gave way to lesser hills. An industrious people must have settled Minnesota; the towns and farms looked more mature than I had expected to find in so young a country. Rivers gradually became less frequent, more sluggish; hills had a meager growth; no more large trees. The beautiful dress Mother Nature had been wearing was exchanged for a drab, plain homespun.

Westward. Imperceptibly Minnesota faded into Dakota Territory. It was early summer; swales still held a little water; otherwise, the eye was met with green prairie grass extending as far as one could look—in any direction. We were in the Dakota prairie.

At each train stop I looked for Indians. In Canada we heard a great deal about their cruelty and treachery; they were always pictured in gruesome warpaint, with tomahawks, and bent on massacre. So far I had not seen a single Indian so I questioned a fellow passenger.

"Indians? Been pushed back west. Didn't you ever hear of Custer's Last Stand?"

I decided not to voice my ignorance again. I would keep my eyes open and get my answers from experience or books.

The infrequent small towns were dusty, buildings weather beaten; storm and wind had left them defeated. Occasionally a building newly painted stood out in glaring contrast. From the train window we saw a line of covered wagons in the distance. This was the life about which I had read. Here was the glamour of pioneering, at least from my green plush train seat.

A flashily dressed, self-important fellow passenger also watched the covered wagons. "Too poor to come by train," he commented. "A whole family, their kids and all their possessions in each wagon. But I guess it takes all kinds to make a new land." He stuck his thumb under his suspenders, puffed out his chest and was about to launch forth upon his own accomplishments— I had heard him off and on all the way from Minneapolis—so I withdrew by myself to let something of these first impressions sink in. I reminded myself that when God looked upon the earth it was still far from perfect, but He found it good and I had something of the same feeling toward my new country. Wherein lay its merit I could not say, but I knew that it was good.

And so we arrived in Aberdeen. On a Saturday in June, 1886, I set foot for the first time on Dakota Territory. Dr. Traveller had written that he would meet me in Aberdeen so I was looking around for him when I felt a tap on the shoulder.

"My boy, is your name Hyde?"

I nodded, noting his black Prince Albert coat.

"Is your name Traveller?"

"That's my name. Your train was late. We leave in five minutes on the other line. I am going with you the twenty miles to Groton. That's where you will be located. This is the last stage of your journey."

Here was the man responsible for my appointment to Dakota. He must have been in his late fifties but he had had no time to grow old. His hair was graying, his blue eyes twinkled, but his mouth was serious. His whole manner was one of urgency, under control. He was not a man of many words but he spoke in a friendly way.

We crossed the tracks together to a waiting train and backtracked about twenty miles east to Groton. Ours was a mixed train, part freight and part passenger coaches. There was no stop on the way.

I wanted to ask many questions but it seemed more important to listen to Dr. Traveller and he told me much during our short ride. The Methodist Conference had decided to open up work in Groton because it was the junction of the Chicago, Northwestern Railway and the Chicago, Milwaukee, and St. Paul Railway. The town was in good wheat territory and should have a promising future. There was already a grain elevator and another soon to be built. Groton was a one-street town but it was the trading center for miles of homestead land with sod houses and a few frame houses. Prairie schooners passed through it— some to remain to open new claims and others to head on farther west. I caught something of Dr. Traveller's enthusiasm for the country and the work. As we were pulling into Groton he said, "Go to the hardware store and introduce yourself to Mr. Axel Johnson. You will make friends. It is that kind of a country."

As we jerked to a stop I picked up my hand trunk. Although Dr. Traveller was continuing on this train to keep a preaching appointment for the next day he stepped down to the depot platform with me while the engine switched off a few freight cars.

"All aboard!" called the brakeman.

As Dr. Traveller swung onto the train he waved me the high sign and called out, "Dig or die, Brother Hyde."

I stood on the platform of that little depot. I did not have to hurry. No one expected me. I had no place to go. I looked around.

Flat. That was my impression.

I stood under a hot sun and looked down the tracks, which contrary to the geometry book seemed to meet at some interminable distance. I looked in the other direction. A tall grain elevator rose at right angles to the flat earth. I looked at the town. One flat dusty street with a few stores and a few houses on each side. If any direction presented any slight undulations my hill-trained eyes failed to observe them.

Then a startlingly beautiful bird call. A meadow lark! Meadow larks and sunshine, and here I stood dwelling on the flatness of the landscape. I laughed and whistled in imitation of the bird call. Now I felt more at home for I had whistled with the birds for years in the Canadian woods. Now I would learn their calls on the western prairies. Life was good!

I left my trunk at the depot and walked down the street to the hardware store owned by Mr. Johnson. When I entered he was busy uncrating a stove and did not hear me until I was well toward the back of the store. Then he turned and straightened up, a well-built, large-framed man, middle aged, with sandy hair and a ruddy complexion. His eyes were friendly, though not too communicative. After all, this was Saturday morning and he was busy.

"How do you do, sir?" he said.

I acknowledged his greeting.

"Is there anything I can do for you?"

"I don't know."

"You are on business?"

"Yes sir, I am."

He adjusted the black apron he was wearing and looked at me a little quizzically. "What is your business?"

"I am here on the most important business in the world."

"I don't think I understand you."

Then I took from my pocket the credentials which had been given me by the Methodist Presiding Elder in Ontario.

Mr. Johnson looked at the papers. He held them for a minute as if uncertain then folded them and handed them back to me.

"I am sorry that you have come."

It was my turn to be surprised. I replied, "Sir, I have not come."

"Well, again I think I do not understand you."

"What I mean is—I have been sent. Anybody can come, but I am commissioned." There was an almost imperceptible deepening of the wrinkles around his eyes as I added, "I am commissioned by the greatest Protestant denomination in the United States."

The wrinkles produced a smile. He pulled out a heavy gold watch chain and rested a large key-wind watch in the palm of his hand. "H'm, almost time to lock up for noon and go home to dinner." He was completely cordial as he hastily added, "Would you go along with me?"

The Johnson home was not far from the store. As the houses of Groton went it was a good-sized house and had been painted. There were several trees in the yard which were responding to the daily attention given them by the family. I was still to learn how much a tree meant in Dakota Territory.

We entered the house by the side door, stepping right into the dining room. At home we had always used the kitchen door excepting for formal occasions. I took our entrance through the family doorway to mean that I was being accepted as something less than a stranger.

"Karin, come meet our friend. I have brought him home to dinner with us."

Mrs. Johnson appeared in the doorway leading to the kitchen. "Heavens, and I hadn't expected company. But it's all right." Something in her voice made me know it was all right, too.

More from embarrassment than from necessity she wiped her

hands on her apron which was bordered with a heavy band of Swedish needlework.

"This is William J. Hyde. He has come . . ." His voice broke off into a hearty laugh. "No, he has been sent by the Methodist Conference."

"It is a long time since we have had a Methodist preacher in our home. You are many times welcome. Would you want to wash before dinner?"

Mrs. Johnson was a rather heavy-set woman, but she moved easily and more quickly than one would have expected. From a drawer she took out a white towel, this also bordered with bright colors. Her zinc sink shone from polishing. The kitchen was clean and inviting.

"Where is Bessie?" asked Mr. Johnson.

"She'll be back in a minute. I ran her over to the Hansens with a pudding for Sarah who's sick and her appetite isn't good." Mrs. Johnson turned to me, "Sometimes a change of cooking is good for a soul, just like a change of preaching." I knew we were going to be friends.

"I will dish up if you men will please go into the dining room."

As I passed the door I looked out and saw Bessie coming up the walk. Although it was a warm day she looked remarkably fresh, "unwilted" is the word that flashed through my mind. Heavy braids of blonde hair circled her head with not a stray lock to look damp and hot on her neck. Her blue calico dress fitted her well and just missed the dust as she came briskly up the walk.

"Papa, already you are home?" She greeted him before she noticed a stranger with him.

"This is Brother Hyde, Bessie. He's going to start a Methodist Church in Groton."

"How do you do, Brother Hyde? I didn't know we were to have a Methodist Church here."

Mrs. Johnson brought in several steaming dishes of food, then seated us at the table. Mr. Johnson asked me to say grace, which

I did with deep gratitude to God for both food and friends. The conversation soon relaxed into an easy mood. Among themselves the Johnsons relapsed a little more into their Swedish idiom. It was not really broken English, just a good flavor of their native tongue.

Through the door into the living room I could see a piano so I asked Bessie if she played.

"Oh yes. As a little girl, back east in Minnesota I took some lessons but out here there hasn't been anyone to help me."

"But Bessie plays well. She's the organist in our Presbyterian church." Her mother was rightfully proud.

"You see, Brother Hyde, we have a good Presbyterian church here," added Mr. Johnson. "The last few years it has been doing good work."

"Papa is superintendent of the Sunday School." The announcement was again made pridefully by Mama.

"I think Dr. Traveller told me you had been Methodists." I began to feel my way.

"Yes, way back East in Minneapolis . . ."

I did not mean to interrupt Mr. Johnson but this was twice that they had mentioned Minnesota as if it were as far removed as England. I laughed the least bit.

"It's just that in Canada we always thought of Minneapolis as being way out *west*, but here you talk of it as being way back *east*."

Mrs. Johnson answered first. "You have been here not two hours. Wait till it is two years and maybe your geography will change, too. Minnesota is 'back home.' "

Bessie explained, "Mama always makes a difference between 'home' and 'back home.' They all do. You will get to understand—if you stay long enough."

"I was going to say we have this Presbyterian church here," continued Mr. Johnson. "And a good preacher. Dr. McLean gives us a good sermon every Sunday. The expenses of the church are paid by the Home Board of the Presbyterian denomination.

That makes it possible to have a good building as well as a good preacher."

Mr. Johnson inspected the food on his plate rather deliberately as if he spoke to it, rather than me. "I suppose the Methodist Board is starting a church here for you?"

"No, sir. I have to start the church."

"But your salary is paid by them?"

"No, sir, I have to raise my own salary."

Mr. Johnson forgot his food for a moment. He raised his fork in an agitated motion. "Brother Hyde, that is impossible."

"Brother Johnson, that is why I am sent here."

"Mama, that was a good dinner." Mr. Johnson pushed back his chair. "Bessie, don't forget the rehearsal for the sociable. I think Brother Hyde and I will go call on Dr. McLean. Jerry can open up the store."

We walked the short distance to the Presbyterian parsonage and were cordially received by Dr. McLean, a scholarly-looking man and a gracious gentleman. He was about forty-five years of age. One would have known he was a Scotsman; he had that delightful burr in his voice.

Sitting in his study, I, an upstart of twenty-two, felt somewhat awed in his presence. The room was lined with bookshelves filled with volumes whose very bindings intrigued me. My eye turned to them even while I listened intently to all the things he told me.

"Come and borrow the books whenever you want to." My warm appreciation for this man almost consumed me at that moment.

Dr. McLean told me about the Presbyterian college which the denomination was in the process of founding in Groton. He was acting president during the time the plans were being worked out.

"The work is too much for one man. Groton is a small community but it serves a large area. You cannot see much of the development around—the houses are little sod shanties miles apart. But this is a big land, and everything in it is going to be bigger; bigger families, bigger farms, bigger businesses. We will need bigger churches. Brother Hyde, I am glad that you have come."

I was happy at that moment. There was to be no jealousy here; no fighting of Presbyterians against Methodists.

"Thank you."

"Yes, I am more than glad you have come." He rubbed his chin and smiled wryly. "I have been here about three years and many times I have wished the Methodists would move in. You know, there are some things the Methodists can do that the Presbyterians never can."

I found that time interpreted this remark.

3

Digging In

A FTER introducing me toDr. McLean, Mr. Johnson had excused himself to go back to the store, so when I left the Presbyterian parsonage I stopped in at the Johnson home to thank Mrs. Johnson for my first meal in Groton. As I stepped in the dining-room door Bessie's voice called to me from a room that looked like a small alcove.

"Come in and see my office."

I crossed the dining room and looked in on her. There she sat at a large roll-top desk with ledgers and day books spread all over it.

"I keep the books for Papa," she explained. "Over at the store there's an office that Peter Cook, the bookkeeper, used. But when Peter went to Aberdeen to work Papa couldn't find another good bookkeeper so I asked him why I couldn't keep books."

Mrs. Johnson came in from the kitchen. "Her Papa didn't like the idea at first," she hastened to add.

"He really didn't," Bessie smiled as she continued. " 'Why, Bessie, you're a girl,' he'd say. 'You can't go to the store and sit on a high stool. Besides, bookkeeping is a man's work.' " She laughed, half in pride.

"Is this a sort of compromise then?" I asked her.

"That's about it. I was always good with figures and a couple years ago when I finished the two years of high school here I almost went to Yankton to college. But Papa decided it was too far for a girl to go alone, and Mama thought it wasn't really necessary for a girl to go to college."

39

"So you stayed here and turned business woman?"

She nodded. "At first I thought it would be dull living here and not be in school, but since I have kept Papa's books I don't mind it a bit. In fact, I like it. I just love bookkeeping."

"Can you cook as well as your mother?" I asked her.

She shook her head. "Mama's such a good cook that she doesn't want me messing around the kitchen. It doesn't seem to come as natural to me as to her. So this arrangement gives us each something special to do. And all this," she indicated the papers and the books on the desk, "isn't as much work as it looks."

As I looked at Mr. Johnson's bookkeeper I thought she would be quite an asset in the store. I could imagine a young man stopping in to buy an ax head just for the sake of passing a word with the bookkeeper. But, of course, Mr. Johnson had a point; girls didn't work as office force, not right in the store.

While Bessie and I were talking Mrs. Johnson had a slightly worried look on her face.

"I been wondering where you are going to live? Do you have any arrangements?"

"No, I don't, Mrs. Johnson. There must be a boardinghouse in town."

"That there is, but I don't think McCleary's would be quite the good place for you, do you Bessie? With the saloon next door it gets pretty noisy and they have a lot of riffraff coming and going at McCleary's."

"Mama, tell Mr. Hyde what you and Papa thought."

"Well, Brother Hyde, we thought if you didn't want anything too fancy maybe you could just stay right here with us. We have a room upstairs that we never use. We finished it off when we built the house thinking my sister might come out to live with us, but she got married and stayed back in St. Paul. As I say, it isn't fancy but we could put a desk in there. There's enough room for that, and you could feel like a preacher."

"There really aren't many places in Groton for a person to live, except McCleary's," added Bessie.

Only a man who has been in similar circumstances can know what a wonderful joy this welcome into a home gave me.

"I'll show you up to the room and you can decide," offered Mrs. Johnson while Bessie turned back to her ledgers.

The room was very inviting. The bed was covered with a blue and white spread and the pillows were well plumped up under the bolster. The commode set was also blue and white, each piece shading from white at the top down to a very deep blue at the base. Mrs. Johnson had already put warm water into the big pitcher and nothing could have looked more inviting on that hot afternoon after the long train trip. Hooked rugs were scattered over a spotless pine floor. A small table and two chairs, one of them covered with a flowered material of some kind, completed the furnishings.

"It's wonderful, Mrs. Johnson, and you're wonderful to give me a home." Her round face beamed and I know mine did too. "That east window just suits me," I told her. "Most mornings I'll greet the sun. I'm an early riser but I'll try not to disturb the rest of you."

"That doesn't need to worry you, Brother Hyde. Papa gets up early, too. He says when you've been raised on a farm like he was back in Minnesota you never get out of the habit of waking up at milkin' time. Now Bessie, she says she could do with a little more sleep and a little less milkin' time, especially since we don't have any cows. We always have breakfast at half past six. That's about as late as Papa can wait. Will that be all right with you?"

All right? At the thought of breakfast with the Johnsons instead of at some dusty restaurant, I would have been glad to eat breakfast before I went to bed at night if that had been part of the family schedule. And I determined that I would surely pay them something for their hospitality even though they would likely object.

"You just go get your trunk from the depot. Sam at the livery barn can take a buggy and go with you. Tell him I sent you."

"Thanks, Mrs. Johnson, but my trunk isn't very heavy. It's just a hand trunk and I can handle it myself."

"Then you just make yourself at home, and I'll get back to the kitchen and get the baking done for tomorrow."

In a few minutes I was back "home" and unpacking my possessions. It didn't take long! Two nails in the closet held everything that had to be hung up; one dresser drawer more than accommodated the rest of my things; the table top was still somewhat bare after I put out my books. But the room looked wonderful to me, and as a last rite of settling I took the tintype of Minnie and placed it in front of the books. The picture had been taken two years earlier when Minnie was a senior in high school. Of course she looked a little older now, but we country folks didn't take pictures very often; there had to be a real occasion before people felt justified in the luxury. Anyway, I liked this picture of Minnie because the photographer had caught just the shade of a smile. Her face was naturally rather serious, and when she smiled it really meant a smile.

My reverie was interrupted by Mrs. Johnson calling up the stairs, "Tonight when Papa gets home, he can help you move the desk in. It's up over the rafters in the barn now."

"That'll be fine, Mrs. Johnson," I called back. This was just like home!

Along in the late afternoon Bessie called me downstairs.

"Dr. McLean's here and wants to see you."

I met the Doctor in the living room and he was all apologies.

"I don't know why I didn't think of it while you were at our house, Brother Hyde, but it just came to me that you have no place to preach tomorrow. That'll never do. I want you to preach at our church at eleven in the morning. It'll be good for me to have a little vacation. Maybe it'll be good for the congregation, too." Congenial little wrinkles played around his eyes, but uncongenial big wrinkles played around my middle! Preach a real sermon, tomorrow morning? I was paralyzed on the spot.

"Oh, no thank you, Dr. McLean, you see I—" But why make an excuse to this man? I'd better be honest, and anyway he could probably guess my difficulty even if I could think up a fine-sounding excuse. I could feel my face get a little warm as I said, "To tell the truth, I just couldn't be ready by morning. That's awfully good of you, but I've never yet preached a real sermon in my life. I've done a lot of exhorting—you know us Methodists—but I'm not ready to step into a regular pulpit on such short notice and do justice to a Sunday morning service. I do thank you, though."

"You're being too modest," began Dr. McLean as if to brush aside my objections, which I knew were real. "I want you to do it."

"Maybe you would let me make a suggestion," I volunteered. "I'll attend your service in the morning, just like any other visitor, then at the end I would be happy to have you introduce me as the man sent here officially to represent the Methodist denomination. I would really appreciate that introduction."

Dr. McLean agreed, but added, "I'm also going to announce that for the evening service we will be a Methodist church with Brother Hyde in charge. How's that for a compromise?"

So it was left and I was faced with the necessity of preparing a sermon for the next evening. It should have been easy. Hadn't I anticipated this moment for years? Right after supper I went up to my room, sat down at the table and spread out my Bible, a hymnbook, a philosophy book and two treatises on theology. Here was enough material for years of sermons but no sermon took shape. Maybe that was the trouble, too much material. So I recalled some of the good sermons I had heard. Still no sermon for me. Surely all a person had to do was choose a text and develop a few thoughts in logical sequence.

By the time I went to bed that night I had decided upon and rejected at least twenty possible topics, each one either too complicated or too meager. Finally out of all the chaos one verse of Scripture stood forth clearly. "I am not ashamed of the Gospel of Christ." That would be my text. Way back in high school my first exhortation had followed a sermon on that text. I doubt if any other verse in the Bible had ever come to me with the recurring force of that verse and I wanted it to be the text of my first sermon in the United States.

The next morning Dr. McLean had a good service. He was scholarly and dignified in the pulpit; his theology was a little different from mine with his occasional reference to "election" and "preordination" but still I liked his general idea. There were perhaps forty people in the congregation, most of them middle aged, and most of them looked as if they were business or professional people although a few were farmers of the more prosperous type. At the close of the service, just before the benediction, Dr. McLean said, "The Reverend William J. Hyde has come into our community to open work for the Methodists. Tonight, this will be his church; I don't know what he will do or what he will say, but the pulpit is his and I hope you and all your friends will come out to the service."

That afternoon I sat down at my desk again. Suddenly I realized why my concern had produced so little fruit the night before: I had been thinking in terms of producing a good sermon, not in terms of saying something to help the people. So now I asked myself, what is the one idea I want most to share with these people? If I knew them better I could do a better job of preaching to them, but I knew that all of us face some of the same problems and if I talked about a problem from my own experience I was sure it would reach home to some of the other people.

That Sunday afternoon gave me a wonderful few hours while I really struggled with ideas. I was hardly conscious of the passage of time until Mrs. Johnson called up, "Brother Hyde, won't you come down for a bite of supper?"

Eight o'clock arrived and I entered the pulpit with Dr. McLean. I was glad he was not an exceedingly tall man because I was feeling small enough without matching my five feet seven against a giant. We sang the Doxology and Dr. McLean offered the opening prayer. Then he made a statement similar to the one he had made in the morning, that I represented the Methodists and he very warmly welcomed me to Groton. I was re-

minded of Wesley's letter to George Shadford when he was sent
to America in the early days of Methodism. "I let you loose,
George, on the great continent of America. Publish your message
in the open face of the sun and do all the good that you can."
Dr. McLean took his place in the congregation and I was left
alone at the pulpit.

We sang one of my favorite hymns to give me a chance to
warm up a little. How many times at home we had started our
Sunday evening service with the same words:

> I am Thine, O Lord,
> I have heard Thy voice,
> And it told Thy love to me;
> But I long to rise
> In the arms of faith,
> And be closer drawn to Thee.

We came to the chorus and I waited for them to swell up on the
words, "Draw me nearer, nearer . . ." Back at Belleville I used
to think we would have to lift the roof to make room for the
music, but tonight the singing lacked the fervor I had been
accustomed to. Maybe I had chosen a hymn not as beloved by
the Presbyterians as by the Methodists. During the singing
people were continually being seated by the ushers; whole
families came together, many of them evidently from the country, with their wind-burned faces and plainer clothes. This was a
different group from the morning service, although I saw some
of the same people. I took it for granted that in a little town any
newcomer would be a curiosity, the more so if he were a
preacher. By the time we finished singing all the verses of this
hymn the church was almost filled.

I read the Scripture, offered a prayer and by the time I got to
the sermon everything felt natural—I might almost have been
back in the Brick Methodist Church. I was just talking to people
as I had always done. I repeated the text, "I am not ashamed of
the Gospel of Christ," and then tried to express my ideas simply.
I just told these folks that we all make mistakes and there is

nothing to be ashamed of in making a mistake, if it is an honest mistake. We need only to be ashamed when we know we have done something we ought not to have done; shame follows a sense of guilt, and guilt and shame make cowards of a person.

I told them about one of my college friends who had cheated in an examination. He was a good student and had had a good record, but one day when he was not prepared for a test he had weakened to the temptation to cheat rather than take a low grade. Then the shame of the act began to eat on his conscience so that he avoided other students; he wouldn't take another course under the professor in whose class he had cheated, and before long he decided to leave school. But before he withdrew he repented his cheating, and with repentance came the courage to confess his mistake; and with confession life took on a new look. Just so when we regret our mistakes Jesus stands ready to forgive us and help us start over again with new courage. Shame makes people slink around, move from one community to another, change their names to help them run away from themselves. It is bad enough to be ashamed of oneself but to be ashamed of Jesus is about as low as a person can sink.

Peter was ashamed of being a follower of Jesus, and he denied even knowing Him; but when he regretted his weak action and became proud of the friendship with Jesus, the Master established His church on Peter's confession. After Paul dedicated his life to Jesus he was despised in many towns, jailed and driven out of cities, hungry, hunted and beaten. But it was this same Paul who said, "I am not ashamed of the Gospel of Christ." Every person has to ask himself, "Where do I stand in relation to Jesus? Do I ridicule the church, or take God's name in vile oaths? Would I be ashamed to line up with the followers of Jesus?" Or can you look over your great Territory and see its need for Christian parents, and honest young people, for unselfish teachers and businessmen of real integrity? Can you say, "I will take the message of Jesus into my home, my profession, my business, because 'I am not ashamed of the Gospel of Christ'?"

Dr. McLean closed the service with the benediction. People were in no hurry to leave. A church service was a social occasion as much as a religious experience. Both men and women were cordial and asked questions about my plans and gave me advice on how to start and who to see and some of them offered to help the work along. I decided that they were just right friendly folks.

The next morning about seven o'clock I was out for a brisk walk. Although I had been in Groton a day and a half I'd had no time to take a good look at the town, even though a complete tour from the business district to the residential area and from the elevator to the horse corral took only about fifteen minutes. In front of the feed store I met a man whom I recognized as having been at the service the night before.

"Good morning, Brother," he said heartily. He had a good handclasp along with the blue eyes and laughter of many of the Irish of this community. "My name's Regan, work over in the elevator there, and I heard you preach last night. It was all right, too. My wife couldn't go with me but I had my little daughter. She stayed awake all evening, even if she is only seven. When we got home her mother asked her how she liked the new preacher." Regan began to laugh. " 'Oh,' said my little girl, and she's a smart one, 'that preacher's a crackerjack!' 'But how did he preach?' her mother asked. My little girl began to wave her arms in the air. 'He preached just like a thrashing machine.' "

His wholehearted laugh filled the air as he slapped me on the back. I made a mental note: Watch your arms, Brother Hyde!

While I continued my inspection tour of Groton I kept an eye open for a likely looking building to use for a church. There would surely be some empty store or warehouse; I was willing to convert any kind of a building into a temporary church just so we could get started. However, there were not more than fifteen buildings along both sides of Main Street, and every building was in use. Hardware store, grocery store, general store, newspaper office, barbershop, feed store, buggy and harness shop, land office, doctor's office, pool hall, two or three nondescript cubby holes of whose interior I was not sure, and Dooley's Saloon, already doing business even at this early hour.

"What or where next?" I queried myself and then the sound of an anvil caught my ear. Back of the main street I found a stable connected with a blacksmith shop. Maybe this was Sam's place that Mrs. Johnson had mentioned when she sent me after my trunk Saturday afternoon. Anyway, an anvil meant horses and I liked to watch a smith shoe a horse, especially if he could do a good job.

The big doors of the shop were open and inside I could see the blacksmith working the bellows, fanning the flame in which a horseshoe glowed at white heat. I stepped inside the smithy and looked over the three or four horses waiting to be shod, then I came back to watch the smith shape the shoe to the foot of a big Percheron. He did it quickly, neatly. In a few minutes he straightened up, and I thought he would never stop straightening; he must have stretched to six feet four. His immense muscles relaxed and he wiped his forehead with the back of a grimy hand as he grinned and said, "You bane new preacher, yaas?"

"That's right," I replied, and we exchanged a few comments on the horse he was shoeing. Then the smith went back to his work and I stood watching for a few minutes, occasionally commenting on a girth burn or a nicked hoof or some other thing to make conversation.

"How a preacher bane know so much about horses?"

"I was raised on a farm—in Canada."

"Yaas?" And the anvil rang again. The next time he paused he continued, "Canada, yaas? You bane goin' stay in United States?"

"I certainly hope to," I told him. "That's my plan."

"You bane plan haf church?" He shifted his plug of tobacco contemplatively.

"That's a good question. I've been looking around this morning but Groton doesn't seem to have any empty buildings. I thought maybe I could find something to use while we're getting started. Any suggestions?"

The blacksmith eyed a tin pail several feet away. With accurate aim and gauge of pressure he landed a stream of tobacco juice in it and then looked back at me with the confidence of a man of many accomplishments.

"Yaas, we haf just von empdy place in town." He grinned a grin of the same large proportions as the rest of his anatomy. "Maybe you ask Pate Jensen about it. Pate, he own the building and he work in lumber yard." He grinned even broader as he pointed down the road on the other side of the depot to the lumber yard.

"Thank you, sir. My name is Hyde," and I extended my hand. The smith looked at his, black from his work and hesitated.

"You bane shake black paw like mine?" It would have been better to call his "paw" a vise for it was all I could do to keep from flinching as he shook my hand.

"Yaas, sir, Mr. Hyde. My name Sam Ting."

"Sam Ting? That doesn't sound very Swedish."

Sam sat down on a broken plowshare.

"Yaas, dat name is a gude yoke on me."

It was plain that he was going to relish the telling of this story so I sat on the tongue of an old wagon to listen.

"Yaas sir," Sam began again, "I come to America ven I can't spake gude English like now. On boat I learn few vords so ven we come to Noo Yoark I can get off boat gude. You see, my name bane Chris Larson and ven we line up for inspector-man the guy in front of me he bane a Chris Larson, too. Then inspector come long and say to each man, 'Vat name?' and man in front of me say, 'Chris Larson' and inspector write it down. So then he say to me, 'Vat name?' and I answer 'Sam' t'ing,' and he write down Sam Ting for my name! So America paper say Sam Ting instead of Chris Larson, and yaas sir, that bane my name in America." Sam laughed heartily as he started the bellows again.

I said good-by to Sam and started out to find Pete Jensen at the lumber yard. Pete was a stocky, energetic fellow with a shock of red hair and freckles which had taken over nearly every available location on his face and hands. I told Pete that Sam had sent me to ask about a building that had an empty room in it because I was looking for some place to use as a church, at least for a while.

When I mentioned the idea of using the room for a church I thought Pete became a bit evasive. Finally he said that, well, the room wasn't exactly empty.

"But if it isn't in use maybe I could rent it and clear it out?"

"It's not exactly that," said Pete. "The room's already rented to the G.A.R. even if they ain't used it for a year."

"The G.A.R.?" I inquired.

"Ain't you never heard of the G.A.R.? Maybe you didn't know we fought a Civil War, either?" I was afraid he was about to shoot me for a traitor so I hastened to tell him that I had just come from Canada and had a lot to learn in the States.

"You ain't so bad, at that," Pete conceded. "I bet a lot a folks around here got so in the habit of just saying G.A.R. that they don't know it stands for Grand Army of the Republic."

"Thanks for the information," I said. "Now what about the room?"

"Ya, that's right. Well, Don Smith is head of the G.A.R. Maybe you better see him. He works down at the elevator," and Pete stepped out in front of the lumber yard and indicated the elevator across the track on the other side of the depot.

At the grain elevator I found Don Smith and asked about the hall. Don was covered with wheat dust which he brushed off as he pushed his hat back on his head and deliberated.

"We got a hall, all right. But I dunno about the church business. You know where the hall is?" He looked at me for an answer. I shook my head.

"Well now, I wouldn't want to be the one to discourage you, parson, but you go down the main street till you come to the building between the general store and the pool hall. The G.A.R. hall is up over that."

It was plain that I was being given a go-around, but it was all semi-friendly; so I walked back to the main street and located the building. Then the full humor of the joke hit me. I had been directed to a building with a swinging door, under which saw-dust sifted out; I heard the clink of bottles and smelled the odor of stale beer, and across a dusty, fly-specked window I read the words, originally in gold paint but now partially flecked off, "Dooley's Saloon."

I chuckled to myself and wished Minnie were there to share with me my first impression of what was to become the first location of the First Methodist Church of Groton.

Right back I went to Don Smith and then to Pete Larson and made arrangements to rent the room for five dollars a month; I was to do the heating, lighting and janitor work and any other services needed. I rented it "sight unseen"; Don gave me the key and I went back to look over my new church. For a moment I was glad I had rented it before I looked at it. Too late now to be discouraged.

To reach the hall I climbed a ladder made of boards nailed across two two-by-fours then nailed flat against the outside back wall. This was our staircase! When I opened the back door I was greeted by a musty smell of beer and dust. I stepped inside the room and wondered if I could breathe long enough to get one or two of the small low windows open. The room was strictly under the eaves and the June sun was pouring its heat down on the roof. Not being too tall, I could stand straight to walk down the center of the room, but if Sam Ting ever came to church he would surely have to bow his head! The roof slanted sharply making it impossible for anyone but a child to stand erect if he got far off the center aisle. It was a pretty discouraging room that Monday morning.

When I got home and reported to Bessie and Mrs. Johnson, neither of them took me seriously at first but I finally convinced them that I had actually rented the place.

"Do you suppose I could find someone to help me clean it?" I asked Mrs. Johnson.

"Bessie, maybe you hitch up Queen and go out and see if Mary Wilkins could come help Brother Hyde." Mrs. Johnson turned to me. "Mary's a widow and an awful energetic person. You'll make dust fly like you never saw before if she can come. She's living alone, just about three miles out east, and she can't always leave her place but Bessie can take you out to see."

"I'll be ready just as soon as I make this last entry," said Bessie.

"Why not let me hitch up Queen while you finish your work?" I volunteered. Queen was a dandy little pinto that should have had a name like Pixie or Sprite instead of Queen; but horses, like people, sometimes get the wrong tags at birth; my two hundred pound cousin named Fairie, for example.

Mary promised to come the next day and as many other days that week as I needed her. So on Tuesday morning, bright and early, the skirmish began. Down came the cobwebs, out went the dust, soap suds ran in competition with beer suds, and we came out with floors surprisingly white. When Mary was through, the windows actually let in some light and after much cajoling they opened to let a cross breeze blow through the room. We took down the faded G.A.R. banner and even removed the torn picture of Mr. Lincoln.

Then we were ready to furnish our church. But with what? I had heard a story that the first sermon ever preached to white people on Dakota soil had been at Yankton where the preacher used an upturned whiskey barrel for a pulpit. We couldn't do any worse and with a little ingenuity we might improve over his equipment.

I made a personal tour of the stores of Groton asking the merchants for empty crates and other supports to use in making benches. The merchants entered into the humor of the situation.

"If the pearly gates came from an oyster why can't the mourners' bench come from a nail keg?" Mr. Johnson wanted to know with a humor that surprised me, but it plainly showed he had once been a Methodist or he wouldn't be talking about the mourners' bench.

Charlie Craig, the debonair young manager of the General Store, waved me to a big pile of miscellaneous packing cases out back of the store. "Help yourself to anything in the trash pile, Reverend, and say a good word to St. Peter for me!"

The men weren't jeering, they were just hugely enjoying the experiment of building a church from nothing. To my surprise, before the week was over several of the businessmen made some excuse to climb the ladder to see the progress of the work.

A few of the young boys in town found real excitement in watching me "make a church." I took them into the planning.

"Now what do you fellows think we could use for benches?" Near-sighted little Mike, the postmaster's son, suggested we might borrow benches from the school, but Guy Ricks, who was as keen as he was dirty, guessed the purpose of the nail kegs piled in one corner and suggested, "We could buy some lumber and put across them kegs."

"Those are both good ideas," I agreed. "But it might be that the school would need its benches for a meeting and to tell you the truth, I don't have enough money to buy lumber. We'd better figure some more."

The largest of the three boys had done little talking; mostly he eyed me suspiciously and I had wondered several times if he might be plotting a little trouble. Then he spoke with an air of finality.

"Leave it to me an' him, Mister." With his thumb he indicated Guy. "Me 'n him kin git it fer you tonight. We know where there's some loose boards in the back of the lumber yard shed. It'll be easy."

"I don't believe I know your name, do I?" I asked to give myself time to size him up a bit. "My name's Hyde."

"We know it. I'm Jarv."

"Thanks a lot for offering to help, Jarv, but I don't think we better get the boards that way. You see this is going to be a church and if we swipe those boards we would be off to a pretty bad start, don't you think?"

Jarv made no reply so I laughed and added, "Besides that,

think of all the splinters stolen boards might stick through the seat of your pants when you slide along on them!"

"Aw, shucks, me 'n him, we don't go to church."

"Maybe this church will be different and you might like to come." This idea of mine was met with a laugh.

"I don't guess so," and Jarv closed that discussion.

The two younger boys had set up a lot of the nail kegs in regular rows ready for the planks.

"If I can arrange to get the lumber, any of you fellows want to help me carry it over here?"

The four of us traipsed over to the lumber yard where I arranged to borrow enough planks to put across the crates and kegs to make our benches. It was understood that there were to be no nails pounded into the boards and that if anyone cut an initial or whittled off an edge I would pay for the damaged board. Pete Jensen offered to haul them from the lumber yard to our building without charge. I think it was to ease his conscience a little. Then my self-appointed young helpers helped me hoist the boards up the ladder and into the hall.

Interest in the venture grew. Several times strangers stopped me on the street to ask about our progress and tell me they planned to be at church the next Sunday evening for our first service which I had hopefully advertised in the *Groton Sentinel*, our weekly news sheet. Bessie went to her father's store with me and helped select some lamps for the room and I used some of the Belleville farewell gift money to pay for them. We fastened six lamps along the walls and with their reflectors they gave enough light so that people could recognize one another almost any place in the room! For a pulpit Mr. Johnson gave me a fine stove crate and enough brown paint to make it look quite like a piece of furniture. On that I would put my own Bible, open.

By Thursday night the room was ready for use and we surveyed it proudly.

"I think it looks right smart, if I do say so myself," contributed Mary.

"Sure thing," I agreed. "You'll feel pretty good sitting right here on the front row, won't you?"

"Me?" she asked in surprise. "Nope, Mr. Hyde, I ain't been to church hardly since I kin remember."

"Too bad, Mary, you're missing a lot of joy. Why don't you come?"

"I don't hardly remember what it was made us quit church. Honest now I don't. But it was a long time ago and I guess I'm out of the habit."

"Too bad again, Mary. You know the Lord hasn't got out of the habit of looking after you, has He? Think it over. We'd like to have you here."

That was all we said then as we proudly looked over our finished job.

When I got home that evening I clipped the notice of the service out of the *Sentinel* to send back to Minnie. "Preaching services will be held at eight o'clock in the G.A.R. hall . . ." I was careful to use that name for our room. The Methodists were not going to give the saloon any free advertising! And fortunately for us, the saloon was closed by law on Sunday so we didn't have to compete for our clientele.

Friday afternoon Mr. Johnson loaned me Queen and I made my first horseback excursion over the prairie. I had heard about a family of Perkinses who had been Methodists back in Ohio so I decided to make my first call on them. They lived twelve miles northwest of town. A native of the country would have made the trip in a little less distance because he would have struck out right across the prairie. There were few well-defined roads but such as there were I stuck to, for my first trip. I reached the Perkins house and found it was a real sod house, the first one I had ever seen close up or had a chance to enter. Sure enough, it was made just as the books said, from slabs of prairie turf piled one on top the other and tightly chinked with mud mortar. It had a thatch roof and the whole thing was surprisingly weatherproof. I don't know exactly what I had expected to find on close examination, but accustomed as I was to a good log house in even the most remote areas, a sod house had always sounded like something that would run off in a mud puddle at the first rain. For one thing, I had not realized how the roots of the prairie grass tied themselves tightly together in the dirt and made a solid mat.

I left a close inspection of sod construction for a later date and gave my attention to the Perkinses which was certainly not hard to do. They were a lively group. Mrs. Perkins was small and quick of motion; I suppose about thirty-five, although I found the prairie gave the women a certain agelessness that made them look about the same from twenty-five to forty. Mrs. Perkins' hair was streaked with gray, pulled back from her face and held securely in a knot at her neck. She looked worked down to the bone, but seemed to have more energy than any half dozen ordinary women. Her husband was tall and slightly stooped. I learned later he had been a clerk in an accounting office back east; his better-than-average education had paid off when he brought his family west for he had worked in an office in Aberdeen for the first six months while his wife held down the claim by living on it with the two babies. The Perkinses now had three boys, Matthew, ten; Nathaniel, eight; and Bartholomew, six.

"We got tired of the ordinary Bible names so we up and took the unordinary ones, but we call the boys Matt, Nat and Bart."

As I was introduced to each boy he came up and shook hands, somewhat painfully and I knew how each felt, and then with a whisk they all skidaddled out to play again.

Mrs. Perkins settled down with her knitting for a few moments' chat.

"Land sakes, think of having a Methodist preacher right here in our house. I guess we haven't had one since we left Ohio. I lived with my aunt there and she used to have lots of them stay at her house when they were riding circuit."

We talked about Ohio a few minutes. Both Perkinses had been born on farms in a prosperous part of the state.

"Our first years out here were pretty bad," Mrs. Perkins admitted, "but now we been here seven years and it's home. I guess when you're in your twenties you want things to come easy, then when you find they don't you settle down to take them as they come. We've got along better than lots of the others."

Before I left the Perkins home we had arranged that on Sunday morning I would come back and hold a preaching service at their house. They had a good sized kitchen-dining-living room in addition to the bedroom. "Besides, there's the whole outdoors," offered Mr. Perkins. They promised to get word to some of their neighbors and were sure that whenever I could get out to preach they would have some folks there to listen. So we set ten o'clock as service time.

"You don't suppose, Brother Hyde, you could go home by way of the Owens, do you? Tilly Owen'd just be tickled out of her mind to see a Methodist preacher. She almost married one back home and she thinks a lot of them in general. Besides, things for Tilly and Walter aren't doing too good and it would please them a lot to have you call."

John Perkins gave me directions for cutting across the prairie so that it took only three or four miles extra riding to visit the Owens. I found Tilly and Walter Owen were younger than John and Pearl Perkins and they were evidently of different stock. A general air of shiftlessness pervaded the poorly constructed buildings; the cattle were thin and the house was dirty. I was glad I had seen the Perkins home first for it gave a better impression of the possibilities of a sod house. Walter slouched when he walked, and his feet dragged with aimless indirection. Yet there was something about him that made me feel he could be much more active if there were anything that made him want to bestir himself. I felt the same about Tilly. Her dress was torn and pinned together where the buttons were gone; her hair had loose wisps straying; dirty dishes stood on the table and uncovered food was open to the flies. But in spite of it all, there was something very appealing about Tilly. I knew that if someone would slick up the house, clean up Tilly and set her down behind a table of coffee, cakes and cookies, Tilly would grace the occasion.

I told them that I had come to see them at the suggestion of the Perkinses where I was going to hold a service the next Sunday morning.

"A real church meetin', with singin' and prayin' and preachin' and all?" Now I knew what was so appealing about Tilly—it was her voice. She had a little of the drawl that the Negroes used to have who escaped into Canada. I asked where they had come from.

"Ohio," said Walter. "Just before we come here. But our kinfolk they all live in Kentucky." That explained it.

"Brother Hyde," said Tilly, "if you could give us a preachin' service right here we'd sure do our best to get the neighbors out. Walter and me ain't been in a church since the day we were married and our two kids ain't never heard a real sermon."

"Your children? Do you have some?"

"Oh yes, Bethie is six and Cora's five. They're over to the Jacobsons this afternoon. One of the Jacobson youngsters, I forget now which one, they're ten of 'em, is having a birthday party and our young ones are over there."

"I tell you, Brother Hyde, if you could come over here Sunday afternoon," Walter got up enough ambition to take the piece of grass he had been chewing out of his mouth, "we'd be right obliged and we'd have some of our neighbors here, too. Maybe not too many folks . . ." His voice trailed off in a defeated tone.

"I'd like to come, Mr. Owen. It doesn't make any difference how many people there are. If you want a service I'll surely be here. About two-thirty in the afternoon?"

So I had three services lined up for my second Sunday in town. I reached home that Friday night, a preacher whose weary bones felt more than their twenty-two years when he dragged them into bed.

Saturday I gave to putting the finishing touches on my talks for Sunday. Even this first week at my new job I had set aside two hours, and soon lengthened it to three, for study and meditation in the early morning before the strenuous activities of the day began. The eastern bedroom window was already associated with the inflooding of sunlight for the physical day and strength and direction for the spiritual day.

And so I finished out the first week in Dakota Territory and Sunday arrived. As I climbed onto Queen's back and put my Bible and sermon notes in a small saddle bag I experienced a great thrill—I had joined the long procession of circuit riders who from the days of Asbury, through Shadford, Peter Cartwright, Eggleston and others had carried the Message out beyond the confines of established churches. It didn't make any difference if I was the last and the least of them all, I had a tremendous sense of "belonging" and that adds immeasurably to a man's own slender resources. Where some earlier circuits had been two hundred miles in extent, mine would be twenty; where some preachers had passed through treacherous wilderness and hostile Indian territory, I would travel through uneventful prairie; where some circuit riders had converted their thousands, my converts would probably be numbered by the tens. But I could make of my job what I would and I found deep gratitude in riding out across the country that morning.

At the Perkins place, long before time for the ten o'clock service, there was a happy hubbub. The opportunity to attend a church service, I soon discovered, was only part of the explanation for this good gathering, for there must have been twenty-five or more people. Just the chance for a group of neighbors to get together was enough to make a lively time for everyone. I met everyone, of course, and immediately got woefully tangled up as to which children were whose and where each family came from, but a good memory for names and faces made it easy for me to call each individual by name within the first few minutes.

An alert reporter could have taken notes for a whole edition of his newspaper in a few minutes here! Politics—those rattled-brained Democrats at Washington, did the scoundrels think they could hold up statehood for the Territory forever? Local news—Gibbs had bought a new-fangled Cassidy plow; Simms

were thinking of moving on west if they could trade their two
cows in on a good wagon; I got lost in the names of people who
were sick or who had babies or whose crops looked good, or
didn't look good. Always the latest wheat quotations from
Minneapolis.

Then as if by common consent the group quieted down, the
women sitting on benches or stools inside the door of the sod
house out of the sun, and the men standing or sitting on the
ground outside, while I stood near the doorway. We held a
short service. The hymns they asked to sing were "What a
Friend We Have in Jesus" and "There Is Sunshine in My Soul
Today." I wasn't much help with the singing but I noted a good
voice here and there and knew we could improve on our music
as time went on. We had a prayer, Bible reading and a very short
talk. Even in this informal setting I could feel something draw
the group together as we worshiped. An occasional tear was
wiped away and I knew that some woman's mind was far from
the Perkins sod house and far from the words a young preacher
was saying. What were the memories of these people? Were
they recalling the last time they went to church, a funeral, a
wedding, the old family pew back home? No one but God Himself knew but I am sure He was there in the little sod house to
hear the unvoiced murmur of each heart.

The service over, horses were brought around for families to
start back home. No one was in a great hurry and before the
first families left we had planned to hold services again the
next Sunday and to add a Sunday School class for "all these
heathens around here," as Mrs. Perkins put it, to which some
voice outside drawled, "And they ain't all kids, either."

The Perkinses invited me to have dinner with them, and then
I went on to the Owen place. Again I was struck with the difference between the Perkinses and the Owens, reflected in the
group of neighbors gathered for the afternoon service. I suppose
the difference was explained in part by the fact that the prairie
land was of unequal fertility; some stretches produced more per
acre than others, and if a family drew poor land as their home-

stead they either tried to make the best of it, and often failed,
or they had to pick up and move on and such a move took both
money and courage.

Topics of conversation were the same as we had in the morning at the Perkinses; politics, people and crops are of universal
interest in a sparsely populated farming country. But under the
sociability I felt a strain of depression. Here were the Hogans;
Pat and Nora had walked six miles and brought two little children with them. Nora's dress was an evident combination of two
old ones, both faded before they joined forces. There were about
fifteen people who grouped themselves in the sparse shade on
the front side of the sod shanty, the Owen house being too small
to accommodate them inside. Just as our service was about to
start someone called our attention to another family off in the
distance, so we waited till the Higginses arrived. I found it hard
not to stare in open astonishment at this family. Their equipage
consisted of the running gear of a lumber wagon, but instead of
the wagon box there was one long plank between the front and

rear axles. Swinging from this plank was a row of bare feet, very dirty and dusty. Hitched to the wagon were a mule and a cow! No wonder the family was late in arriving. I was introduced to the Higginses—father, mother and ten children. They had traveled since ten o'clock that morning and it was now after two-thirty. We took time to welcome them and the Higginses, since they had their cow with them "allowed" they might as well spend the night and go home in the cool of the morning. I almost lost the thread of my sermon wondering where they would sleep but I decided the haystack would probably serve. Before I left the neighbors at the Owen place we had made arrangements similar to those made at the Perkinses so I was all set for the next Sunday's round.

I was back in Groton in time to clean up from my horseback ride, eat a bite of supper while I told my experiences to the Johnsons, and make ready for the main service of the day in our new church room. I didn't know how many people would come nor how they would act, worshiping over a saloon. I wondered about a lot of things, but I didn't worry about them—this was God's venture as well as mine. So I climbed the ladder at the back of Dooley's Saloon at seven-thirty that Sunday night.

Already the room was nearly filled. People were greeting one another in a most friendly way; there was some jesting, of course, but nothing loud or out of place. By the time the service started the room was packed. I had figured that the improvised benches could seat about sixty—I was planning for an optimistic future but every seat was taken and a few men were standing at the back. It was suffocating with so many people packed under the rafters, but once in, there was no hope of anyone's getting out unless a whole benchful slid off to the middle aisle!

To open the service, I announced a hymn, but of course there were no hymnals excepting the one I held. And I couldn't sing! I started, from force of habit, to indicate that the congregation should stand while they sang, then I remembered the low roof.

"Just remain seated," I announced. "I'll recite a verse of our hymn and then you sing it after me."

I read the words, then waved my arms in what I hoped was

some kind of time to keep the audience together as they sang,

> There's not a friend like the lowly Jesus,
> No, not one; no, not one.
> There's none can heal all our soul's diseases,
>
> . . . .

The people sang pretty well. "Diseases" came out "dee-zeezuz" with a good slur on the "dee," we flatted the high notes, dragged the time, gasped for breath in the wrong places, but we loved it and accomplished the entire hymn with gusto. Our first hymn was hardly finished when from the audience I heard a voice start up, "I am Thine O Lord, I have heard Thy voice." This service had a real Methodist flavor, with testimony by hymns at the very beginning!

During the singing I scanned the audience. Sam, the blacksmith, was there, a cud of tobacco in his cheek; I am sure he wished for his pail at times but he swallowed frequently and wiped his mouth on the sleeve of his blue shirt. On the first bench, right in front of me, sat "me'n him" who had offered to steal the planks for our benches. Flanking Jarv on each side were several of his cohorts and I wondered if they had come to disrupt the service. I looked for Mary, but I didn't see her although I felt her presence in the cleanliness of the room. Bessie was there and a real help on the singing. I spotted a few others I knew, some of them the merchants who had provided the crates and nail kegs, and some of them people whom I had met the previous Sunday night at Dr. McLean's church. Most of the people were the very common working folk and families who had driven several miles across the prairie.

From the first hymn to the benediction, it was a good service. I think we worshiped in the beauty of holiness, although we were lacking in the beauty of any other appointments. God was in Groton that night where the people sat on planks across nail kegs in the room over Dooley's Saloon.

As the crowd left that evening I heard Jarv proudly proclaiming, "Me'n him, we helped build this church!"

4

Prairie Preacher

THE days of terrific summer heat were upon us. The thermometer climbed into the nineties, hit a hundred and I thought it had stuck there irretrievably. Then it pushed its way to 107 degrees before it retreated to the coolness of the eighties. The nights gave little relief. However, we knew it was the golden sun that put the gold on the ripening wheat, which in turn, put gold into the wallets in the fall. We accepted the heat.

The days were too short for all I wanted to do. So much needed to be done all at once—or so I thought. Then too, prairie life was new to me; there was adventure and excitement in it; I didn't want to miss anything.

There was a feeling of unsettledness in this country. The prairie schooners pulled into Groton at intervals; a few remained, others headed on beyond the railroads. Most of the land in Brown County had already been filed upon under the Homestead Act of 1862 which granted one hundred sixty acres to any citizen who qualified for the grant and then "proved up" by living on the land and cultivating it for five years. This part of Dakota in the James River Valley was fertile soil easily worked up for wheat and good for cattle raising. By 1886 the earliest arrivals considered this "settled" territory!

At every opportunity I talked to people. That was one of the best ways to learn. Mr. Judd, the kindly gray-haired banker, knew to a penny the financial assets of each homesteader. He told me that a few of these men had more money than appearances indicated. But as was customary in a new country everything they earned went into more land and more stock to earn more money for more land and more stock. Barns came before homes and the needs of the stock often before the needs of the family. "But where there is one who makes money there are twenty who can barely live. Things are getting better, though." He pushed his steel-rimmed glasses back up on his nose confidently.

I talked with land agents, some of them tricky; and claim inspectors, most of them honest. I heard stories of claim jumping and illegal proving up; of doors and windows that were borrowed before the visit of the claim inspector and then returned the next day or hurried on to another homestead before the inspector arrived there. I liked best talking to the folks who lived on the earth itself. These settlers were young people; the old people stayed "back home." They were young people whose parents had homesteaded Ohio, Iowa and other midwest states, or they were young people who had come with one of the waves of migration from Scandinavia, Ireland or Scotland. This was a land of young people looking to the future, although a few of them had a past they were eager to escape.

Each day brought its new experiences. I saw the roots of the thick buffalo grass parted by the plow for the first time. Then I helped a family build its first sod house. In early August, Ernie and Mary Laws came from Iowa, eager to start proving up on their claim which was located in the general direction of the Perkins place. Ernie had been a farm hand back in Iowa, and Mary was the village milliner, a gay little blonde who chattered easily with all the new neighbors. When she and Ernie, who by contrast appeared slow and awkward, got to discussing their plans, I was convinced that Mary had some real brains tucked behind her curls. From the day of their arrival the young Laws were popular and while they were making the final arrangements to build, a group of settlers out their way decided to organize a "house raising" which I judged was always a gala event.

By eight o'clock on the morning of the appointed day the neighbors were arriving from miles around—whole families. They brought their implements and tools with them. Two plows turned up the sod in long strips which the men cut into rectangular slabs. The location for the house was staked out by another group and the corner uprights were put into place. A few more two-by-fours were set in between these uprights and the plate laid across. With the framework up, the sod slabs were then laid, one on top of the other as a mason lays bricks, the slabs of one layer laid over the cracks of the layer below; then the cracks were chinked with damp earth forming a thick, solid wall. Space was left for a door and two small windows. As soon as the frame was secure the carpenters moved to the roof. Rough boards were laid, sloping gently from the front of the house to the back, assuring drainage. Then the roof surface was covered with a sod thatch.

That day I was thankful for my farm experience for as I worked along with the other men they began to joke. "Wouldn't expect a sky pilot to know so much about the earth, would you?"

"How'd you learn to swing an ax at one of them preacher schools?"

"Hey, parson, kin you swear in Greek so as to make it polite?"

It was all in fun and would remain so as long as I could work as hard as they did. So I pushed a little harder.

"Why don't you men do something?" I chided. "A person would think this was an aid society the way you talk and forget to work."

The fact was that I had not done outdoor labor for months and was soft; by early afternoon I felt like dropping in my tracks but if anyone slowed up, it was going to be the other fellow first.

"You're sure a devil for work," said the boss of the day. "I'll come around and see if you kin swing your texts as well as your ax."

The men stopped only once during the day and that was for the noon meal. Home-smoked ham, eggs, coffee, biscuits. This was company fare on the prairie. The talking, joking, laughing were a greater treat than any elaborate menu could have provided. By four o'clock families began to leave for home. The women were quieter as they climbed into their wagons or onto their ponies. They knew it might be weary weeks before they would have such companionship again.

It was good to share the social gatherings of the people but I realized that I must know them individually before I could really serve them. For instance, one night when I was caught in a bad storm and had to spend the night at the Perkins house Mrs. Perkins told me about her first reaction to the great prairie. For the first six months her husband had tried to work in Aberdeen, while she stayed on the claim to satisfy the requirements of the law. She said she used to stand at the doorway and pray for a "miracle of shape."

" 'God, let just one thing rise up and have some shape!' I used to pray. Everything was so flat and stationary! Couldn't God raise up a tree? Couldn't He heave the earth into just the smallest hill? But the land lay there motionless and flat. The only thing that ever rose was the horizon, and when it began to weave you knew you better look away before you went mad. Back east in Wisconsin I used to be alone but there it's different. Here it isn't so much that you *are* alone as that you *feel* yourself alone." After a little pause she added, "But if you live it out long enough you come to like it."

That night I thanked the Lord for the memory of trees, the companionship of the forest, the lap of the waters of the Bay which still sounded in my ears. And I asked him to show me how to bring to these people that more abundant life which He had in store for them. Before I fell asleep my sermon for Sunday came to me, as all good sermons do, from the needs of the people. Unconsciously the words of the song were going through my mind,

> No, never alone.
> No, never alone.
> He promised never to leave me,
> Never to leave me alone.

I would tell the story of God's promise to Jacob and my text would be, "Behold, I am with thee, and will keep thee in all places whither thou goest . . . I will not leave thee. . . ."

I was encouraged by the number of requests to come out to some home where there was illness, or where a baby had been born, or where plans for a community gathering were under way. Dr. McLean was especially busy that summer because of the many hours he was putting into plans for the proposed Presbyterian college. I was usually free to go where I was needed at a moment's notice. Sometimes if I heard of a family where I thought I might be of help I went without an invitation, usually with happy results, but sometimes the reception was a little dubious. One of these visits was to the Quiggs family. I heard about them in the General Store which seemed to be the clearing house for general information. While purchasing some kerosene for the church lamps one Saturday afternoon I heard the assembled male loafers elaborating on the Quiggses; potato peelings strewn on the floor for carpeting, the brood sow and the cow brought into the house for warmth in winter, eight Quiggses unbathed from September until May. Mr. Quiggs had the habit of being "took" to his bed for months at a time and just as suddenly being "untook" when his fancy dictated. But he never worked; Mrs. Quiggs ran the place and the family.

One of the male gossipers turned to me. "You believe in prayer, Elder?"

"That I do."

"Might try it on Old Man Quiggs." Several loud guffaws. "Bet my plugga tobaccer 'gainst yer alpacky coat you can't pray him into liveliness."

In those days, when I was addressed as Elder I never was sure whether it was a mark of respect or a jab at my youth, but it always made me realize that something was expected of me. I decided to look in on the Quiggses the first time I was out their way.

It was not long before the opportunity presented itself. As I approached their shanty I heard shrill voices screaming at one another, and above them all a female siren. Then a barking dog announced my arrival. When I appeared at the door children scampered from the middle of the room but watched me from behind chairs and cupboards. In one end of the room Mrs. Quiggs was churning.

"C'm in and set. I cain't stop now; I'm about ter git butter. You kin take some buttermilk home with you."

Continuing to churn with one hand my hostess used the other one to shoo some chickens off a chair so I could sit on it.

"You're the preacher, ain't you? I heard tell that the Methodists brought in a young chap to start a church. Hope you're gittin' on well."

I started to thank her for her interest but before I could speak she was indicating a far corner of the room where her husband was lying on what was supposed to be a bed.

"He's took," she announced.

One of the little girls, perhaps four years old, although thin and puny for her years, came over by my chair and stood staring at me. I am sure I have never seen such dirt as was on that little girl; her hair was a dark, matted mass, but I had a feeling that in its natural condition it would be soft auburn ringlets. It was the child's eyes that held me—enormous brown depths that seemed lighted by some hidden fire.

"That's Delsie," said her mother. "Delsie's not quite right. She ain't lively like the others and sometimes she even goes and sets over there by her Pa as if she liked it."

Delsie stood there, her eyes fastened on me; she didn't smile, she didn't move, she didn't speak; she just looked.

Suddenly there was a commotion by the kitchen table as one of the other children knocked over a pan of green beans. Mrs. Quiggs hurried over to administer punishment but the culprit rushed out doors, his mother tossing harsh words after him. I think if I had not been there something more substantial might have followed him.

During this absence of her mother, Delsie walked a little closer and put one hand in mine; then she continued to stand. Again my attempt at conversation was thwarted—this time by the cat which had hitherto been peacefully sleeping on the kitchen table. When it was awakened by the commotion of the spilled beans it gave one frightened leap and landed right in the uncovered churn.

I jumped up to rescue the cat but Mrs. Quiggs, as if powered by a high voltage electric current, sprang back to the churn, grabbed the cat by the nape of the neck in her left hand, and with her right hand scraped the buttermilk down the sides of the dripping creature back into the churn. She threw the bedraggled cat out the door after the children, sat down and resumed her churning.

"It'll all come out in the buttermilk," she remarked complacently.

The situation had about got the best of me but I managed to stay long enough to approach the bedside of Mr. Quiggs and ask about his condition and promise to return before too long. It was a pretty weak pastoral call and I left without prayer—or buttermilk. As I turned the buggy away from the house I saw Delsie standing in the doorway so I waved her good-by and I thought I detected a tiny smile as she limply waved back.

Driving home I tried to figure out Delsie. I was sure her condition was not a matter of "not being all there," but I didn't know how to explain it. Then I began to chuckle over the buttermilk experience. After all, Mrs. Quiggs had quite an adequate philosophy. Inconveniences, troubles, catastrophes—they all do have a way of working themselves out. They do all come out in the buttermilk!

That first summer Dr. McLean was a continual source of inspiration. An occasional drive into the country with him was a rare treat; he raised my sights from the immediate problems around me to a longer range. One day I accompanied him into the country where he visited a family I did not know. Their son had gotten into some kind of a scrape and had been sent to jail.

"Hyde, the church is falling down with the young people. What are we doing for them in Groton? Why are we Presbyterians having to struggle so hard to start a college? Why are you Methodists having a hard time at Mitchell getting Dakota Wesleyan underwritten? Where are we going to get preachers for our new churches? What are we doing to produce Christian young folks to become businessmen and politicians? That's our problem, to awaken the people to their responsibilities."

Unexpectedly he stopped his horse, climbed out of the buggy and began to dig around in the dirt. His prairie-trained eye had noticed a white point reflecting the sunlight. In a few minutes he had unearthed a pair of buffalo horns, bleached white in the sun and then partly buried in the dirt through the years.

"We don't find good ones like these very often; mostly they've been picked up and sold and the poorer ones go for fertilizer. You'll see people bringing them in for shipment this fall. A man could get fifty cents for a specimen as good as this. These horns should teach us a lesson. Fifteen years ago buffalo roamed this land by the thousands, but they're gone now. We used poor judgment. The Indians roamed here, too, and we made enemies of them. Massacres and wars. We used poor judgment there. It would be a great thing, Hyde, if we would bring the judgment of the Lord into the judgment halls of this state—for we will be a state before long. We lost out last year because the Democrats in Washington wanted only one Dakota—they were afraid of two extra Republican senators if the Territory came in as two states. Poor judgment again."

I realized the truth in what he had said about our not doing much for the young people in our town. I admitted to myself that I just wasn't adequate for all the jobs that should be done. Minnie would be a big help if only she were here with me. She had a way with girls—and boys, too! Maybe when winter came and I couldn't spend so much time getting acquainted in the country I could do more for the young people in Groton. But for the summer I knew that my big job was visiting the people.

One afternoon as I was returning from a service at the Perkins house I cut across the prairie at a different angle from my usual route and came upon a scene that saddened me. At some time there had evidently been a sod house here. The thatched roof had fallen in and the sod walls, encouraged by the rain and the wind, had tumbled inward forming a mound. The prairie grass had licked its way to the base of the walls, then had grabbed footing inch by inch up the sides. A great green grave holding the remains of Hope. Smaller hillocks, which I took to have been a cattle shelter and a root cellar, stood as head and foot stones but carried no dates and no epitaphs.

The experience had left me with a haunting depression and that evening at supper I told the Johnsons about it.

"It was the Wilsons," Mama Johnson said the name simply but with feeling.

Mr. Johnson wiped his mustache very deliberately as if to gain time to organize his words. "We loved them. Mama and Bessie especially, because of the children."

Between them they told me that the Orville Wilsons had been a young couple; she was fairylike as if she could walk on air, and he was handsome, clean cut, but not vigorous. Orville had been a clerk in a railroad office back in Ohio when the doctors told him they suspected consumption; that he should leave his desk work and take up something outdoors. So they sold everything they had accumulated in ten years of married life, joined a western migration group and eventually reached Groton. Their resources were soon exhausted and because of Orville's health their claim was slow in its development. Trips to town became less frequent; usually some neighbor did a little shopping for them leaving the purchases at some appointed place for Orville to pick up. Their shanty was isolated. With the work of summer no one noticed how long the intervals had become between any news of the Wilsons.

One day the land inspector came to town to report to the doctor that he was needed at the Wilsons. Not wanting to make the trip alone Doc asked Bessie to ride out with him. They found Orville so weak that he had to rest after crossing the tiny sod room. Daisy, his wife, sat on the edge of their straw mattress, staring into space and apparently unconcerned about the family around her. She was holding a pair of worn-out baby booties and on the table were two little shirts and a faded baby dress. It was evident that she was expecting another baby. Her two children, a little girl about five and a boy, perhaps two years old, were pathetic, unkempt and starving.

"We brought them home," said Mr. Johnson, as if it were the only natural thing to do.

Bessie took up the story. "The doctor said we'd better get them both to the hospital as soon as possible. The nearest hospital was in Aberdeen, twenty miles away. We put blankets in the back of Miller's democrat to make it easy for Daisy to ride. Orville was so weak we had to prop him in the front seat for the long drive. The town people took up a collection. Three days later the baby was born dead. But Daisy won her way back slowly. They stayed on in Aberdeen and by the end of the year Orville was able to take some work with the forestry service and Daisy went back to schoolteaching. We had the children here for six months. We almost felt they were ours."

These wonderful Johnsons!

That night, I pondered the question, "Was the mound on the prairie a grave to lost Hope or a milestone on Life's highway?" The prairie posed many questions and I earnestly sought to find their answers.

Preaching services took on added meaning with each Sunday. The Lord had much to say to these people and how patient He was with me as I fumblingly tried to say it. I realized over and over again that He was teaching me more than I was yet able to teach them.

During these weeks I often spoke of the time when we would have our new church, and I was surprised that I seemed to be the only person thinking in such concrete terms. They thought of a church as something in the vague and distant future. I was hard put to "bide my time" as one of our old Scotch neighbors used to say. I could see the church as plainly as the early settlers saw mirages as they came across the prairie. Many times a wagon train of settlers would see an entire city in the distance, tall buildings, streets, trees and flowers, even a lake near by, where actually only the bare prairie existed. But we would make this mirage a reality; with a word here, and a word there, I would plant the idea in the minds of the people. As harvest time approached I reminded myself that the wheat seed had been planted months before. It was still planting time for the seeds for a church; more time and more work were needed before we reaped.

But I was impatient. I wanted more hours in the day, more days in the week, more miles covered, more people visited. Life was wonderful, wonderful! I began to get up earlier; I never needed much sleep so I pushed five o'clock back to four o'clock. I read late into the night. I worked in a feverish excitement I could hardly control.

Then one morning the smell of baking bread lured me into the kitchen where Mrs. Johnson was at work. She was just taking six loaves out of the oven, big, well-rounded and evenly-browned loaves.

"They're real works of art, Mother Johnson," I said.

"Now you just sit down and I'll cut a nice fresh heel for you." She knew my weakness. With a sharp knife she cut the crunchy crust and went to the cupboard for a plate and some butter, chatting along as she worked.

"Breadmaking is good for the soul. You can have a good yeast and well-ground flour but you can spoil your bread if you try to hurry it. Take this baking, the bread turned out a lot better than last week when I tried to get it out in time to go early to Aid. Then it was a little heavy. It's got to have just so long to rise— twice, mind you—and so long to bake or it isn't fit to eat."

"H'm," I said.

"Maybe a little more coffee with it?" she asked, and without waiting for an answer she was pouring it out of the never-empty pot. As she set the pot back on the stove she asked casually, "Will, do you read your Bible?"

I looked up quickly. That was an odd question. She knew I did. Then I saw the twinkle in her eye.

"Well, son, there's something in it about 'he that hath ears to hear, let him hear.' Now whoever thought I'd be making a sermon—and to a preacher at that."

So Mrs. Johnson had read my impatience. I went to my room. And to my knees. "God, put a bit in my mouth and hold me back when I want to take the reins and run. Keep me from the sin of impatience." It was not an eloquent prayer but I was to repeat it many times in the days to come. I needed to learn to work with God and not run ahead of Him. "In all thy ways acknowledge Him, and he will direct thy paths."

August. My first Dakota harvest season was over. A good rainfall during the summer of 1886 made a bountiful harvest. Tired bodies and worried faces relaxed with the knowledge that there would be food for the winter and seed for another spring. Maybe a new thatch roof, or even fresh whitewash for the inside of some plastered shanty; or for the more prosperous, the possibility of a "real" house. A bank account here and there. I could share something of the people's happiness but not all of it because I had never yet experienced a bad season with its attendant horrors.

Fall was coming. And so was the Annual Conference of ministers to be held in October—three hundred miles away—at Watertown. Throughout the summer I had continued my studies which would eventually qualify me as a full-fledged minister. While I was in college I had taken my examination and had been ordained a deacon. That examination covered my religious experience but it did not go into theology. "Deacon" was my official status now. The Methodist Conference had a two-year course of study to prepare a deacon to become a minister. Also there was the regulation that a preacher had to become a member of a Conference before he could perform certain ministerial duties. As a deacon I could not administer baptism nor officiate at weddings and could only assist at the Lord's Supper. It was necessary that I attend the Conference to be received into it. But how? Three hundred miles and I had no money.

Depending on how I looked at it I could figure my first three months in Dakota were a financial success or a financial failure. My first lesson in church finance had come the morning after the first service in the G.A.R. hall. I had met one of my future parishioners who gave me a bit of advice.

"Elder," he began, "I was up and heard you last night. It was a good service. But you made one serious mistake."

"Thank you, sir," I replied. "You know I'm a beginner in this business. I'll appreciate your suggestions."

"Well, Elder, we all expected you to take up an offering when you got through preaching. You never mentioned it. That was your first mistake."

"Thank you again, sir, I'll make you a pledge here and now— I will never make the same mistake again as long as I live!"

The next Sunday evening I told this incident from the pulpit. It opened an easy way to let the people know I would welcome whatever they chose to give. For myself, I needed only enough to pay my board and room and the few necessities of life. But the church would have some expenses to meet from time to time.

I kept an accurate account of every dime I received from the three church groups to which I preached. Above my room and board, at the end of the three months I had exactly three dollars. One dollar a month! That is why the expense of going to the Conference began to press me. I knew I would go—but the "how" was one of the "impossibles" that I was here to solve. And as usual God did the solving for me, working through others.

Two nights before I would have to leave for Watertown I returned to my room. In my mind I was raising the question of using the remainder of the money given to me before I left Belleville, but I hesitated to do this because I had told myself that this money would be used for the church work and not for me personally. I was still undecided when I entered the house and found one of the businessmen of Groton waiting to see me. He handed me an envelope. "Some of us just took it on ourselves to ask the townsfolk to chip in a little. You can't do your job right unless you go. We want you located here in Groton as an official member of the Conference so we figured we better

help get you to the meeting. We hope they will send you back."
The envelope contained twenty-five dollars and thirty-two
cents.

At Conference I would see Dr. Traveller again. During the
summer he had dropped in on me once between trains. At that
time I confessed to him that I had no official church members
yet.

"No members, but a lot of sinners," he remarked. "They'll
make good Methodists if you get them converted. That's why
you're here."

At Conference I would meet other preachers who were just
names to me now. One also meets missionaries and hears, first
hand, their thrilling stories; he listens to the reports of all
churches in the state; and last, but far from least in importance,
the appointments for the coming year are made at Conference.
Each man's fate hangs in the balance as that final moment
arrives. At Conference preachers are feasted and feted; they are
the "visitors" for whom the fatted calf is slaughtered. In fact,
Conference is the high point of the year in the eyes of every
Methodist minister.

So I went to my first Conference in the United States. It was
pure exultation. Two days were filled with speeches and reports
from the foreign field, the home field, then from the local
churches. For these latter reports the secretary would call the
name of a church and the preacher or some appointed official
would rise and give a statistical report of the progress of the
church during the past year.

I was at the bottom of the list, the newest man in the area,
not even a member of the Conference yet. I listened to the other
reports: Sioux Falls, Watertown, Yankton; an impressive list of
new buildings, additions and converts. Finally, it was my turn. I
stood up.

"My name is W. J. Hyde. I have been in Dakota since June.
We have three Societies in Brown County (I followed John
Wesley's custom of reporting small groups as Societies until
they were large enough to be called churches), the largest at

Groton. There I can report five members, two men and three women and they are all on the official board."

I sat down. The Conference broke into shouts of laughter.

Bishop Thomas Bowman—the first Bishop I ever laid eyes on—rose. "My boy, that is the most unusual Conference report I ever heard in my life." And he was an elderly man.

I received a unanimous vote into the Conference which allocated one hundred dollars annually for missionary work at Groton. They advanced me twenty-five dollars to carry me through the next months.

I stepped off the train at Groton for the second time in four months. Groton had not changed but I had. I was reminded of our kitchen door back home; there were perhaps fifty marks, each scratch indicating how much one of us youngsters had grown since last measuring day. We were seldom conscious of our growth until we looked at the mark—a half inch, an inch— but we actually felt taller after the measurements were recorded. I measured myself against the June day I had first stepped into this community: I had grown in my understanding of people; I had grown in my sympathy for others; I had grown in my knowledge of the country and its effects upon the inhabitants; I had come to realize that there was infinitely more to know that I would ever learn; I had come to the knowledge that God was indeed gracious to entrust his work to a blundering young upstart like myself. I paused momentarily while now, in October, I recalled the last words Dr. Traveller had spoken to me as his train pulled away that Saturday in June, "Dig or die, Brother Hyde." I was prepared to dig for another year.

Again in my study at home I itemized my needs: a horse, a wife, a church, and the most immediate need was the horse. During the summer my work had been hampered because I did not own my own horse. Mr. Johnson was exceedingly liberal with his; others in the community loaned me their horses; I rented ponies at times from the stable. But to make the coming year count as much as possible I needed a horse.

At the edge of town there was a sales barn. Every few weeks

wild horses from the prairie were brought in for sale. I often visited the corrals, studying the horses, watching the habits of unbroken animals, fascinated with the way the cowboys handled them. In fact, watching horses was part of my recreation.

Having made the decision that I had to have a horse in order to do the Lord's work, I went to the sales barn to look over a new bunch of wild animals recently brought in. There were a dozen or more, all beautiful, branded horses. I selected one which I judged to be four or five years old, brown with white stripings. His name would be Prince.

"How much do you want for this fellow?"

"One hundred dollars. Cash deal."

"I'll take him if you will come to the bank with me while we complete the transaction."

Business is much like preaching: too many words cloud the issue. Minnie had often told me that I could use a few more words at times, "just to ease things along," but that way of doing never came naturally for me. I liked to get to the point.

The banker, Mr. Judd, was a member of the Presbyterian Church. I told him I had just bought a horse for one hundred dollars. "But," I hastened to add, "it is a cash deal and I do not have a cent of money."

He looked over his steel-rimmed glasses.

"Well, what do you want to do about it?"

"I would appreciate it if you would pay this man the one hundred dollars." It sounded a little more brash than I had expected.

The banker hesitated scarcely a moment. "Such procedure is somewhat outside our business regulations. But give me your personal note and a mortgage on the horse."

"And if the horse dies tomorrow the mortgage will still be settled," I said.

"I am sure of that. You understand I'm doing this both for you and for what you represent, something much bigger than any individual. The Methodist denomination doesn't want you to fall down, and neither do we."

The man got his hundred dollars. I got something more valuable—the realization that the church I represented gave me a standing in the community I would not otherwise possess. It was good that I learned this lesson early in my ministry.

I now owned the horse. But what good was a horse without a buggy?

Across the way was a dealer in buggies. Within the hour I was looking over his display. "Are you interested in a buggy?" He smiled and I grinned a little sheepishly.

"Well, I've bought a horse, so I suppose I need a buggy."

"I know you got a horse, I heard about the deal already. Your credit is good here, too. I'll make a special bargain with you because you do a sort of special work. A man bought a buggy here some time ago and paid several installments on it but was unable to finish the payments. You can have the buggy for what is still due on it." I signed the note.

I now owned a horse and buggy, but what good were they without harness? That afternoon I went to the harness shop and told the owner my plight. "I won't see you stuck," he laughed; "go over there and pick out some harness for your horse."

I still needed one more thing—someone to share my joy. So I went home and got Bessie to come inspect the half-day's work.

"What are you going to do with them now?" she inquired. "Did you ever break in a horse?"

I realized that although I had handled horses since I was a youngster I had never broken a horse to driving.

"No, but I guess we can."

We climbed into the buggy and the horse took off. We drove twelve miles over the prairie that afternoon without one difficult moment. Driving the horse proved as easy as driving the bargain to get him.

That fall I worked out a schedule for myself. Mornings I devoted to study. There was still that two-year Conference course to complete and take an examination on. There were sermons to prepare, three each Sunday, and I did not repeat the same sermon three times a day. By this time I also had a Sunday School established in connection with each preaching place. Further, I needed the stimulation of books, those great minds and person-alities made available for all men during all time. So I took up Dr. McLean's offer to borrow liberally from his library. Occa-sionally I allowed myself the luxury of buying a new book so that I could keep abreast the thinking of the best men in the country. Afternoons and evenings I gave to calls in my boundary-less parish and to church meetings of various kinds. Except for emergencies I tried to adhere to this routine. Sometimes I wondered if emergencies were not more routine than routine itself!

Before winter set in I had at least a slight acquaintance with every settler within driving distance of Groton. Calls for the services of a preacher became increasingly frequent. Sometimes it was illness in a family or death in a little sod house. Many nights I sat beside the bedside of someone whom the doctor had given up and for whom love and prayer were the only cords that could hold him to this earth. Both cords pull strong and frequently I walked out under the paling morning stars knowing I had witnessed the miracle of returning life.

Many nights I sat up with the body of some neighbor whose soul had crossed another frontier into a land where there would be no more night or sorrow or sighing. These experiences were a test of my own faith as well as a test of my ability to be of help to a person struggling with sorrow. A man doesn't just mouth words when he is face to face with the elemental facts of life.

There was the time I sat up with Bert Uhlam's body hoping that Molly, his pretty dark-haired Irish wife, would let her pent-up grief break and get some rest. But she sat bolt upright on a hard-seated chair. Attempts at conversation failed. Finally, about two o'clock in the morning I said to her, "Molly, you aren't playing fair. You are not giving God a chance."

She turned on me with such anger as I have seldom seen.

"Give God a chance! What chance does He deserve—except the one He took? He has stolen Bert from me without giving *him* a chance! He doesn't need Bert as much as I do. God's got millions of people but Bert was all I had. God gets him for eternity but I had him only three short years. I hope God is happy up in His golden heaven. If He had to live in a sod shack alone He'd know how much I need Bert."

"Molly, God did not take Bert."

"He didn't? Well, I would like to know who did then. It wasn't the devil. Bert was too good a man for the devil. Only God would want a man like Bert."

"That's right. God would want a man like Bert. But God needs him here on earth as much—maybe more than He needs him in heaven."

"Then why didn't He leave him here?"

"Molly, come over here and sit where you and Bert and God and I can talk this out."

She hesitated.

"You don't have the reputation of letting people down," I said.

She pulled her chair over nearer to the bed.

"This is the way I look at it, Molly. Bert loved horses, and he liked them full of life. He handled them well but he always wanted horses that were a little too full of life for the average man to handle. Spot and Spray were a good team but they shied easily. Do you hold that against God?"

She didn't answer.

"Bert used harness that was not good. He had mended it several times, himself. So when the team was frightened and bolted the harness broke in one of the mended places. Do you hold that against God?"

She spoke suspiciously, "Do you hold it against Bert?"

"No, I don't. He'd done an honest job but there was a weakness in it that he didn't know about. So he was thrown out of the wagon and died from the injuries."

"Other people have been thrown farther than he was, and they didn't die. Why didn't God save him?"

"Molly, what kind of a God would it be who ran around saying, 'I will put soft ground under this man and save him,' or

'I will put the wagon seat where this man will land on it and break his back'?"

"He takes care of the sparrows—they say."

"And he takes care of us. But that does not mean we are kept out of all harm. Even the sparrows battle the storms and die in the blizzards. But He cares for them. The weak harness, the frisky team, whatever it was that frightened them—those things are a part of the daily hazards of life. Hazards are all around us. We use our best intelligence and avoid most of them. But sometimes our best intelligence and our best intent are not enough and the hazard overtakes us. It is like a person running from an approaching storm; sometimes the rain starts before he reaches shelter."

All Molly answered was, "Bert and I drove five miles in a pelting rain one day just to go to a party. We had—good times—together." It was the first time she showed the least sign of emotion—other than anger at God.

I went on, "Now I look at it this way. God has made a good world. And God has made fairly smart people. But because both the world and the people are not perfect there are mishaps. Disease—God does not send it. His part is to help us use all our resources to fight the evil combinations that make disease. God does not manufacture tragedy. And when it comes he tries to reach us, to help us through it. God works for the good. He is working tonight to help you find some way to go on living a beautiful life without Bert. God is nearest when He is needed most. Would you like to speak to Him now?"

Her voice was a bare whisper. "You do it."

So we prayed. Molly's head went down to the edge of the bed. She cried those silent tears that are the harbinger of calm. After a little while she looked up at me.

"Do you honestly believe what you have said—God does not send death to punish us or show His greatness or something?"

"I honestly believe it."

"Why doesn't someone tell us that sooner? I never heard it before. Lots of people don't know it yet."

"I've dedicated my life to telling people about a God of love, a Father who does for His children far more than any earthly father would—or could—do for his family. God could use your life in His work too."

"Mine? What could He use me for?"

We talked. We talked about Sunday School teaching; about caring for foundling children. We talked about missionary work; and about nursing. We talked about the effect of Christian homes in a community. We talked for hours.

As morning breathed softly on the little window in the sod house Molly got up to turn out her kerosene lamp. For the first time she looked a long, full look at Bert. The look was prompted by something deeper than courage.

"I loved him. And I don't hate God like I did before."

She moved around the room. We heard hoof beats in the distance, and I knew that a neighbor, the nearest one four miles away, was coming to do the morning chores for Molly. I knew some of the women who had helped her during the evening would return. So I climbed into my buggy and the horse took me home while I wondered what should be the next move to help Molly.

One morning, soon after my return from Conference, I was sitting at my desk studying when Mrs. Johnson knocked on the door.

"I'm sorry to interrupt you, but there are some people here and they say they have to see you. They can't let me give you the message."

I glanced out the window. There was a hayrack to which was harnessed a mule and a horse. That gave me a clue to the financial status of my visitors but not to their mission. I hurried downstairs. Sitting bolt upright on the edges of their chairs I found a man of about sixty, a woman at least thirty years younger, and four individuals of an older generation.

The man stated their business directly.

"I want to be married."

He then indicated the other people, "That's my ma and pa,

and them's her ma and pa. They all live with us so we thought we might as well all come along. Well, let's get at it. Stand up, Stelly, and let the preacher do his job." With all his gruffness he didn't sound unkind.

"Sit down a minute, please," I said, "I'll get my book of discipline and a wedding certificate."

I was glad to have a moment in my room to collect myself. I had always heard that the bridegroom was the one who was nervous at a wedding, but this time it was the preacher. I finally found my book but my fingers were all thumbs; as I tried to locate the wedding ceremony the pages stuck together. "Get ahold of yourself, Brother Hyde," I admonished myself. "All you have to do is read the words!" But I knew that marriage was more than reading and repeating words. It was the solemnity of the occasion, even under crude conditions, that affected me. "You are doing this in the name of the Church. Do it right."

I took my book and returned to the parlor. The couple to be married were already standing by the bay window. The groom's elderly mother rocked in the platform rocker which squeaked a little with gentle regularity, furnishing the music for the occasion. The ceremony was soon over and the bridegroom turned toward the aggregation of family.

"Let's be on our way. It'll be past dinner time when we get home."

While I signed the wedding certificate he fumbled in his pocket and brought out a half dollar which he laid on the table. His new wife eyed the piece of money momentarily then reached into a pocket someplace in the folds of her skirt.

"I wouldn't want you to think I married a cheapskate," and she laid a quarter on top of his half dollar. Then they all trooped out, climbed into the hayrack and drove home to dinner.

New Year's Day arrived, a good time to take stock of the accomplishments of my half year's work. The "Societies" which had been organized at the Perkins and the Owens sod houses had outgrown their original quarters. Each group had moved into the nearest schoolhouse, for the schools on the prairie followed the old New England pattern and were used for anything the people needed them for, from church to polling places and town meetings. By January we had added several Sunday School classes at each place and changed our schedule so that I met with the outlying churches on alternate Sunday mornings which gave me more time with each group.

In Groton we were outgrowing our quarters too. During the fall I held a two-week revival meeting with preaching every night except Saturdays. The revival service added about twenty new members, mostly young married couples. It was not a mass movement. How could it be when only one person at a time could walk down our aisle? We replaced most of the benches with chairs bought for twenty-five cents each. We also bought second-hand hymnals that cost us ten cents each. Joking about the "perpendicular stairway" continued but the room was usually filled to capacity so I knew the jibes were more in jest than in ridicule. Then when we put up a stove for the winter we were so cramped for space that it added real meaning to the matter I had been talking about for some time.

We had to have a church.

5

A Spire on the Horizon

BUILD a church at Groton? Was I crazy? They didn't say it in those words but I could see what was in their minds. "Sure, it would be fine but—" "Yes, sir, someday—" or "When we get around to it—" So I decided I would have to play the ignoble role of gadfly and prick the people just enough to get them into motion for I was convinced that a church was possible. In this country no one saw much money but the country was reflecting prosperity. Business was good: the land business, the cattle business, the implement business. Frame houses were replacing sod shanties. There was talk of another grain elevator. The newspapers referred to the "Dakota boom."

If everything else could boom, so could the church. When the merchants boasted of their increased turnover of stock I said to them, "Wonderful, wonderful! You'll be wanting to help with our new church, won't you?" When the real estate agents bragged about their fine business I rejoiced with them. "Nothing increases the value of land like a good honest town for people to live in and trade in. Right?"

"Right you are, Elder. Keep up your good work."

"Yes sir, we're going to expand it, too. About ready to build a new church. That'll help your business, won't it?"

They were all pretty well committed to the worth of the project before any organized move was made to raise funds. In the background I had been doing some correspondence with the Methodist Church Extension Society and they had agreed to pay half the cost of the new building if the people would raise the other half. The official board took heart when they received this news. They knew and I knew that our church members did not represent wealth; that the work the church was doing for the community would be the biggest selling point in raising money from non-Methodist people. These board members had pride. If the Methodist denomination could back them like that they would surely show what the folks of Dakota were made of.

The women took the first step. While the men were still figuring how many bushels of wheat equaled a thousand running board feet of lumber the women served a chicken dinner to raise money for the First Methodist Church of Groton. With the women behind the project success was practically assured.

There were some logical questions to be answered. The most frequent one was, "Do we need two churches in a town this size?" I always answered the questioner that we were not running in competition with the Presbyterians. One church could not till the ground for God any more than one farmer could farm all of Dakota Territory.

Or, "If we contribute to a Methodist Church maybe you'll think everybody ought to become Methodists."

I could laugh at this. "Do you think if I preached in a beautiful church I would be more narrow minded than I am up over the saloon?" And the people laughed too.

There was one thing about the Methodist Church that made it a good church for a frontier country. It had no confession to which a church member had to subscribe. That is one thing Dr. McLean had in mind when he told me on our first meeting that the Methodists could do some things the Presbyterians could not do. An individual could believe what he wanted to about the Lord's Supper, about the form of baptism, about the inspiration of the Scriptures; if he gave his life to God and desired to live after the teaching of Jesus he could be a Methodist.

So I answered questions. And I asked one, over and over again. "Has the Methodist Church justified its existence in the past six or eight months?" We took good will for granted, and set to work. We were democratic: we asked everyone for a contribution. The money began to come in, but not always on the first visit. One real estate man put me off several times, so I decided to let him wait, knowing he would finally convince himself. When I got back to him a few months later he gave me a pledge for five hundred dollars, the largest single pledge we received.

The winter busied us with work and buried us with snow. Sometimes the soft Chinook winds deceived us into thinking we were going to miss the severe cold of other winters. But Sally Jones, the town seamstress who could tell about the weather from her corns, always said, "Those winds, they're just weather breeders." And, sure enough, without warning the thermometer would start to drop as my Canada sent its worst blasts to sweep unobstructed over the prairie.

"It ain't nothin' like the winter of 1880," the old timers said with an air of superiority and recounted tales of animals and people found a few feet from their houses when the drifts melted in the spring.

We had our fun. Town people met in one another's parlors for parties. Country people had sociables in the schoolhouses. Young people, warmly booted and mufflered, piled into bobsleds with heated stones for footwarmers and heavy buffalo robes wrapped around them. What if the temperature did flirt with fifteen below zero?

Because Bessie was a gay and friendly person and because there was a piano in her home it was natural that the young folks of the community gravitated to the Johnsons. Doctor Burns, commonly called "Young Doc" because when he first came to town he had taken over the practice of an older man, dropped in frequently. Doc wasn't married and "batched it" with another young bachelor, Red Furham, who was a land inspector, out on the road a good deal and located in Groton only temporarily. Because I enjoyed the constant hospitality of the Johnson home I knew what a treat it was for Doc to stop in and enjoy the entire family. Doc and I discussed medicine at length, new vaccines, new treatments for consumption, new almost everything in the medical world where progress was being made at a rapid rate. Doc could have been a really great doctor, I think, if he had only put a little more energy into his practice, but he was never one to go far out of his way to treat these frontier settlers nor to sit up too late at night doing any study or research. Maybe he couldn't be called lazy, but certainly he was not consumed with ambition. But he was an easy conversationalist and well liked among the people in town.

Max Elder, a young schoolteacher, was another of the frequent visitors at the Johnsons. Max and Doc cooked up an idea that I should join them and the three of us would move into our own bachelor quarters. If they had been living at the Johnsons they might not have found the idea of a new location so intriguing. I certainly did not want to change my residence; where else would I ever find such good friends or consistently enjoy such good food? Doc and Elder tried renting a small house to share but Doc's irregular hours bothered Elder, and Elder's desire for quiet so that he could study toward his degree cramped Doc's style, so the combination soon broke up.

Of course a lot of girls were always in and out of the Johnson home. Bessie did most of her bookkeeping in the mornings so her afternoons and evenings were filled with some kind of an "Old Maids' Club" and church work for she was working in both the Presbyterian and Methodist churches. Our new and growing work captured her imagination and she gave countless hours to drilling the choir or planning with a group of young girls we were organizing into a club. Rather frequently Bessie would ride with me on some of the afternoon calls out across the prairie.

That winter it was the social occasions that made me realize more than ever my need for Minnie. I needed her for a wife and I needed her for the preacher's wife. Bessie and a young businessman were "interested in" each other. The three of us frequently sat around the Johnson living room, talking and singing. Vera, another of the young women who worked in the church, began to drop in frequently. Then she would invite us to her house a few nights later. Her mother, an excellent cook, often asked me to dinner. Vera was goodlooking in a dashing brunette fashion. She took a Sunday School class and needed frequent help with her lessons. Then one morning I came home to my room unexpectedly and heard a neighbor in the kitchen with Mrs. Johnson. "What does that flirt mean, setting her cap for the young preacher like that?" I stole out the door and the two women never realized they had given me a valuable hint.

Everyone knew there was a "girl I left behind" but I had tried not to bore them with constant talk about her. The next several times I was around Vera I let Minnie fill a good part of my conversation and was very soon rewarded by hearing Bessie recount, with great glee, that Vera had gone "completely daffy" over the new land agent. I was convinced that a minister needed a wife.

In January that winter I took out my first citizenship papers. Having always felt myself a citizen of the Territory, it seldom dawned on me that legally I was not. But I would be, as fast as the law allowed.

It was the evening that I got home from the trip to Aberdeen to file papers that I found Doc at the Johnsons and for the first time since I had known him he was really worked up over a case.

"Hyde, why couldn't you get your confounded old carcass here sooner? You choose the one day you could be of some use to get out of town."

The fact that Doc was "talking rough" made me know he was covering up his real feelings.

"What's the trouble?"

"It's little Delsie Quiggs. She's got rheumatic fever in that filthy hole her family lives in. I spent all night and a good part of the day out there—you better not come near me, no telling what you might catch. It's clear we've got to get the child out of that place. Her mother says that Delsie keeps asking for the 'Jesus man.' I suppose that's you."

"Hospital?" I asked.

"I don't know," Doc answered. "This will be a long siege. Rheumatic fever takes good care for months. I've been talking to the Johnsons and they would bring Delsie here only Mrs.

Johnson isn't too well this winter and I don't think it would be right. Bessie is willing to take care of Delsie but it would still put too much responsibility on Mrs. Johnson, I think."

"Who else is there?" I asked.

He shook his head. "We've tried to think of everyone. I don't think we could ever take care of the hospital expense at Aberdeen, even if we could get Delsie in there."

I had an inspiration. If it worked it would be the salvation of two people; if it failed we would have only lost a few hours and would work faster to make them up.

"Bessie!" I know I shouted loud enough to be heard around the block and she was only in the kitchen fixing a bite for me to eat. She came running into the living room.

"Bessie, you've got to go with Doc out to the Quiggs place and help move Delsie. Put on all your warm clothes; it's a cold night but I don't think it is going to storm. I don't know whether Mrs. Quiggs will object to our taking Delsie out of their house, but I don't think so. She seems almost afraid of the child. Use any argument you need to use."

"I'll go, but where are we going to take Delsie if we get her out?"

"You're to bring her to Molly Uhlam's house—I hope."

"What do you mean, Hyde?" the doctor broke in. "Molly doesn't know anything about this and you can't—"

"You may be right, Doc," I agreed; "the plan may not work, but I have a hunch it will. You take Bessie and everything you need to move Delsie and get right out to the Quiggs place. I'm starting for Molly's and I think we will be ready for you and Delsie when you arrive."

"I don't exactly get it but I won't wait to argue now," Doc said. "I'll be back to pick you up, Bessie, as soon as I can get a fresh team and some blankets."

Mrs. Johnson made me stop long enough to eat a big ham-and-egg sandwich and drink some hot coffee, then I was on my way to Molly's. The winter night was black which made the stars stand out like gold studs on deep velvet. It was winter cold but not bitter, so the ride was beautiful, eight white miles out across the prairie. As I pushed the horse at his best speed I also pushed my prayers straight through the stars to the listening ear of God and asked His guidance in this venture to help both Delsie and Molly.

As I neared Molly's house I realized that it might frighten her to have someone appear at her place in the middle of the night so for the last mile of the trip I whistled as loudly as I could, one hymn tune after another, so she'd know that it was a friendly visitor putting in at her port. Then I saw her light move past the windows so I knew she was up. As I climbed out of the buggy I heard Gyp, the dog, growling just inside the door, and then I heard Molly's quiet voice, "Be still, Gyp."

"Molly," I called out, "this is Hyde."

The iron bolt on the door was pushed back, then the door opened and Molly said, "Come in, Brother Hyde. Whatever is wrong that you're out this time of night?"

"I hope I didn't frighten you."

"You didn't. The first sound I heard was someone whistling 'What a Friend We Have in Jesus' so I decided it was no ordinary night prowler coming this way. But what is it?"

"Put the lamp down and sit there by the table, Molly, because I have a big favor to ask of you and it may take me a little while to explain it all. Did you ever know the Quiggs family?"

"I know a lot about them," she answered, "and I've seen Mrs. Quiggs. That was enough!" She said it jokingly rather than critically, but I knew the mental picture she probably had.

Then I told Molly about my one visit to the Quiggs family and the danger that little Delsie was facing now. I had to hurry the last part of my story before my courage failed me.

"Molly, I've come to ask you to take care of Delsie."

She looked at me till I thought her deep blue eyes would bore clear through me before she spoke. Then she said just one word.

"Why?"

"There are two reasons, Molly. I want Delsie's body to live

and I want your soul to live. You need someone who needs you.
All that love you had for Bert can't stay cooped up forever.
You've got to pass some of it on to someone."

"I wouldn't know what to do—"

"Doc'll take charge of the case and I'm sure Bessie will
help you as much as she can, but Delsie's recovery depends on
the love and care of one person who will live for nothing else
for the next few weeks. It won't be easy—"

"Who cares about that?" asked Molly with a little contempt
in her voice.

"I'll have to tell you, Molly, that I've sent for Delsie, and
Doc and Bessie should be here with her within an hour, if she
is still able to be moved. That doesn't commit you, though. If
you can't take her we will head right for town and work out
some other plan."

The future of two lives waited in the eternity of the next few
seconds.

"I'll do it," said Molly.

We went to work, built up the fire, rigged up another bed
frame out of some boards stored in the barn and then used some
heavy binding twine to weave rope springs. When Doc and
Bessie arrived with Delsie we were ready. Toward dawn I took
Bessie back to town and left Doc for a few more hours'
vigil.

During the next weeks we kept moving a steady stream of
food supplies, medicines, friendly visits. By spring it was not
unusual to find the two, Mollie and Delsie, playing games together or sitting on the grass talking. To our mixture of horror
and delight, the Quiggses showed no interest in Delsie's return
home.

"We got so many young ones under foot that it's kinda good
to have some of them clear out. Matt, he's gone to work, but we
don't know where he is. Her Pa misses Delsie sometimes but he
says it's one less to feed if anyone else wants to feed her." The
maternal in Mrs. Quiggs had been worn out, I sometimes
thought, in producing her brood.

"Leave Delsie with me through the summer, anyway," urged Molly, "and then we'll see."

The work of the church went on, at times slowed by the weather and at times speeded up with the excitement of the building project. We drew plans and plans. We got estimates. We discarded ideas, began again. Everyone seemed to remember something fine about his church back home and wanted to incorporate it into this one. I think I grew a little in diplomacy that winter.

When spring came we moved out of the G.A.R. hall and into a tent for our services. It was much better during the hot summer weather. Harvest came early that year. It always seemed to me, with a Canadian background, that wheat harvest came too early to make sense. The waving green grain so soon turned into a golden rustle, and harvest was on.

This was perhaps the most exciting harvest of my life in Dakota. It helped me harvest a church! As I watched the constant procession of wagons loaded with wheat pull up to the elevators I realized that here was the wealth of the country. On the side of every elevator was posted the market quotation for the day. As each man brought his wagon into the line waiting to unload he would hurriedly jump off the seat, look at the posted listing, then climb up and settle back to wait his turn, or perhaps stand, chewing a piece of straw as he talked over his harvest prospects with the other men.

I formed the habit of spending part of each day at the elevators. At times I joined in the conversation, especially if it took a turn toward what was good or bad in the community. Many times I jumped up on the wagon seat beside the owner and told the farmer that we were going to build a church in Groton, that the church would make the community a better place for him and his family. Everyone knew this was so true that not one man turned me down. They seldom gave less than five dollars; sometimes ten or twenty-five and several gave fifty dollars in cash or pledges. I had to work fast but I found I had the best product in the world to sell.

One morning I fell into conversation with a man whom I knew only by sight and by reputation; a man known to be a miser. After I talked to him a few minutes he pulled his wallet out of his pocket and handed me five dollars. "My old woman was a church member in Minnesota. It's for her."

Then his mellowed spirit suddenly hardened. Pointing with his corncob pipe to a wagon several feet removed from us, he said, "Young man, any money you git out of that customer over there, I'll double."

"What's his name?" I asked.

"O'Malley." He said it with a mixture of spite and delight.

I knew I was on the spot. I walked over to O'Malley's wagon, made some comment about the weather and climbed up on the seat beside him.

"I'm something of a stranger here," I said. "What's your idea of the country?"

He launched into as bragging a sales talk of eastern Dakota as I ever heard, ending, "What's your business, young man?"

"I am a preacher with the Methodist Church."

"Well, I'll be—" and he launched into another flow of language that was a masterpiece of its kind. I gathered that he did not fraternize with preachers as a daily occurrence. "What you settin' here by me for?" He paused.

"I am raising money for a new church in Groton." He did not explode but for a minute I was fearful. I continued, "I understand you're a good farmer and a good businessman. I was sure you would know a good investment when you saw one. A lot of your neighbors feel the same way you do about their community, so they're contributing to a church for it."

"Young man, do you see that critter sittin' over there on the wagon the third one in the second row?" It was the man I had just left. "Talk to him and I'll double whatever he does. Guess that's fair enough and then some!" He settled back, safe in the assurance that I would not trouble him again.

This kind of buck-passing was giving me a workout but it also had an element of sport. I walked back to the prospect. "Your friend will double whatever you do."

His jaw dropped. "Well, I'll be horn swaggled and tied for a colt. Did he say that?"

"That's what he said." I grinned. "But I didn't wait to get it in writing."

"I bet you didn't!" To my surprise the humor of the situation struck him more than the fact that he was being relieved of some money. "How do we figger this out now, Brother? I'm aiming to make him pay as high as I kin."

I climbed up and sat down beside him again.

"Let's see. You gave me five dollars. Then you said you would double his. He said he would double yours. Altogether you are going to pay me fifteen dollars. If he doubles that, it will be thirty for him. How about it?"

"That's pretty mixed up but if it means that ornery cuss has to dig up thirty dollars, it's a good way to figger. I'd like to see his face when he hears what he's stuck for."

"Come on along," I said.

"No sir, we ain't on speaking terms. We got a bet, goin' on two years now, that neither one'd be the first to speak to th' other. He cheated me one time." His fury spurted up.

I returned to the "party of the second part," and showed him fifteen dollars.

His face went from red to purple. He stood up and waved his fist in the air as he shouted to his prodding enemy, "You great big lunkhead you—" Then he stopped dead still. His arms dropped. He sagged onto the seat.

"Would you call that speakin' to him, parson?"

I hardly had time to assure him that I would consider he had spoken when the driver of the first wagon reached up over my shoulder and grabbed O'Malley by the hand. "Mike, we are speakin' agin'!"

"Shure and that's what me big mouth got me in for. Now I have to pay the bet as well as fergive you, and you know, Pete, as well as I do, that you were in the wrong." He began to get slightly worked up again.

"Mike, we will each pay half the bet and pay it to the preacher for his church."

"And how much is it costing me now?"

"I think it was thirty dollars before," I volunteered.

"Ye just wait, young man, till I git weighed in and I'll pay you out. But I think, parson, ye missed yer callin'. Ye would have made a land agent."

"Mr. O'Malley," I said, "this really went farther than I thought it would when I first spoke to you. If you feel it's not quite right, just say so and I'll call it all off."

The easily angered, hard-talking Irishman relaxed. "You did me a good deed, today, parson. Maybe a little more religion would help us all."

Two friends united and fifty-five dollars for the building fund —not a bad hour's work.

We continued to hold services in the tent while the building got under way. A frame structure, forty by forty-five feet, had been decided on. There would be a large room for worship; a smaller lecture room for prayer meetings; downstairs a kitchen, dining room and Sunday School rooms; for good measure, up under the eaves we finished a room, while we were at it, for any purpose it might be needed; and rising above it all a belfry with a spire. A stone foundation, of course.

Those stones! Eagerly the church members offered to contribute their services to the work of building. Just as eagerly I volunteered to get the stones. But whoever counted the number of stones in a foundation? It isn't just the stones that show above the ground, it is the tons and tons that are buried below the surface of the earth that count.

"Gotta go six foot down, below the frost line," said the contractor.

The nearest stones were twelve miles away, out across the prairie. I borrowed a horse to team with Prince, hitched them to an old wagon and we spent most of the summer (or so it seemed to me) under a blistering July sun. There never was a sun as hot as the Dakota sun of 1887. I was just stubborn enough to do the job myself after having offered to take it on but I was thankful it wasn't the walls of Jericho I had contracted for! By

October the foundation had begun to rise upon those stones and we had raised all but eight hundred dollars of our share to match the equal amount from the Extension Society.

Conference time again. My second one. The report this year was different from my first. We now had a church roll of fifty. We had a new building under way. I had received in salary, one hundred dollars from the Home Board and three hundred and seventy-five dollars in collections from the churches.

At Conference I thrilled to the reports of all the activities of the denomination—new churches, just like mine, being established; new missionaries sent to the foreign fields; the work under William Taylor in Africa had a great appeal to me. There he was at retirement age, after a spectacular ministry beginning with the Gold Rush and building the first church in San Francisco, now developing a whole chain of foreign mission stations. I looked over all the new books and allowed myself the luxury of buying three, and I renewed by subscription to *The Western Christian Advocate*. But under all these interests I kept wondering if I would be transferred to another circuit. I'd been in Groton more than a year and it was customary to move preachers often. But I wanted to stay to finish my church—and to have Minnie see it!

The last day of Conference arrived. I schooled myself to receive with Christian grace any appointment I was given.

"W. J. Hyde, Groton, Brown County."

Those were beautiful words. I could hardly wait for the final benediction; I wanted to get back home.

That winter a store was vacated which we promptly hired for a church until ours should be completed. Our membership kept growing. I held another revival meeting that year. It was not the highly emotional spree these meetings sometimes are. I determined when I first started my preaching that I would teach as I preached, and teaching is a slow job. But a series of meetings gives a minister a chance to work intensively and it keeps the church constantly in the minds and prayers of its members. It is the best way of working the field unto the harvest.

My letters to Minnie were full of church building. She wrote that she was sure she knew the location of every nail in the church. She shared our progress as eagerly as if she were with us. And in many ways, she was. When I drove the prairie alone, Minnie frequently was there giving me good advice. When I watched some woman shriveling under her prairie loneliness I would ask myself, "If that were Minnie what would I want someone to do to help her?" The answer was always a safe guide for me. When we had our church sociables I could see Minnie moving around among the people, her voice, her soft laugh, they exhilarated me and they haunted me. I wrote her that I would be home before the dedication of our church so that we could be married and together we would share the joy of our first accomplishment.

Almost feverishly we rushed toward the completion of the building, still carrying on all our services and other work. Finally it was near enough completion so that only the few last details and finishing up around the grounds remained to be done. I could go get Minnie and be back for the dedication.

That afternoon I took Prince and drove the twelve long miles to the rise of ground from which our foundation stones had come. I drove out alone to this place where my vision had so often urged me on to harder efforts—and more blisters. Arriving at the familiar spot Prince stopped of his own accord and I got out of the buggy. I was looking off toward the west. The Psalmist had once sung, "I will lift up mine eyes unto the hills." Deep joy must have prompted those words for hills are a natural symbol of stability and strength. Here I had no hills but I had the long, long view to the rim of the world where the sun set. To myself I repeated:

> So be my passing
> My task accomplished and the long day done,
> My wages taken, and in my heart
> Some late lark singing,
> Let me be gathered to the quiet west,
> The sundown beautiful and serene.

18657

Then I turned toward Groton and my eye scanned the skyline. Yes, there was a spire on the horizon! I was flooded with a sense of gratitude.

"I thank Thee, Father of Heaven and earth . . ."

6

The Preacher Takes a Wife

I WAS back in Belleville, Ontario, again. Two years is not a long time but enough changes can take place in that short span so that it takes a while to find your place again. Here was Albert, my youngest brother, now a husky high school fellow, taller than I. And Harry who had always been my closest pal had a girl and was too busy with his own work and courting to have much time with me. A new niece or nephew here and there in the homes of my married brothers and sisters. The Hydes were quite a clan by now!

And Minnie! She both had and hadn't changed. When she stood beside me she still came just to my eyebrows; her eyes still sparkled with concealed joy over amusing ideas that passed between the two of us; at other times they were calm with understanding and appreciation. It was hard to put a finger on the changes in her. There was a new confidence in her manner and a new poise. I noticed in her home that she had a casual way of easing her mother out of the kitchen for a rest or of assuring her father that the produce was ready for market whenever he wanted to start to town. When guests dropped in Minnie seemed to find it not too difficult to keep the conversation going or to help make plans for the church meetings to be held in the late summer. Yes, this was the same girl I had left behind, the same girl I had thought about and dreamed about for two years—only lovelier.

The days passed swiftly. I renewed acquaintances around Belleville, beginning with the members of our Hallelujah Band. Asa Vermilyea was doing well in his boot business and while I bought a pair of shoes from him we recalled the days when he helped put me through college and our Band, of which he was leader, covered the churches of the countryside. I found Willie Finkle who had been our tenor soloist busy with the music in one of the local churches, and Enos Farnsworth was in the east studying for the Methodist ministry.

"Now tell us about your work," each one would say and we would be off on stories of the prairie, politics, business, living conditions—the frontier held a fascination for everyone.

Afternoons, Mr. Grills let Minnie and me use Bird, his finest horse, to cover my old Smith Company route and visit with some of the families I used to serve during the summers. In practically every home we stopped in there was one question asked of Minnie over and over again, with slight variations. "How can you go so far from home and leave all your family?" The question disturbed me but it was good for me to hear it asked so frequently because it gave me a new realization of the sacrifice my girl was making to become my wife. Mrs. Fletcher even added, "You'll only know one person in the whole United States!"

Minnie flashed back, "But he's quite a person!"

Bless her soul, she never once mentioned the possible loneliness but instead always expressed such confidence in me that I actually felt capable of taking care of both of us—not realizing how much care she would take of the caretaker.

During this visit at home, in the few days before our wedding, I spent some of the most precious hours I ever had with my mother and father. I appreciated them much more now that I had been away for two years. I knew that hereafter my visits home would doubtless be separated by increasingly long intervals so I wanted to absorb all I could from these two wonderful parents. To them I owed a happy childhood and a fine religious background. I urged my folks to talk about their younger days: Father's life in London, his dissatisfaction with the Church of England, his early interest in the Wesleyan movement, his exhorting with the Salvation Army; Mother's girlhood when she was Sarah Watt London, brought up in a strict Scotch Presbyterian family. I saw the whole panorama of their lives: Old

World, New World, always in search of that indefinable "something better" for their children; land clearing in the wilds of Canada—how they regretted the custom of logging off only the biggest trees and then burning all the others to speed up the clearing process; their first log house; the succession of children— one left buried in England, one in a little Canadian cemetery and nine others crowding the house with work and laughter, problems and family love; their moves from one farm to another and then a final move into town so the children could have a good grade school and a high school; their constant activity in the work of the church. And running through the whole story was a great zest for living and loving.

Why shouldn't I be a happy person? While I was home on this visit I was impressed with the fact that I came naturally by a faith in the eternal care and goodness of God. All my life I had heard it preached and all my life I had seen it quietly demonstrated in our home. Sometimes when I was younger Ma would chide me a little, "Willie, you take everything so natural. You don't ever seem to be bothered when things go wrong. I hope you won't be like your Uncle Dan." Later I learned why Uncle Dan didn't worry—he just ran away from difficulties. But there is also a freedom from worry that comes from stepping out to meet difficulties and getting a grip on them before they get you in their clutches. It was this kind of assurance that I hoped to achieve.

With all the wedding preparations in the Grills household there was constant activity and a mere male sometimes felt in the way. Mr. Grills said he was glad he had a barn to escape to and get out of all this female fury. Every time any of the women sat down there was a hem to turn or a sleeve to adjust on Margaret's or Mattie's dress for the wedding. Minnie's had been finished before I arrived and was safely hanging in the closet upstairs, and I could not have even a peek at it until the day arrived or eternal bad luck would attend my bride.

Minnie had to give time to packing her trunk with countless hand-embroidered sheets, pillow cases, towels, aprons. We didn't have prospects of owning much furniture but I could see there would be gay touches to whatever kind of house we lived in.

As the wedding day drew near the activities in the kitchen increased. There were chickens to be dressed, beans to be baked and potatoes prepared for salad. And cakes? Margaret baked her special sunshine variety and Mattie made dripping pan cakes with fancy icings, always joking—"That'll fool 'em. The fancy icing will cover up the fact that the cakes are very ordinary." In reality nothing that Mattie did was ordinary. The neighbors followed the country custom of sending in cakes, each proud to provide the best sample of her specialty—angel foods, devil foods, marble cakes, pound cakes. The big pantry off the kitchen was a notable display of culinary art, alas! so soon to be demolished.

The house had to be spotless. I thought it was always so clean it shone, but I was told it was miserably dirty and with all those people coming! When I expressed the opinion that with a hundred people crowded into the house no one would be able to see if the far corners were clean or dirty, the answer I got was that I talked just like a man! Window panes had to glisten, every curtain had to be freshly laundered. A wedding, after all, is the biggest event not alone in the lives of two people but in the social calendar of a rural community where all events are dated in relation to births, weddings and deaths. Minnie moved through the excitement of which she was the center with a wonderful balance between walking in a dream and keeping her feet on the solid earth.

At last The Day arrived. July 4, 1888. In Canada we celebrated the date in royal style as Queen Victoria's birthday. In the United States we celebrated it as the nation's birthday. But for us—it was our wedding day. Mrs. Grills had arranged flowers to bank the bay window in the living room. Behind this bower the eye could catch the changing lights of the water of our beloved Bay of Quinte. In this setting Minnie and I repeated our vows after Brother Edwards, the Grills' family minister.

Minnie as a bride was beautiful, her dark hair and queenly

bearing accentuated by the pure white of her soft voile dress. Every detail of my bride's attire is indelibly stamped in my memory, although I had to learn the correct dressmaking words later. Besides, I've heard the wedding dress described many times. It had a wide yoke of alternate rows of lace insertion, line-narrow tucks, and embroidery; the billowing skirt repeated the pattern of the yoke; and full sleeves finished out the effect of sheer loveliness.

The Grillses carried out all the gracious acts of good hosts for a merry group of neighbors, and never once let the sorrow of sending a daughter so far from home mar the complete joy of the occasion.

When train time was approaching Minnie changed into her blue "going away" dress. Our trunks had already gone to the depot. We took our hand baggage and while all the neighbors called out their best wishes we climbed into my brother Dan's rig and he drove us into Belleville to catch the late train for Toronto—and points west.

We followed the route I had taken alone two summers before. How much more interesting this trip was with Minnie to share it; the colors were brighter, the clouds were more feathery, the hills more rolling, and the flat less monotonous. Companionship is an intensifier of beauty. For the first time in two years Minnie and I had time to talk over all those things that seem too insignificant to put into letters but which are very important in welding two lives together.

And so we reached Groton. Half the town was at the depot to meet us; most stores had closed so that everyone could turn out. It was a homecoming such as I had never anticipated. After all, how was I to know what to expect? This was the first time I had ever brought a wife, and a new one at that, into a parish. We were escorted to the Johnsons for a big dinner and a pantry shower for the preacher and his wife—jams, jellies, smoked ham, pickles, fresh bread, and a miscellany of kitchen utensils that Minnie knew how to appreciate in approved fashion.

Before I left for Canada the Johnsons had urged me to bring

Minnie into their home with me for the few weeks we would be in Groton, for although no announcement had been made of the fact, I knew that when Conference time came I would be transferred to some other town. Having been in Groton more than two years and having completed one good-sized job, I knew without being told that October would find us locating in some other place. Minnie and I appreciated the Johnsons' offer but we had decided that we wanted to start our married life alone. However, we felt it was rather foolish to try to rent a house and set up housekeeping for the short time we would be in Groton. So it came about that it was to a somewhat unusual location that I took my wife after our homecoming reception. We moved into the church! Our parishioners had had a good laugh about my plans but I think they approved because the men hurried to get the well sunk before I returned from Canada with Minnie. It may have been a church, but it was a brand new church and no place in the United States was as dear to me as this building. Our living quarters consisted of the extra room we had finished off under the eaves; it was furnished with Sunday School chairs and one of the tables from the dining room and a few other pieces of furniture supplied by friends. Mrs. Johnson and Bessie had even put curtains at the window and moved the bed and blue commode set from my bedroom to give the place a finishing touch. Our "parlor" for important guests was the ladies' parlor which was usually used by them on Aid Society day only. Our cooking was done on the stove in the church kitchen.

When we finally found ourselves at home alone we were tired. We sat down on our Sunday School chairs, folded our hands in proper school style, looked at each other and broke into a good laugh.

"I'll always have something to talk about when conversation gets dull," boasted Minnie. Then she added more seriously, "We'll be spending most of our lives in church, so we might as well get used to it."

Surprisingly enough we found our quarters very adequate. But then, we didn't have much time to spend at home. I do believe

every family I had ever visited invited us for dinner. The Mc-
Leans, the Perkinses, the Owens—life was a continuous celebration in which I now frequently took a back seat. Topics we had
never touched upon in my former visits consumed much of our
visiting time—clothes, babies, recipes, wallpaper and cooking
utensils. The preacher very definitely had a wife!

The remainder of the summer we were kept busy with finishing the details of the church and making plans for the dedication. We thought the building was beautiful with its clapboard
walls; tall, graceful cathedral windows; and the vestibule
mounted by the belfry, topped by the spire.

One evening soon after moving into our "home" Minnie stood
outside the church examining the basement wall.

"Anything wrong?" I inquired.

"No, I think it is beautiful, but I was just wondering which
of these stones raised the largest blisters." She turned to me
with mock seriousness. "I'm glad, Will, that you have a trade
you can fall back on. 'W. J. Hyde, stone hauler.' You know you
could someday be fired as a preacher. Sometimes I think you're
not entirely orthodox."

We were almost up to dedication Sunday but in one respect,
and only one, I was disappointed. The women had bought fine
carpeting for the aisles and pulpit, the pews were well varnished,
the hymnals had all been repaired; but every time I stepped into
the church I wondered how the battered old organ was going to
look when we moved it over. We had got used to it, worshiping
in the vacant store, but in this beautiful auditorium against the
lovely windows, how would that scratched and wheezy organ
look and sound? However, the people had responded so liberally
to every call for money that I hesitated to ask for another cent.

Finally, however, I got my courage to the point of calling a
meeting of the Building Committee and the Official Board,
and that night I learned a mighty important lesson. I found that
they had been wondering why *I* had not done something about
getting a new instrument! They were as embarrassed over the
old organ as I was but they hated to push the preacher. If I were

going to draw a moral from that meeting it would be, "Expect great things and great things happen." But the next day we were far too busy to moralize.

First thing in the morning the chairman of the board got busy and by noon he had enough money pledged to guarantee payments on a new instrument. So Minnie and I were sent to Aberdeen to see what the music store could do for us. When the manager heard about our new church and the two old buildings we had used while we were getting organized, he became enthusiastic about our plans and made us a very good offer—on a piano! Whoever dreamed of such a thing?

"Maybe we better dream a little more," was Minnie's response to my question.

We went back home a very elated pair and found it hard to wait the two days before the piano would arrive. It came on the noon way freight and it was Jarv who brought us word that it was being unloaded at the depot. We arranged to have it hauled immediately to the church where it stood at the bottom of the steps for uncrating.

"I'm glad it came during the noon hour," said Jarv as he began to pull nails and loosen boards with great care so that nothing could scratch the instrument.

It took no time for a crowd to collect and everyone had an admiring word to say.

" 'pon my soul, if it isn't mahogany!"

I thought I recognized the voice but turned quickly. I was right. Here was Mary who had helped me clean the room up over the saloon for our first church service. I tried not to show surprise as she continued, "My old man used to do some cabinet work and he thought mahogany was wonderful to work on. He was always going to make me a mahogany table. But then he died."

The noise of removing the crate made any comment from me impossible. Then Mary spoke again, "Brother Hyde, don't you think I ought to get a soft rag and polish up that piano?"

"That would be fine, Mary. Maybe Mrs. Hyde has one."

While some of the men carried the crate out back of the church to make kindling for winter fires Jarv stood and looked at the piano.

"Say, Reverend Hyde, remember the day we carried the planks up over the saloon to make benches? We've done things since then. You know, I've been thinking a lot this last year. Say, did you know I've worked for the elevator for six months straight? Pretty good, eh? But if a feller don't want to do cheap work all the time, how does he go about bein' something different?"

"That's a mighty important question, Jarv. Come on up this evening and we'll talk awhile."

"Gorsh, I mean golly . . . I mean . . . Oh pshaw, sure I'll come up. I ain't terrible busy."

I made a mental note to ask Minnie to make a chocolate cake. Minnie was a good cook and cake does wonders in breaking down a boy's self-consciousness.

By this time we were ready to carry the piano into the church. Four husky young men picked it up and moved carefully up the steps, through the doorway, down the aisle and finally set it in position in the choir loft. Mary appeared from the back room with her cleaning rag and lovingly wiped the beautiful finish till it reflected the light to her satisfaction.

Then everyone just stood there waiting for something to complete the occasion. Bessie sensed their feeling for she sat down on the piano stool and began to run her fingers over the keys, playing little snatches of one thing after another. Then she drifted into some hymn tunes and I drifted to the back of the church. Minnie stood at the end of the piano watching Bessie and soon she began to sing. And I am told on good authority that the preacher wiped a tear from his eye. He was just that happy!

Dedication Sunday was an all-day celebration. The two outlying churches joined the Groton congregation for the day. Families arrived in their wagons from distances up to fifteen miles. The morning worship service was a time of high and solemn dedication of both the building and the lives of the members to the ongoing work of Christian fellowship.

Sunday dinner was served in the church, every family having brought its contribution to this meal which was almost like the love feasts of the early Church. A period of relaxation followed while neighbors held reunions, older children played and small children slept on their parents' laps or on hay in a wagon box. A three o'clock service of song and praise completed the day and sent everyone to his home with a warm glow of accomplishment and fervor for the future work of the church.

The Conference in the fall of 1888 was the third I attended in Dakota and it was by far the most rewarding. I had been in the Territory long enough to know a number of the preachers so I could grasp a fellow worker by the hand—just like all the other preachers did—and ask, "How's the work going at Pierre?" or "What's the news from Watertown?"

For another thing, there was a good fight on in the denomination and we in Dakota did not escape the controversy. Across the country Methodists had a question to argue and a "cause" to defend, and it concerned the women! At the recent Quadrennial Conference, which is international in scope, four women delegates had arrived, each representing a mid-western church. A fifth woman from India registered a little late after the uproar had subsided.

The right of these women to be seated as official delegates was challenged. The cry went up, "Women as official delegates at a Methodist Conference? Certainly not!" A large part of the convention favored their recognition, contending that Methodist procedure called for clergy and lay delegates in equal numbers and "lay" had always been interpreted to mean any adult church member in good standing who was neither a minister nor a member of an "order." Most surely women were part of the lay group. The opposition argued, however, that such an interpretation of "lay" was proper for all local participation of laymen, but that the idea had never even been considered that women would be sent as possible delegates to an official legislative body. Women were lay members of the church at home, but they did not qualify as voting delegates at a Quadrennial.

Arguments on both sides of the question had many ramifications. Several unofficial ballots were taken, one by the bishops, one by the clergy, one by the laymen and in each balloting the vote was nearly a tie. Finally the delegates were asked to cast their official ballots and the cause of the women lost by a small margin. The Conference proceeded to its other business but the issue was far from closed.

It is true that the temper of the times was against the women; they had not yet come into their rights. But it was also too bad for Methodism that it took refuge, even temporarily, behind a slogan, "We have never done it that way before." It was only natural that in the ensuing months the local churches, state conferences, the Methodist press, all the official denominational groups should air the question and when four years later it was again brought before the Quadrennial Conference at Omaha the delegates favoring the admission of women as voting members won out. Of course our young Dakota Conference fought the battle in miniature, but along with most of the mid-western states we lined up with progress rather than with tradition.

The last day of our Conference arrived and under the surface was the tension which always existed as we reached the final business of the convention—the preaching assignments for the coming year. Feeling sure that I would be transferred I shared in the apprehension of the other preachers but I found myself anticipating the announcement as one looks forward to a new adventure.

That morning as we were entering the Conference hall Bishop Fowler stopped me with some passing word of greeting, then after a moment asked, "You're expecting to be moved, Hyde?"

"I've taken it for granted. Right?"

"That's right and I'm pleased over your new location. I want to express my appreciation for the fine work you've done at Groton. I've never told you but I've had many a chuckle over Dr. Traveller's report of the way he left you alone on the depot platform with the encouraging admonition to 'dig or die.' You hardly look like a corpse!"

Bishop Fowler's fine sense of humor was one of the characteristics that made him a good man to work under.

"It seems to me your new building at Groton and your new wife have earned for you a county seat appointment," he continued. "A town of about a thousand and a much better salary."

The gavel of the presiding officer called the Conference into session and we all settled down for the work of the day. The first order of business consisted of the reports of the local churches and I laughed to myself as I recalled my first report of two years ago. Then came the reading of the appointments for the coming year. I was so interested in watching the expressions of some of the men—relief, disappointment, satisfaction—that I only half heard my name read, but in a fraction of a second I was giving close attention.

"W. J. Hyde. Faulkton, Faulk County."

From Groton to Faulkton was a big jump, professionally more than geographically. Faulkton, about seventy-five miles southwest of Aberdeen, was a much talked-of town because there had been a big fight between it and La Foon, five miles distant, over the location of the county seat. The fight built up a great deal of animosity between the two towns. But when both the Northwestern and the Milwaukee Railroads ran their lines through Faulkton, this bypassing of La Foon sealed its fate; people soon moved out and La Foon was one more ghost town on the prairie.

It wasn't easy to leave Groton but we made it a happy time in spite of the tinges of sadness. A Methodist minister, especially in the early days, had to steel himself for frequent farewells; most of us were transferred after one or two years in a town, and three years was the absolute limit. It was part of our philosophy that when you leave a community you leave friends to come back to; when you move to a town you have new friends to make. We made arrangements to move quickly—not a difficult task with our few possessions—to avoid any lingering sighs over the departure. The church people got together for one grand evening of fellowship. People are so wonderful! After a few speeches and much good food Bessie sat down at the piano and Minnie stood beside her and we sang. My, how those people had learned to sing in two years! We began with "Count your many blessings, see what God has done." We sang along to "What a friend we have in Jesus," and then,

> Blest be the tie that binds
> Our hearts in Christian love:
> The fellowship of kindred minds
> Is like to that above.

As we sang through the verses, one by one the hymnbooks closed; no one needed to read the words.

> When we are called to part,
> It gives us inward pain;
> But we shall still be joined in heart,
> And hope to meet again.

That's a happy song. We followed it with the benediction, "The Lord bless thee and keep thee, the Lord make His face to shine upon thee and be gracious unto thee; the Lord lift up His countenance upon thee and give thee peace. Amen."

Our work at Groton was finished.

7

Blackballed

OUR move to Faulkton was easily accomplished, since we hadn't been married long enough to accumulate all that miscellany which makes moving hard. We decided to ship Prince with us; he was too much a member of the family to leave behind.

At Faulkton we were met at the train by Mr. Cowles who represented the official board of the church as chief welcomer. He was a talkative individual, inclined to be paunchy and the front of his vest would have profited from the use of a little water and a stiff brush. But he was a genial host and gave us a good reception. He helped us into his surrey which was drawn by a fine pair of bays and as we proceeded down the main street he gave us a passing introduction to each building of importance, pointing with a flick of the whip.

"There's the newspaper office. Ray Tipton's a good editor but he doesn't come to church. His wife's a hard worker though. Ray says he's going to get into heaven on her record, but I tell him he's kept records long enough to know you got to make your own entries—even in heaven. Ha!"

I hardly thought this a good enough joke for his explosive laugh but I soon found that he punctuated all his important statements with this mark of self-appreciation.

"That's the court house. Fine building, eh? We made fools out of La Foon on that score. Ha!"

"I've heard about the fight over the location of the county seat," I said.

"Yep, it was a good one. General store," he continued, "high priced but honest. Now down the street there, at Wally's you

115

got to watch their weights. Old Wally puts his thumb on the scales. Tricky that way."

Our personally conducted tour of Faulkton came to an end at the church. "Pretty fine building, eh?" Mr. Cowles continued his monologue which had never grown into a conversation. "Yep, I was chairman of the board all the time we were building it. Takes a lot of work, Brother Hyde. How d'you like it?"

I expressed real admiration for the building completed just three years previous. My predecessor had left me a good place to work in and I was grateful to him. We did not pause long because Mr. Cowles wanted to get back to work.

"Perhaps the Missus would like to look into the parsonage next door."

We stepped across the little plot of yard connecting the church and the parsonage.

"Two trees!" exclaimed Minnie with delight.

"Yep. The other preacher had that notion. I always said they were more work than they were worth. Trees don't come natural to these parts so I always say why bother with them. But the preacher's wife sent clear back to Northrup, Braslin and Company in St. Paul for some seedlings and these two lived."

"They're lovely, Mr. Cowles," Minnie complimented him.

On the steps of the parsonage Mr. Cowles paused. He looked at the new preacher's wife and then at the parsonage. "For a young thing like you, Mrs. Hyde, I'm afraid this house don't look so good. Didn't realize before how it needs paint. It's a little run down, perhaps."

I suggested somewhat briskly, "It's always a good idea to have a few jobs which show they need to be done. It's fun to do work that appears to the eye. Don't you find it so, Brother Cowles?"

Brother Cowles took off his hat and scratched his head contemplatively. "Now, Brother Hyde, might as well tell you, we've been pressed pretty hard for money, what with building a new church and all. Might have to go a little slow on suggesting any more financial outlay."

"You've done fine work, too, Brother Cowles. Your church is

a real credit to the Methodists and to Faulkton. But how would you like to show off your town to newcomers and say, 'Now, here's our parsonage'? People judge a congregation a whole lot by the kind of house they put their preacher's family in."

We stepped into the house and walked through the rooms. Faded wallpaper, peeling paint, sagging back stoop. Minnie took it all bravely. I resolved that for her sake we would fix up this place in a hurry. Also I really did have a conviction that church property should be kept in good condition.

"Thank you, Mr. Cowles, for giving us so much of your time this afternoon. We like Faulkton already. And it has the reputation of being an up and coming town. We're mighty happy to be sent here. Now I guess we better go to the hotel till our things arrive by freight."

"No sir, Mrs. Gardner, she wants you to stay with her. She's had the preacher stay with her while he's gettin' settled for I don't know how many years. Lizzie Gardner's crippled and don't get out much so she has lots of folks in. Ha!"

Mr. Cowles drove us to Mrs. Gardner's house, a neat, attractive, two-story home.

"Her husband was in the elevator business before he died. Made a little pile, I guess."

Mrs. Gardner met us at the door. It was love at first sight between her and Minnie.

"You're so young, so nice and new looking," she beamed at Minnie. "And the preacher's wife! We hope you'll like it here, Mrs. Hyde."

She held out her hand to me. "Gracious, you're young, too. Isn't this wonderful, Mr. Cowles? Young folks have so much energy. Now your room's right at the head of the stairs. You'll excuse me if I don't go up with you?"

We expressed our appreciation and then I said to Mr. Cowles, "I suppose you have a board meeting tonight?"

"Well, now, I suppose it is customary but I just haven't got around to call it."

"Now, Ben, you know it won't take you long to get word to

the men." Mrs. Gardner gave him a gentle prodding. "Of course you want a board meeting so Brother Hyde can meet our officials. You know, you're the acting chairman while Ed's out of town and they can't move without you."

Brother Cowles straightened up and beamed at this recognition of his importance. "Guess we can make it about eight o'clock, Brother Hyde. Over in the church office."

Cowles said good-by, leaving us in the comfortable care of Mrs. Gardner. We stayed with her a week while a cleaning bee was in progress in the parsonage. When we moved in, the house still smelled of fresh paint, the wallpaper still crackled a bit with drying, the cellar shelves were still damp from scrubbing when Minnie put out her fruit and jelly brought from Groton. And Prince was bedded down on fresh straw in a clean barn.

In addition to the Faulkton church I had a small preaching place eight miles out across the prairie. The work was similar, in many respects, to the work at Groton only on a stepped-up scale. The biggest difference was the fact that now I had someone to work with me. Minnie was my constant companion in visits in town and around the countryside. On a moment's notice she would pick up to drive anyplace we were needed. From the first minute she arrived in Dakota, Minnie caught the spirit of the prairie. She found it easier to be away from the hills, woods and streams of Ontario than I had anticipated. She missed them, but she did not mourn for them. Life was full of joy and work for both of us. Minnie taught a Sunday School class, worked in the Aid Society, sang in the choir. She seemed born to the job she had accepted—a preacher's wife.

Life moved at a swifter pace in a county seat town, especially a county seat in the late 1880's when the Territory was in the grip of riotous political tensions. Agitation for statehood continued. And with it the more hotly fought battle for the location of the capital. Nationally, the Democrats still battled for the admission of the Territory as one state—those two extra Republican senators stuck in their craws! The Republican Convention of 1888 made statehood an issue so when the party was continued in office it had to make good its campaign promise. On Valentine's Day when we all love each other for twenty-four hours, the Enabling Act was passed, and on Washington's birthday the Act was approved, adding three hundred thousand South Dakotans to the century-old family of the Father of our Country.

Although North and South Dakota were calling themselves "Sister States" there was an undercurrent of jealousy over which one would be considered the older of the twins. President Harrison, with the wisdom of a Solomon, solved the difficulty by signing the papers without knowing which one he signed first; the space for his signature was all that was exposed. Then the papers were shuffled by another person, so that no one but the recording angel knows to this day which sister was born first.

The fight for the capital city became hotter. A half dozen cities put in their claims and were backed by local citizens, industries, the railroads, and by politicians who sold themselves to the highest bidder. There was Huron, the center of population; Pierre, the geographic center; Aberdeen, the railroad center; Sioux Falls, the largest city; these and others juggled the map of the state to make hamlets appear metropolises, to make railroads appear to run through every town with enough population to help swing the election. Free talk, free food, free transportation, free promises—an orgy of liberality to entice voters.

One day while the contest was at fever heat I met a flamboyant politician who accosted me in a loud voice, "Reverend, why doesn't the church get in on this momentous problem?"

"You're right," I agreed. "I'm planning to discuss citizenship from my pulpit Sunday morning and I'll expect you there."

"Well, I—"

"Sure, I know you're busy but this is a momentous problem!"

He was there. I took for my text Ephesians 2:19: "Now therefore ye are no more strangers and foreigners, but fellow-citizens with the saints, and of the household of God." I reviewed the amount of time and money that had gone into getting our state into the Union, reminding the people that every person in the Territory automatically became a citizen when we became a state. Many of us, including myself, were proud to be new citizens. I reviewed the honor and the benefits that accrue from citizenship in the United States. But, I asked, how much time had these same citizens given to preparation for citizenship in the community that transcends all earthly communities? The ultimate citizenship of all Christians is in the kingdom of God. While the people of South Dakota were squabbling over designation of a capital city, were they not forgetting the one great City that had a prior claim to their loyalties—the New Jerusalem?

After the service my politician friend shook hands with me heartily.

"I asked for it," he said. "Now I know what one of your parishioners meant when he said that wherever Brother Hyde starts he always ends up in Heaven. I'll remember your sermon when I challenge a preacher again."

That same sermon was the source of one of those temptations that Satan delights to put in the way of preachers, a better paying job. Among the strangers in the audience that morning was a representative of an old line insurance company from St. Paul. On Monday morning he called on me.

"If you can spare a few minutes," he began, "I want to talk to you. I want to lay before you the great future of the insurance business and offer you a job with our company. Anyone who can sell the Gospel like you sold it yesterday morning would make a whiz of an insurance agent. Our company would start you at an annual salary of twelve hundred dollars beginning next week."

I knew he meant this offer graciously so I tried to receive it in the same spirit.

"Thank you. I appreciate your offer. I really do. The salary is much more than I am getting now, but if you could raise it to twelve thousand dollars it still would not tempt me. This is my lifework. I know of nothing that could call me away from it. Absolutely nothing."

He shook hands cordially. "I was afraid of that. But I thought it was worth a try. When I'm out this way I'll see you again."

After the insurance agent left I sat alone for a long time, thinking. A man goes along taking his profession as a matter of course until some experience checks him up short. Whether or not I would ever be what people call a success in the ministry I did not know. But I did know I was glad I had come to Dakota when I left college instead of going east to some established parish. I knew that for me the ministry was the only profession to which I could give myself unreservedly. I thought about the folks in this town and their need for those things that only the church can supply. The men engaged in growing wheat for the mills to turn into flour for bread—how much more they yearned for the Bread of Life. Engineers were talking about irrigation projects—how useless if the Water of Life did not flow freely, too. The merchants—how paltry their wares unless they realized they were secondary to the things of the Kingdom. People came to church because it had something unique to give them. I felt new joy at being one of the servants—even if the least—who served from this bountifully laden table.

At the lunch table I told Minnie about the insurance offer. I will admit I built up a little false enthusiasm for it just to see the effect on her.

"Willie, you know you didn't even consider it." That was all she said. Where do women get their sixth sense?

Although the church at Faulkton had been built three years before we took up our pastorate there, a considerable debt remained, so we began working on that immediately. Before the year was over we were glad we had not delayed. The summer of 1889 was a hard experience for everyone in Dakota. The season began as usual and the black earth was prepared for the wheat. Great tracts of land were plowed for the first time. Expansion! That was the cry of the Dakotas. Then we waited for the rains—

rains that never came. Each day the blistering sun shone down with increasing heat. The parched earth bore a pitiful stand of wheat, not enough to tie the soil down. The winds of summer which usually played over a shimmering sea of green that changed to gold as the season advanced, instead, blew across arid black ground, picking up the fine soil and piling it around like evil snowdrifts. That summer we had black blizzards. The dust-filled air irritated the nerves as well as the flesh. Families began to leave for back home and were written off as weaklings by the farmers who remained. Other farmers came to town to borrow money to tide them over till the next harvest. Interest rates went as high as 12 per cent; but, the people argued, you could easily make up for one lost season.

In the Hyde household life took on new meaning that year. I could say it became third dimensional for it was at Faulkton that our first child, William Clifford, was born. A baby has a peculiar way of changing the focal point of life. There is a constant temptation to center all the family activity around the little blond or dark, or bald head in the cradle. But we were prevented from complete reorganization—or disorganization—by the fact that this baby had a popular mother; she was in too constant demand to drop out of circulation just because there was a baby to care for. In those days parents either stayed home or took their babies with them, so we rigged up a basket that was easy to handle and the baby went to Sunday School, to church, prayer meeting, choir practice, and frequently on our Sunday afternoon circuit trips where the women in the country church "couldn't abide not seeing the Missus."

The town of Faulkton and especially its Methodist church owed much of their thriving success to one man, Major Pickler. In the Civil War the Major had played a prominent military role and in 1890 was still in the prime of physical strength. He was tall, broad shouldered, walked with erect carriage and a spring to his step. Through his law office he had helped bring the county seat to Faulkton, but in contrast to many lawyers of this period he was scrupulously honest in all his dealings, which the people rewarded with complete confidence in his word. In addition to being a lawyer, Pickler also was a real estate agent. I doubt if there was a family within a radius of twenty miles which the Major did not know personally; he also knew the value of their land, how far they had proved up on their claim or how large a mortgage was held against it; he knew the size of every family and in many cases he knew the ambitions of every youngster growing up in a sod house. The Major spent much of his time counseling the pioneers who were ignorant of the legal loopholes that gave unfair advantage to claim jumpers or unscrupulous agents. It was men like Major Pickler here and there throughout the Territory who gave it a substantial feeling of integrity and morality.

The Major worked as hard for the church as he did for his other interests. Countless times when I greeted some stranger at the door after morning worship he would say, "Give the Major credit; he told me I ought to support the church and encourage the new minister. But I'll be coming again on my own hook now." Perhaps the Major never knew how much good he did me but after all, preachers are human beings, very human in many ways, and a trickle of praise gets more work out of them than a deluge of criticism.

Soon after coming to Faulkton I had an opportunity to meet Ray Tipton, the newspaper editor whom Mr. Cowles had mentioned on the morning of our arrival. Ray made a great contribution to the joy of living in Faulkton. He was a level-headed editor and in knowing Ray I had my first opportunity to get well acquainted with a newspaper office. Regularly I read the St. Paul *Pioneer Press*, to which I had subscribed ever since coming to Dakota. Now at Tipton's office I had an opportunity to follow the editorials of some of the other leading dailies, especially the Cleveland *Plain Dealer* and the St. Louis *Post*. But in some ways the most important part of my newspaper education came from the behind-the-scenes information that Ray gave me. Our talks might start with the price of wheat on the Minneapolis market and end up with American foreign policy in dealing with

Japan. Or we might start with the wisdom of creating a new cabinet member for agriculture and ramble through Hamlin Garland's new book of short stories and end up with a discussion of religion. We frequently talked about the church but Ray was always noncommital concerning his personal relation to it, although he beamed with pride whenever anyone mentioned his wife's able leadership.

The second winter we were in Faulkton I held the usual series of revival meetings for three weeks. One evening Ray was there with his wife. She told me afterward that she never knew what prompted him to come. When she was getting ready to leave the house that evening she had said to him, "Ray, don't forget to close up the base burner if it gets to going too hard." He put down his newspaper, picked up his coat and hat. "I'll shut the damper now. I'm going to church with you." After the sermon, when the invitation was given, Ray came forward and dedicated his already fine life to the Master.

A preacher sees many kinds of conversions: the hard, rebellious soul that has thwarted God's plan for years; the person sunk in sin who literally grasps the Rock of Ages as his one hope; the man in whom good and evil struggle so that to "tear the evil from his breast" is a real and violent battle; then the man like Ray Tipton who has thought out the meaning of commitment and takes the step as an honest and logical process in his life. Which way is most important? Every child of God is important and the manner of the birth is not essential. However, there is a stability that comes with the conversion of a man like Ray which makes a preacher know that he and the Lord have someone substantial to build with.

In Faulkton there was a small church of another denomination whose farmer-preacher was not yet ordained. I was reminded of my early days in Groton and was always glad to help him out as Dr. McLean had often come to my rescue. One day in January the young preacher, Guy Hibbs, asked me to assist with a funeral.

"I don't know the Carriers," he said. "I think they needed a preacher and I was the first one they thought of so they sent for me."

It was a bitter cold day; the wind howled across the prairie and the swirling snow was already settling into drifts. We knew it was a treacherous day for an eight mile drive into the storm. Hibbs borrowed a powerful team from one of his church members; we heated stones for footwarmers, put on our heaviest coats and wrapped ourselves in buffalo robes. Pushing the team against the wind we finally arrived at a small isolated frame house, so cold we thought the marrow of our bones was surely frozen.

A few neighbors had gathered. The storm plus the fact that "Uncle Joe" who had died was only a distant relative of the family and practically unknown to the neighbors, kept the gathering from assuming the proportions usual to a country funeral. Because of the heavy wind we arrived a bit late, and most of the friends were already in the living room. However, in the kitchen there were a few of the men who were not interested in joining the mourners until the preacher arrived. While Mrs. Carrier took our coats and made room beside the kitchen stove to warm our heavy robes before the return trip, one of the men picked up a big coffee pot from the back of the stove.

"Take time for some coffee, Reverend," and he offered Brother Hibbs and me each a big cup of steaming coffee such as never warmed a preacher's insides before. I thought I could feel each drop radiate heat through my whole body. Hibbs and I sat down at the kitchen table and drank a second cup.

"I'm still too stiff to start the service," said the young preacher; "just another half a cup, please."

He held out his big bone china cup for more and I decided he must have been chilled worse than I, for by now I was glowing. Finally Brother Hibbs put his cup down, picked up his Bible and little black book of *Services for All Occasions* and started to rise from the table. But his legs wouldn't hold him and he sank back onto the chair. The men looked at one another with horror and Brother Hibbs looked at me scared stiff. He tried to speak and his bewilderment increased.

"Brother Hyde," his voice was thick and his words a little jumbled. "I guess I'm th-thick. I th–think, Brotherrr Hyde, you better sthart the th–thervice for me." His shoulders drooped and he half closed his eyes.

"Don't let him fall asleep," said one of the men in a too loud voice. He stepped closer and began to shake Hibbs.

"Hey, parson, all that's the matter with you is that you're drunk. That coffee was half whiskey!"

This brew was not uncommon but usually was not served to ministers. We kept the young preacher awake, assisted him into the living room and I began the service. Hibbs paid strict attention to every word I said and by the time we were ready for the obituary he had recovered enough to read it and pronounce the benediction, although he spoke with unusual deliberation and concentration. After brief commiserations to the family for the loss of this uncle whose body they now had to ship back east I drove Hibbs home and asked his wife to put him to bed—he had had very severe exposure that day!

Two years at Faulkton brought us to the beginning of the last decade of the nineteenth century, a good time for the Hyde family to take stock of itself. My wife and I decided that financially we had nothing to complain about. Our salary was eight hundred dollars a year, plus parsonage. Four years before I had had no church, no house, no wife, no baby, no horse, no salary. Also we had the extra money that came from weddings and other services for which I never charged but none-the-less grateful people used to pay at times. This money amounted to about one hundred and fifty dollars a year, and as is customary it went to the preacher's wife. But actually we fared even better than our financial record would indicate. We shared the good fortunes of our parishioners. Every garden, every canning season, every hunting season yielded a contribution to the manse. As for chickens, we frequently received six or eight at a time. Beef, mutton, pheasants, vegetables, cakes, pies—it is really a provident relationship that exists between the small town preacher and his flock. We learned the art of receiving as well as the joy of giving. It was no lack of appreciation that prompted the mistress of the manse to remark one fall that she wished everybody had not had an excess of beans that year. What would we do with forty-five quarts of beans? However, our only real complaint came when the price of beefsteak went up to twelve cents a pound!

By the time Conference met in the fall of 1890 I had completed the job I had been sent to Faulkton to do. The debt on the building was paid and the membership of the church had increased enough to make the congregation self-supporting, so I had an idea we would be transferred. And I was right. For one real reason we hated to leave—too many people were already moving out of Faulk County. A second summer of drought had cleaned out almost half the settlers. The saga of Dakota had proved a sad story with the same theme repeated page after page.

But I was a Methodist preacher so we accepted the invitation to go to St. Lawrence, a thriving town somewhat southeast of Faulkton. St. Lawrence was a good town. The area around us was more highly populated than at Faulkton; the countryside more rolling than at Groton. This was my first church without a circuit of outlying points. Because it was the only Methodist Church in this area the membership was largely composed of farmers although there were a fair number of businessmen, schoolteachers, and other professional people. Most of them were alert, young, strong. Dakota was still too young to have an elderly population. The church at St. Lawrence had a good building, the main auditorium seating about two hundred and fifty people while another fifty could be accommodated by opening the Sunday School rooms which circled this main room. It was a fine place to work.

Prince continued to take Minnie and me—and now the baby —on long afternoon drives into the country. I cultivated the farmers while they cultivated their crops. Because of the continued drought and repeated crop failures many of the families who clung to the land were reduced to abject poverty. Malnutrition was prevalent; throats and lungs burned from the continued heat and dust. Children suffered most and too many little cradles were left vacant those years; too many parents carried aching hearts within their aching bodies. The church was needed desperately in this land of increasing despair.

Frequently Minnie and I went into homes where parents, such as Amy and Ben Merritt, were beside themselves with grief because a child had died before it was baptized. Since coming west Amy and Ben had been so busy with all the work of getting started on the prairie and then the worry of keeping going that their religion had taken a back seat. They kept promising themselves that soon they'd do the proper thing for their two little girls. But pneumonia came before the convenient time arrived. Amy had come from an Old World German background and the church of her childhood had taught that an unbaptized child went to hell. Now she looked at her curly-haired four-year-old Sarah, two days ago a laughing youngster; today dead.

"And I've doomed her forever," wept Amy almost out of her mind with sorrow and remorse.

"Don't say that," I told her. "Don't grieve because Sarah wasn't baptized. There is nothing magic in baptism and there is nothing in the Bible that tells you that Jesus damns little children. What a different story you find! Jesus loved them; He called them to Himself and delighted in their company. He blessed them and He told them that 'of such is the Kingdom of Heaven.' Little children are beautiful and pure in His sight. They do not need the regeneration of baptism. God isn't interested in the sprinkling of water; He is interested in what happens in people's lives. The essential beauty of baptizing a child lies in the dedication of the parents and their consecration of the child to the Christian way of life. Your little Sarah is with Jesus. You have reason to be happy over that."

Happy? The word had fallen out of their vocabulary. In the weeks and months that followed it was our job to bring it back again.

During our winter at St. Lawrence the fourth member of the
Hyde family arrived, a brown-eyed, brown-haired little girl.
William Clifford and his young sister, Florence Mae, made a
juvenile twosome that took an increasing amount of their
mother's time and energy. Papa Hyde more frequently made his
longest trips into the country alone, but there was the compensation of coming home to a tiny baby girl, a boisterous two-year-
old boy and a wife who was never too tired to seem glad to see
him. Our life was supremely happy excepting for the one draw-
back that Minnie was beginning to feel the physical effects of
the dry, hot climate.

The thriving state of our own family added a more poignant
sadness, for me, to the condition of the homes I visited. Hardly a
day went by without uncovering some hardship. One afternoon
while making calls on the edge of town I came upon a family
who had lost everything during the drought and had moved to
town into a very inadequate shack. Winter was nearly upon us
and the day was bitter cold. The children were wearing all the
clothes they possessed and were huddled around a tiny stove in
which the mother was burning whatever material the children
could find in the alleys, including old shoes which she soaked in
kerosene. After visiting a few minutes I asked one of the older
boys to walk with me to the church a few blocks away and we
soon returned with two large buckets of coal. The mother's
gratitude was pathetic even though it was such a small thing I
had done. It has been the mission of the Church through the
ages to give the cup of cold water—and the cup can take the
form of a coal bucket. When I left I went immediately to the
relief commission and told them the needs of the family.

"We'll look into the case," they promised.

"That's not what I want," I told them. "I have looked into it.
Here are the facts. The family is in immediate distress."

"Yes, Reverend Hyde, the coal will be sent today."

For the hundredth time I realized the authority that comes
to any individual who ministers "in His name."

Minnie had the reputation of being the best cook in the

church. I thought her the best cook in the world. She could do wonderful things with food and the church women got the habit of looking to her for new ideas or for tasty ways of preparing the "same old things." I had an inordinate pride in her cooking and was exceedingly happy whenever we had guests for a meal. In fact, it was this pride that led to our first marital difficulty. One morning a wedding party came to the parsonage, a young man, his financée, her parents and two attendants to stand up with the young couple. I had never met the people but they were such a gay wedding party that it seemed too bad to have the whole affair over in the few minutes it takes to perform the ceremony. I thought it would be wonderful to have a real celebration so I invited them all to stay to dinner—it would be good for this young bride to see the kind of meal a real cook could turn out! I suppose I was unconsciously prompted to this generosity by the mouth-watering savor of food already coming from the kitchen.

I thought Minnie did not seem too enthusiastic over the improvised dinner party but she "did herself proud." We had two beautifully roasted pheasants, potatoes, vegetables, hot rolls and coffee, topped off with two cream pies. As I watched the sumptuous meal progress I wondered to myself how even Minnie could produce a dinner of such proportions on so short notice. Then like a bolt from the blue it struck me—much of this food had been prepared for the church dinner that evening! I had completely forgotten about the dinner. Suddenly the food lost its charm for me and I had a difficult time keeping up conversation.

Finally the wedding party left and I went into the kitchen to make amends to Minnie. She was washing dishes and didn't stop as I laid the wedding fee on the sink drain. Minnie was the most generous person in the world; there was no streak of the mercenary in her. But she had a sense of reality about finances that I sometimes lacked.

"How much is it, Will?" I was surprised at the question because she had never asked me that bluntly, just as if the amount made a difference.

"Two dollars and a half," I replied.

"How much did the wedding certificate cost?"

"Twenty-five cents."

"How many horses did you feed?"

"Four."

"And six people," she added.

"From a business point of view, maybe I wasn't too smart," I confessed. "I guess I let my enthusiasm run away with me and I'm sorry, Minnie. But what a wonderful memory of a wedding feast that young couple will have."

"That's all right, Will. We are not in the ministry as a money-making venture. My real worry is the church dinner this evening. You better go to the cellar and bring up some sauerkraut so I can fix something."

I went to the cellar convinced that my wife was not too happy over my morning's work, and I didn't blame her. Neither was I. But Minnie's rebound was good and by the time she reached the church she was explaining the absence of the pheasant and the pies in such a humorous way that the whole church had a good laugh at our expense.

We stayed just one year at St. Lawrence but it was a happy year. The drought continued, which made money tight, but there was a liberal friendliness among the people. We would gladly have worked there longer but the Presiding Elder asked us if we would be willing to transfer to Parker, so of course we went. Parker is in the southeastern part of the state, near Sioux Falls, Dakota's largest city. This move took us out of the flat prairie into the more hilly region of the Sioux River. Parker was a thriving town and we felt quite metropolitan.

Soon after coming into the community I was appointed chairman of the County Prohibition Committee. Both of the Dakotas had come into the Union as dry states, but that did not mean there were no puddles here and there. It had been my custom during the few years I had been preaching to give an occasional temperance sermon. During the Territorial days I often talked to the saloonkeepers and many of them agreed that liquor was a curse to any man, woman or community. One of the men even went so far as to say he would never let his son come near the saloon; he didn't want the youngster mixed up in that kind of business. After we became a dry state it was part of the work of our committee to weed out places where liquor was sold illegally.

There were two men who gave us a lot of trouble in Parker and some of the neighboring towns. Cy Brown was an almost illiterate person who looked like a crook in every inch of his short anatomy. Vernon Talbott was a tall, fairly well-educated man, handsome in a superficial way and very smooth in all his dealings. One member of our committee once commented that "Talbott could quote Scripture and at the same time steal your watch out of your vest pocket."

One of my early tussles for temperance was occasioned by these two men. Our committee caught them in so many evasions or open defiance of the law that we finally brought them to trial. As chairman of the committee I had to take a fairly prominent part in the proceedings. When both men were sentenced to two years in the state penitentiary Brown was so angry that he shook his fist in my face and swore he would "get even with that Methodist preacher," whom he decorated with several red hot adjectives. Once closed, the episode took its place in the background of my mind and although two years later I heard vague rumors of their release from prison the men did not cross my path again and I had no reason to think they ever would.

Then I was invited to join a fraternal organization. Several of the men spoke to me about membership but it was Ed Holmes, the station agent, who was most insistent that I join the Order. It seemed to me that I was busy enough without adding lodge meetings to my schedule, but I recognized that the organization did some fine things and stood for high ideals, so I let Ed present my name.

The morning after the lodge meeting the station agent came to me again, this time very long-faced and ill at ease. He fumbled around trying to make a little conversation and I, not knowing

the cause of his embarrassment, couldn't help him out. Finally
Ed blurted out the truth. I had been blackballed! The men had
voted three times and each time there were two blackballs. He
was all apology; such a thing had never happened before and
everyone was dumbfounded. The only way he could explain it
was that there were two men present that night who had not
attended lodge for months, in fact, for about two years. Like a
flash it came to me. Just a few days previous I had heard that
my two "friends" had been seen in town. Could they possibly
be members of the lodge? I threw back my head and laughed.

"If Brown and Talbott are members," I told Ed Holmes, "I
know why I was blackballed, but don't let the action worry you
and I won't let it worry me."

Ed was tremendously relieved when he left me—only to return two nights later, this time looking really worried.

"I'm afraid we're letting you in for trouble, Brother Hyde.
Brown and Talbott are telling all over town that they're going
to go to church Sunday morning and sit on the front seat. They
sound as if they planned to give you a bad time."

"Thanks for the warning, Ed. Of course I don't know what
they plan any more than you do, but I'll be prepared with my
own plan and we'll see who comes out ahead."

Sunday morning arrived. As the church bell finished ringing I
stepped into the pulpit and had just started to read the opening
words of the service when down the aisle came Cy Brown and
Vernon Talbott; Cy was a little the worse for his last drink and
walked clumsily. The two men paraded to the front seats. Then
I noticed something that had escaped my eye. Although I had
been conscious of an unusually large audience I now discovered
that the first two or three rows of seats which were customarily
vacant were well filled today. Every lodge member in town was
in church sitting right there as near the front as possible.

I had given a great deal of thought to the sermon for this
morning. This one hour might be my only chance to reach these
two men and I prayed that I would be guided in saying something that would be helpful.

I took for my text the words spoken to John while he was acting as a kind of private secretary for Jesus who appeared to him on the Isle of Patmos. "To him that overcometh I will give . . . a white stone." At the time these words were written they had great meaning for the people although today we pass over them without a thought because they do not represent anything in our experience. But in Biblical times the white stone had tremendous emotional significance. Imagine a court hearing: there sits the judge, holding the power of life or death over the man on trial; below him is the culprit, who knows that the decision of this judge will determine his fate; there are the enemies pressing charges; there are witnesses for and against the accused. Finally the testimony is all over, there remains only the final decision. The tension in the courtroom grows as an attendant brings to the judge a bowl containing white stones and black stones. The judge receives the bowl and in secrecy takes out a stone, writes upon it the name of the accused, and then drops the stone into an urn. The courtroom is tense. If this is a black stone, the accused dies; if it is a white stone, he has been judged innocent. The attendant lifts the stone from the urn. It is white! Life flows again through the breathless crowd; the accused man lifts his head and looks upon a seemingly new world. He has been saved!

Jesus offers this forgiveness, this salvation, to every man. "Whosoever will." We only have to desire a better life and promise with His help to try to lead it and He gives us this new chance. Jesus invites *every* man to join the Order of the White Stone, the Church. The emblem of this Order stands for purity; it says to the world that your sins have been wiped out. Membership in the Order brings joyous freedom to the soul. Jesus offers membership today to anyone who would join His Order and receive the White Stone. If anyone here this morning would accept the invitation, let him come to the altar while we sing,

> Just as I am,
> Without one plea,

But that Thy blood
Was shed for me.

The choir and the people rose; their voices swelled with a new realization of the joy that comes from belonging to Jesus. As they sang I watched the ultimate in tragedy and the ultimate in joy in human souls. Brown walked noisily out of the church and slammed the door behind him. Talbott looked after him, hesitated before taking a step, then turned toward me and his hard face broke like a child's about to cry.

Quietly I said to him, "Yes, Jesus invites you, too."

He sat down, too weak to stand. The congregation sang to the end of the hymn, "O, Lamb of God, I come, I come." Mr. Talbott looked up at me and I took his hand; in front of this church full of people he rose to his feet, and it was as a new man in Christ Jesus. The love of Jesus had brought us into the same order of brotherhood.

While we were living in Parker two family events of importance took place. The major event was the birth of our second daughter, Clara Alberta. Clara was another Grills with her dark eyes and soft brown hair. We were happy that Florence would have a sister near her age. There is a close companionship between sisters not duplicated in any other family relationship. And the way their big brother was developing it would take two girls to balance his masculine energy.

The other event was the death of our beloved horse, Prince. We had always taken a lot of pride in Prince, kept him well-groomed and fed him well so as to keep his coat sleek and shining. In spite of all our care, one day we found him dead in his stall. We called a veterinarian.

"Too much fat around the heart," was his verdict.

Our loving care had been the cause of his death. It was a tragedy to our children and our household was sorrowful. Word got around town that the preacher had lost his horse. A few days later while the family was still mourning the empty stall two men drove up to the parsonage in a carriage, leading a horse behind them.

"We hope you like this animal, Brother Hyde. He's to replace Prince. We figured it never would do for a preacher to be without a horse. He's from all your friends in town."

Our family felt complete again with a fine horse in the barn.

By the time we were established in Parker, after six years in Dakota, I was feeling like an old-timer for I was invited back to Groton and to Faulkton to hold revival services. The visit to Groton was heart-warming. I stayed with the Johnsons and at times the years rolled back and I was the country boy far from home on his first mission. But time allows only momentary lapses. I was here on a new mission, to add souls to the church I had built.

The old friends? Jarv was a fine young man teaching a Sunday School class. To my surprise I heard him referred to once as "Mr. Sylvester"; it was the first time I was conscious of his having a last name. I decided Jarvis Sylvester was a fine-sounding name and it looked as if its owner were going to live up to it. We had a good laugh about the boards we had hauled up into the attic over the saloon to make our first church.

I wasn't surprised at the continued good reports about Molly for I had heard several times of her fine record as a nurse in Aberdeen and I had seen her there once, soon after she had made arrangements to keep Delsie and rear her. The Johnsons were older, of course, but still the same big-hearted people who could take all the world under their wings including their young grandson. One by one I asked about friends. Many had given up their land and their hopes—burned out by the sun that had once transformed the wheat into gold for our church.

I also spent two weeks holding a meeting at Faulkton. Here Minnie joined me for a few days and we relived the first year of our married life. With a borrowed horse we rode out across our favorite stretch of prairie at sunset. We viewed the past and contemplated the future. The irritation of the dust and wind were wearing Minnie down very visibly. Our children were feeling the effects, too, so we knew our next move had better take us east, not west.

Conference time, 1892. With two years at Parker completed I had an idea we would be sent to another charge. We were advanced to Dell Rapids, a beautiful location on the Sioux River just a few miles above Sioux Falls. While living in this community we completed our triumvirate of girls, adding Ethel Grace to the family. She was a slender, fine-featured child with blonde hair and gray eyes in contrast to the three older children. Dell Rapids gave some relief from the heat and dry prairie air of the former locations but the doctors still warned us that Minnie would have to leave the prairie. So nine happy years, and five thriving churches after I had been left by Dr. Traveller on the lonely depot platform to "dig or die" we knew we would have to seek another garden plot and ask the Lord to let us labor for Him there.

8

Saints and Sinners--Ohio Style

IT WAS settled in our minds that we would leave Dakota, but where would we go? We couldn't spin a bottle and follow the direction it pointed. We thought about several states in turn; we liked Minnesota as we had seen it from the train window; we loved Wisconsin when we passed through it. Illinois? Indiana? For some reason our minds did not take root in any of them. Ohio sounded best to us. It takes a lot of thinking, talking, weighing of assets and liabilities to decide where to move a family, but I was convinced that if we did the best planning we could the Lord would guide our moves. We have always had reason to believe that "in all thy ways acknowledge Him and He will direct thy paths" were not words idly spoken.

There were two attractions which helped us decide on Ohio. A few years previous some of the Hyde relatives had moved from Canada to Cleveland, so that the state did not seem entirely strange. Perhaps more important was the fact that Ohio was recognized as a strong Methodist state; the names of several great clergymen and some outstanding lay workers were linked with Ohio. From Dakota friends who had migrated from the Buckeye State we often heard stories of famous people "back home."

There were tales about Mary Bird Lake who started the second Sunday School in the United States; which was also the first in the entire Northwest Territory; about Colonel Moore who built the first Methodist meeting house in Ohio from his own hand-hewn logs; of Lorenzo Dow whose fame was almost legendary, a John the Baptist of his time who for forty years, covering the turn of the century, tramped the state, preaching always out

of doors, using fallen trees or stumps for a pulpit and always
eagerly welcomed by the settlers. In his trek of two hundred
thousand miles back and forth across Ohio he preached the first
sermons ever heard by some of the pioneers. There were stories
about John Stewart, a mulatto from Virginia who founded the
mission to the Wyandot Indians. As a young man Stewart held
a grudge against the Methodists until one night in Marietta he
wandered into a Methodist prayer meeting and was converted.
After that he felt a special "call" to preach to the Indians. To
travel with him as an interpreter he found a full-blooded Negro
who had been captured in his childhood by an Indian tribe and
therefore spoke their language.

The more we thought about Ohio the more we seemed
already a part of the state; we felt that somehow we belonged
there. But, according to Methodist practice, there had to be a
vacancy in a Conference before a new preacher could move in
and receive an appointment. It was already early fall and Conference time came in October, so one of my last acts in Dakota
was another "first": I applied for a job! I wrote to the Presiding Elder in Ohio, told him our family situation and ended the
letter, "After you have given all your assignments for the coming year, if there is anything left I will be glad to take it. I do
not care what kind of church it is."

At the same time that I wrote this letter to Ohio I talked to
Bishop Charles H. Fowler who was the Bishop in charge of our
Conference, and one of the men who has contributed most to
my life. Perhaps the fact that the Bishop was a native of Canada
pulled us a little closer together, but he was also a person of
large intellectual accomplishment and with a great capacity for
understanding people. Among his achievements were a successful presidency of Northwestern University, a fine editorship of
the *Christian Advocate*, and the distinction of being the first
grandson of a Methodist preacher ever to be elected to the
bishopric. Bishop Fowler offered to write a letter of recommendation for me and I have no doubt but that this letter helped win
for us a welcome in Ohio. In the last conversation I had with

the Bishop while still in Dakota he said with a hearty laugh, "You're going to a fine Methodist state, Brother Hyde, but don't think you are going to heaven yet!"

An immediate reply from Ohio set us packing. The Presiding Elder's letter was almost apologetic. There was only one appointment open, a large rural circuit of four churches which paid only eight hundred dollars a year. This amount was considerably less than we were getting at Dell Rapids but we decided the Lord had opened the way, the rest was up to us.

So the Hydes moved across the hundreds of miles from Minnehaha County, South Dakota, to Richland County, Ohio. Such moves are filled with mixed feelings. Nine glorious years had been ours in Dakota; the most loyal friends in the world we had known there; four of our children had been born there. On the other hand, the continued drought of the past five or six years had left great stretches of the wind-swept state desolate: closed banks, abandoned farms, bankrupt businesses, ghost towns, dust storms. I have seen the air so black that we could not distinguish the outlines of the house across the street. I have watched people buffet the dust-laden wind against which they had to brace themselves so hard that when the wind let up momentarily they would fall to the ground. But all in all, the state had been *home* and it was not easy to leave.

Nevertheless there was a certain excitement about heading into the sunrise. Back east! The train carried us back into the increasing vegetation of Minnesota, through the gorgeous autumn of Wisconsin, the brilliant reds and yellows of the hardwoods against the dark pines; lakes, rivers, streams—to our prairie-dried souls the world seemed bubbling with water. Somewhere in Wisconsin our train stopped for brief repairs to the engine so Minnie and I left the children asleep while we walked a few turns up and down the station platform. Here we met a man whose west-bound train was taking on water. He was impatient at the delay and finally spoke to us.

"Which way you headed?"

"East," we answered.

"No sir! Not for me again. I'm headin' west and I'm goin' to stay there. I've been to Pennsylvania to work in the mines and I've been to Georgia to work in the cotton and I've been to Massachusetts to work in the mills. Now I'm goin' back to Dakota. Out there there ain't no ocean to slap at you all night and there ain't no hills to shut you in. You kin see your neighbor's lamp ten miles away and know you got a friend over there. Man, I'm headin' fer God's country if this danged old train ever gets rolling."

"Will," said Minnie after the visitor left us, "it's wonderful, isn't it? Where your heart is, that makes home. Who is to say where God's country is?"

We arrived in Richland County, Ohio, in the fall of 1895 and found the towns of Butler and Belleville to be the two largest on our circuit of four not-too-thriving churches. How odd that a Belleville should enter our lives for a second time! We reveled in the grass, the wooded hills, the orchards, all the foliage and vegetation of Ohio. It took a little time to get completely settled because we moved into a rather run-down parsonage which needed the usual fixing up, but we began to get acquainted with our parishioners from the very first Sunday.

How friendly the people of Ohio! Yet the mood of the state was different from any we had known before. Both Minnie and I had been reared in pioneer country and had worked for several years in frontier territory, always in the land of the future. But Ohio had a past! True, it was a glorious past and the people could well be proud of their state's accomplishments but at least half the time they were looking back over their shoulders. Ohio was already planning a centennial celebration for 1903 while South Dakota was scarcely out of the cradle. One was not in Ohio long before he was told that the state had provided the nation with six presidents, two Harrisons, Grant, Hayes, Garfield and McKinley.

Driving through the countryside "old" grist mills were still in good condition but the "old" toll roads were becoming a thing of the past. We found the circuit to which we had been assigned already suffering from the ailments of age—the churches were plain run down. But Christianity is a rejuvenating tonic; a good dose of religion and they could be revived.

To start the treatment I held thirteen consecutive weeks of revival meetings, at least three weeks in each town. We took in one hundred and ninety-five members on confession of faith. By the time we added the new members to the awakened backsliders and the faithful few who had carried on the work for years, the total made a sizable congregation in each community. Through the next months we organized, or reorganized, Aid Societies, missionary societies, Sunday Schools and young people's work. The new Epworth League Movement was a boon to a lot of us preachers who had floundered trying to do a job with our young people without any materials or guidance or supervision. The Epworth League was a terrific stimulant for many churches.

We felt we had hardly got our breath in Ohio before the Presiding Elder came looking over the field in preparation for the coming Conference. The circuit was now so active that it was evident it would have to be divided into two circuits, and the churches were so informed. Then the trouble began. When we got to Conference we found that each of the four churches had sent in a request that Mrs. Hyde and I be assigned to their church. One of them was gracious enough to say, "If you must take the preacher at least leave us his wife!" None of the churches wanted to relinquish its request so there was a stalemate and the matter was laid before the Conference. But the Conference had no good solution so the problem was finally taken to the Bishop himself. He called me into his office and asked me, since I was the person most concerned, if I had any suggestion.

"I think you had better eliminate us from the circuit altogether," I said. He agreed. When the last day of Conference came and the appointments were read he announced, "We are appointing two men to fill the Hyde boots." But the Lord did not leave me barefoot. I was transferred to Centerburg, the center of the state, and the center of a little confusion on my first Sunday morning there.

It appeared that Centerburg had requested a certain minister of some standing in the Conference, which was definitely more than I could claim, having been in the state only one year and in an obscure parish at that. When I arrived for the morning service immediately following Conference, the people were obviously disappointed. I was sorry for them, and furthermore, I did not know how an unwanted preacher was supposed to act. Nothing in my experience had prepared me for this moment. I decided that if I ever wrote a book for young preachers it would contain a chapter entitled "Advice to Second Choice Preachers."

After church I walked home to dinner with a doctor and frankly discussed the situation with him. "I hope you stay," he said. "I don't know what kind of a preacher you'll prove to be but when I heard your prayer I knew I wanted you." That was encouraging, but he was only one member of the church. That afternoon I sent word to the chairman of the Official Board that I would leave the parish as soon as they could make arrangements for my replacement. Before the afternoon was over he called on me with a unanimous request from the other members of the Board asking me to accept the church.

So I moved the family to Centerburg and we entered into a delightful relationship which was strengthened by the fact that our youngest child, Leonard, was born there. We now had a boy at each end of our line of offspring.

Although Ohio boasted of being the cradle of the temperance movement, it was not a dry state. Some communities had no saloons because they voted them out by local option. On the whole, both the liquor interests and the temperance organizations were active. Throughout my life I hated liquor, perhaps because as a minister I saw more clearly than some the terrible suffering which follows in the wake of drunkenness. I did not engage in tirades against drinking but I accepted it as one of the evils against which the church needed to wage a constant battle. Sometimes I felt that the temperance advocates were too sentimental for their own good. It was common practice in summer tent meetings to throw slides upon the screen while someone read in emotional tones the old ballad, "Ten Nights in a Bar Room," with its pleading

> Father, dear father, come home with me now!
> The clock in the tower strikes one.

I never felt this was a very sound appeal.

It was at Centerburg that I had my first skirmish with the liquor interests in Ohio. Centerburg was a dry town and whiskey could be sold only for health purposes and then only on prescription from a doctor. One day a pompous gentleman, representing a patent medicine company, came to town, registered at the hotel in its best room, and began to circulate cards which carried the name of his medicine and also, "Liquor sold only on prescription." But this man was no doctor. However, he was an impressive individual who always appeared on the streets wearing a dark suit with a white cravat, a tall silk hat and carrying a gold-headed cane.

Something phony was in this deal. I watched the hotel and noted the countless people who went in and came out with little patent medicine but with large quantities of wine and whiskey, sometimes enough to last a year "for health purposes." But in a few days they would be back to have their prescription refilled. I discussed the situation with some of the church people and they offered to accumulate evidence against the man whom they dubbed Mr. Prescription Only. We found that he had prescriptions all right, signed by a country doctor not too far from town. When the evidence was collected I went to one of our Centerburg lawyers and he went with me to Mt. Vernon, our county seat, to ask advice of a prominent lawyer there about prosecuting this man.

"You have a clear case," he told us, "but the liquor interests are very powerful. You'll need plenty of evidence and pretty solid public opinion in your town to back you. That will be your greatest asset."

We went back home and I got the church people together. They had some of the fake prescriptions and could get plenty more. Our people enlisted other respectable citizens in the community and we were soon ready to open fire. We had a warrant served on Mr. Prescription Only who immediately hired a well-heeled lawyer from Columbus, the capital city. The Mt. Vernon lawyer offered to take our case without remuneration. Trial was scheduled for a Monday morning, so on Sunday night I opened fire with a sermon which had been well publicized. I chose for my subject, "The Devil in a Silk Hat."

Long before time for the evening service the sanctuary was filled. I used no names—it was hardly necessary—but I reviewed the situation in our law-abiding community. It was not a pretty picture that I painted.

During this time the liquor interests had not been lying down on the job. They had made plans to pack the courtroom on Monday morning. Learning of their strategy I arranged to have the doors opened at a certain time and long before that hour the temperance people were standing just outside in such numbers that the minute the doors opened the courtroom was filled with our group.

The trial started. The judge was a weak-kneed individual who leaned slightly toward the liquor group. Mr. Prescription Only was there with his oily Columbus lawyer; our forces were there, confident in our Mt. Vernon counsel. The first item in the trial was the reading of the charges against the gentleman in the tall silk hat. Then the defense attorney called his first witness.

"I want the Reverend W. J. Hyde on the stand," he said.

I took my place and was properly sworn in.

"Now," said the Columbus lawyer, "I want the Reverend Hyde to tell us what he said in his sermon at the Methodist Church last night."

"A proper question," ruled the judge.

"Your Honor," I responded, "I will gladly accede to the gentleman's request, but the sermon I preached last night took forty-five minutes."

"Shall the witness proceed?" asked the judge.

"No!" shouted the attorney, waving his hand toward me. "Dismiss him!"

The crowd cheered so long that the judge had to rap many times for silence. This setback seemed to break the suave assurance of the Columbus lawyer; he was never able to pull himself together as master of the situation.

After the testimony was all in the verdict was rendered. Guilty! Mr. Prescription Only was sent to the penitentiary to serve a one-year term. Immediately following the trial the doctor who wrote the prescriptions had his license revoked for a time.

The next night the good citizens of Centerburg had a shower on the Methodist preacher—groceries, eggs, garden produce, money and many thanks. Then during the night some of the other citizens of Centerburg showered the Methodist preacher. In the morning he found whiskey bottles—empty of course—strewn all over the front lawn and porch. Everyone had a good laugh. But I laughed last. I closed the deal by having a year's subscription to *The Ram's Horn*, a temperance publication, sent to Mr. Prescription Only while he was serving his term in prison.

Much of our life at Centerburg centered around the lively youngsters growing up in our family. They were no better and no worse, I think, than any other assortment of three girls, an older brother and a baby. But the eternal unexpected in children keeps life interesting for adults. There was the day we bought the new horse. Mother went with me while I closed a deal I had been dickering on. Then to climax the afternoon we bought each of us a new duster, long gray ones to keep our clothes clean during our country drives. When we pulled up in front of our house the children were gleeful in their inspection of the new horse and I made some comment to Mother that we had better water the animal. In no time at all Ethel, about three years old, was back from the house with a small tin cup half full of fresh water. It took some comforting to make up for the laughs of the older children.

Mother liked to keep the girls' hair in curls but the curls

needed the encouragement of being done up on rags every few nights. Ethel's hair usually looked better about the second day. The Friday night before Children's Day Mother fixed Ethel's hair for Sunday, then cautioned her to be careful through Saturday. But on Saturday afternoon our ingenious son decided to play barber with the result that three of Ethel's long curls were sacrificed for the development of Bill's tonsorial art.

Sunday morning Mother lined us up for inspection, a regular ceremony before going to the church. The week that the dress-

maker had just spent at the house paid off because each girl was outfitted in a new "best dress" for the summer while the boys had new shirts and pants (one pair cut from an old suit of mine, of course). Ethel's hair had been reparted in a way to cover up the missing curls. Last, but not least, Mother came to me.

"Will, are you sure there's not a hole in your handkerchief?" Every Sunday since our first year at Faulkton she had asked that question. Mother said I had a peculiar habit of taking my handkerchief from my breast pocket and using it frequently in some odd little gesture, and she was always mortally afraid I would appear in the pulpit and wave a holey rag in the face of the audience.

I took great pride in looking down from the pulpit at my family. Two children sat on one side of Mother and three on the other side. Mother was rather a dignified lady and if the children wiggled or whispered she wouldn't speak to them or even shake her head; she simply looked a little more fixedly at me and reached over and pinched the offending child without so much as moving her shoulders to do it. One Sunday as the girls stood to sing the hymns and again as they sat down, each girl put her handkerchief to her mouth. Standing in front of them as I was, their actions were very obvious but Mother did not seem to notice. I wondered if they could all be getting sore throats; maybe some epidemic had hit the town and they were coming down with a malady. Still, they did not look feverish and they were not unduly restless. At the dinner table I questioned their strange behavior, much to their embarrassment. It came out that they had taken cookies to church and it was only in the confusion of the congregation's standing and sitting that they could get the handkerchief-concealed cookies into their mouths.

That year my brother Harry came to visit us over the Christmas holidays. One night Mother and I had to go to a church function and Harry offered to take care of the children. It was a cold night so we had a big fire in the fireplace. We left the children playing with their new Christmas blocks and Uncle

Harry settled in a comfortable chair with a good book. The next morning Mother couldn't find the blocks. On questioning the youngsters they told her they had burned them the night before. Sensing a degree of unbelief, and certainly disapproval, they all insisted that Uncle Harry had told them they could. All he could remember was an endless series of questions from children while he was trying to read, so he just sat there saying, "Um-hm" to keep them quiet while he finished his story.

The next time we went out we decided Uncle Harry was not too satisfactory as a nursery attendant so we hired Mrs. Carter, one of the church women, to come in. Mother put the children to bed and arranged the neighbor comfortably near the coal heater. In the ceiling just over the place where she was sitting there was an opening covered with an iron grill to let the heat from downstairs help warm the bedroom above. This being a very cold night the children decided to take turns sitting on the grill to warm up for a few minutes. Then they had a better thought; if they took the grill out the smaller children could hang their feet down through the hole and get them much warmer. Suddenly the grill banged down on the floor, missing Mrs. Carter's head by about a half inch. She raced upstairs as fast as her two hundred pounds could make it, but, she reported, when she got up there every child was fast asleep in his right bed!

Mother and I were extremely happy in our family circle and the children apparently thrived under the routine. Family worship followed breakfast, then the children were off to school, or in vacation time each one had some part in the family work. From the breakfast table I went to my study where I maintained the habit of spending three hours in study and meditation, always of course with the understanding I could be called if needed. Books—how much they meant to me! No week was complete which did not include the reading of at least one new book, and when I came home from Conference or camp meeting I could hardly keep from reading up my whole new store during the first few days.

Camp Meeting Time! That was the high point in the year for

many Methodists. During our Ohio days we went to camp meeting regularly every summer. The entire family, Mother, the five children and I, would pack up for a ten-day combination of religion and vacation, camping in tents or renting a little cottage depending on the camp site. Frequently there were two or three thousand people in attendance, many of them coming year after year so that "camp meeting time" was like a tremendous homecoming or family reunion. Sometimes the meetings were open-air gatherings with the evening preaching services conducted in an immense tent, while during the mornings classes would be held and in the afternoons several smaller preaching groups might be conducted at the same time. Sometimes instead of a tent a large auditorium was used for the main services.

The camp meeting has been held in contempt by some religious groups, but it is an institution more sinned against than sinning. In the early 1800's an emotional revivalism swept through Kentucky and Tennessee and was supported by all the denominations working in these frontier states. Presbyterians, Disciples and Methodists were the most active groups among the pioneer people so they were caught in the "peculiar American phenomenon" as some church historians like to call the early emotionalism of the camp meeting. Stories of hundreds of converts swooning to the ground, barking like dogs or jerking with uncontrollable contortions are true, but this was a passing phase of southern American revivalism.

The emotionalism of the early camp meeting was not encouraged by the denominations and the majority of preachers discounted it as a means of true conversion. Of course there were always a few preachers who gloried in the demonstrations they could cause, and there were always camp followers made up of gangs of rowdies who tried to work up the people and haggle the preachers. But on the whole the camp meeting was a spontaneous outburst of real religious enthusiasm, American style.

It had some unique advantages. In sparsely settled areas where distances made "neighboring" difficult, where there were not enough people to form regular churches, where preachers had circuits of several hundreds of miles so that each community had a church service only occasionally, the camp meeting was a wonderful experience. Each family came in its own wagon or buggy, brought its sleeping and cooking equipment, reveled in being with people, people, people, and stored up enough religion to spread over the thin places during the coming year.

Camp meetings fit the genious of the early Methodist movement—its warm insistence on a regenerated heart rather than a well-defined creed, its system of circuit riders established when Asbury first came to America and furthered by Peter Cartwright and other outstanding Methodists of the 1700's. The camp meeting was never a part of the official system of Methodist gatherings, which consisted of conferences on various levels —district, state, and the international quadrennial.

The shores of Lake Erie and Lake Ontario became favorite sites for some of the largest of these gatherings. Chautauqua in New York, and Lakeside in Ohio, are still known throughout the world as centers for religious and educational gatherings of a great variety, and both of these huge institutions have grown from original camp meetings of the Methodists. With the later development of the camp meeting another characteristic of the Methodist Church found full play—its insistence on education for its members. Early circuit riders were also traveling librarians who carried their books—a paltry few it is true—in their saddle bags and loaned them to families on their circuits. The Methodists fairly bristled with publications in a day when magazines were still in their infancy. *Zion's Watchmen, Zion's Herald, Christian Advocate, Christian Recorder, The Methodist Review.* These names attest to the printing proclivities of the early Methodists.

As early as 1773 the minutes of the first Conference held in America record a discussion of the good effects resulting from the circulating of Wesley's sermons, and carry the statement: "It now became necessary for all the preachers to be united in the same cause of printing and selling our books, so that the profits arising therefrom might be divided among them or applied to some charitable purpose." This resolution gave birth to the Methodist Book Concern. In the wake of Methodism camp meetings spread throughout the entire United States and even invaded England. About 1810 old Lorenzo Dow, so beloved by the Ohio pioneers, visited England and took with him the idea of the American camp meeting. However, organized Methodism in England did not take kindly to the innovation brought by Dow.

The Hyde family loved the camp meeting. There were special gatherings and plenty of playtime for the youngsters; there were meetings and conversation for the women; there were meetings and more meetings for the preachers; and at night there was the inspiration of hundreds of people singing together the great revival songs from the Sankey songbook and listening to preachers whom the average Methodist would never otherwise have a chance to hear.

Camp meetings were also something of a workout for the preachers who carried the responsibility of the preaching services, the preacher sometimes being paid as much as fifteen dollars a day, which was very good remuneration. Many times after a ten-day camp meeting our family would go home to Centerburg or Orrville or Berea, tired out but elated, feeling it was wonderful to have had all our good time and a hundred and fifty dollars as well!

During our years in Ohio I preached in camp meetings throughout the state and also in Iowa, Indiana, Wisconsin and South Dakota. One summer when I finished a camp meeting in Indiana I was given a beautiful basket of peaches which I decided to take home to Mother and the children. It was a hot overnight ride on the train. I kept the peaches carefully on the seat beside me so they wouldn't be unduly bumped or jostled. Several times through the night when some man walking down the aisle would stop to smile and say, "Peaches, eh?" I would beam proudly. "Yes, beautiful big peaches from Indiana." In a little while someone else would comment, "Peaches, eh?"

Arriving at our station I lovingly picked up the basket. A sticky stream of juice was oozing out. Afraid the basket might break, I put my hand underneath to support it. The juice oozed a little faster, a little browner. "Peaches, eh?" I said to myself while I waited for everyone else to get off the train ahead of me. Then I dripped out onto the depot platform. When we reached home, we buried the peaches. Forever afterward when the family wanted to do something expecially nice for their father one of them would say, "Let's give Dad a basket of peaches!"

The happy days at Centerburg came to an end when we were transferred to Orrville in Wayne County. This was a delightful town in a part of Ohio that I felt somewhat acquainted with through two groups of people I had known in earlier days. As a youngster in Canada I had known several Negro slaves who had escaped through the underground railroad. Some of them on reaching Belleville, Ontario, found friends in our Methodist churches there. Now I was living in part of Ohio through which they had been spirited. Also this part of Ohio was "back home" to many of our Dakota friends. We thought the world was getting small whenever we found people who knew people whom we knew.

The Orrville church was made up of a group of intelligent people, many of them professional, including the superintendent of schools and many of his teachers. On the whole they were not wealthy, but they lived comfortably, almost every family had its horses and a cart, buckboard, surrey or other vehicle. An inspection of the shed where the horses were tied behind any church gave a good indication of the financial level of the community.

Our family took an interest in the Johnny Appleseed orchards in the area. These orchards were a beautiful monument to the peculiar little man who had an obsession for planting apple trees. In the early days of the mid-west, Johnny was a familiar figure tramping across the country with a supply of apple seeds and a few books tucked into the bosom of his worn shirt. He gave the apple seeds to any pioneer family who would plant and tend them and he shared his literature with any settler who showed a spark of interest in the contents of his beloved books. A one-man traveling library as well as a peripatetic nursery.

Soon we were proudly calling ourselves "Buckeyes" just as if we had all been born in the state. The youngsters were delighted when we visited the historic sight that gave the Ohioans their name. It seems that a Colonel Ebenezer once met an Indian chief and his followers to negotiate a treaty. When the chief saw Ebenezer, a tall, erect man with a gallant appearance, he called out, "Heap big Hetuck!" *hetuck* being the Indian for buckeye, a tall tree, common in those parts, whose nuts resemble the eyes of a buck.

I had now been preaching for fifteen years. It is always hard to analyze and evaluate one's own progress, but as well as I could judge I was developing a more mature style of preaching. Perhaps I was less emotional than in my earlier days; I now tried to remember not to "swing my arms like a thrashing machine"; but I also knew that the heart as well as the head has to go into a sermon even if a slight emotionalism breaks the polished exterior. I believe also that good sermons stem from an occasion rather than from an abstraction. I tried to remember that a church needs a preacher because the people have needs which only a church can minister to. I studied the truly great preachers whenever I had a chance to hear them. Many of them I knew well and we discussed at length the elements of good preaching.

These were the days immediately following the evangelistic fervor of Dwight L. Moody. Thousands and hundreds of thousands in the United States and England had been swayed by his appeal which was simple—Christ died to save sinners, He died for you even if you are among the dregs of humanity. Moody had a passion for men and for his Master and he brought the two together. When he found Sankey, his song leader for many years, he found the other half of a combination that has never been equaled in a Gospel team. Scores of times I have used the Sankey songbook in revival meetings. Moody was the great and sincere exhorter raised to the nth degree but his preaching was not the kind necessary for the Sunday-to-Sunday preaching of a regular pastor.

Then there was Frank Gunsaulus, acknowledged the greatest orator on the religious platform. The rhythmic beauty of his words and the musical cadences of his phrasing gave his lectures and sermons magnetic appeal which held audiences spellbound. Doubtless he was gifted to begin with, but it was encouraging to other preachers to know that Gunsaulus had had to study to improve his technique. As a young preacher he was given to over-dramatization which might have ruined his career had not a wealthy benefactor in one of his congregations called his attention to this defect which he was afraid would become magnified as time went by. To ease the sting of criticism the gentlemen sent young Gunsaulus on a tour of Europe where he would have ample opportunity to study and reorganize his preaching techniques.

I studied Bishop Quayle. He was a tremendous inspiration to me always. A big, unsophisticated-looking man who talked with

a drawl and whose unruly red hair stood out stubbornly. While preaching he would run his fingers through this mop of hair, with no soothing effect. But who cared? The Bishop would stand up to preach. "I saw a flower yesterday. . . ." From such a simple beginning he would build a great sermon.

Bishop McConnell was different; a logical mind, a persevering worker, a fine teammate, but lacking a little in the warm human

sympathy which attracted the common layman. His mother was a member of one of my congregations so I knew Francis Mc-Connell over a long period beginning when he was working on his doctorate at Boston University.

And Bishop McDowell, one of the most beloved bishops ever to serve in the Methodist Church. For four years we were members of the same Conference and I knew his father and step-mother intimately for many years. It is from such contacts that one gets the stimulation to improve, improve, improve. No easy, slipshod methods are acceptable when one is working for the Church.

I also studied men who did not attain the status some of the bishops attained—for status is more than position. One bishop in the Ohio days was eager to impress the ministers with his importance by outlining in detail what should constitute a preacher's program. To carry out his plans would have taken at least three pastors working overtime in every parish. At the end of one very dry and overbearing talk he asked if any of us had any questions. One preacher asked one question, "Bishop, when do you expect us to spit?"

The work in the Orrville area became heavier and I persuaded myself that a faster horse would be an asset so I was soon in possession of a dapple gray, a handsome trotter. He covered ground swiftly but he had one delightful peculiarity, he would never allow another horse to travel in front of him. This idiosyncrasy caused me no inconvenience because even at funerals the minister's horse and buggy led the procession and I could hold him to any desired speed. But occasionally a farmer would turn in from a side road immediately in front of us. He did not long remain there but would find himself behind the preacher and part of the funeral procession.

One Sunday afternoon about four o'clock as I was returning from a country trip a race horse hitched to a jockey cart attempted to go around me. My horse instantly took up the race. Into town we sped, down the main street. People on their front porches, in their lawn swings or hammocks jumped up. "Look at preacher Hyde!" The shouting did not ease our pace! Right past the parsonage where Mrs. Hyde and the children were sitting. I dared not turn in. I was standing, feet braced against the buckboard with all my one hundred and twenty-eight pounds pulling on the reins. "Hooray!" the children shouted, and we picked up speed. Through town and out onto another country road before I could ease Pal out of his excitement.

The children thought it a good performance. I think my wife felt that our next horse should be trained for the ministry.

Every summer since the death of my mother shortly before we left Dakota my father had been visiting us. How our children loved him! They tormented him with practical jokes, and doubtless bothered him with incessant noise, but the greatest treat they knew was to have him tell them stories of his younger days, especially the escapades of himself and his twin brother whom no one could tell apart and how they capitalized on this fact to mix up their teachers, their girls during their courting days, and at times even their parents.

Grandpa had a soft spot in his heart for our girls. As they grew older each one took a part of the housework. On a warm summer afternoon if one of the girls had been ironing Grandpa always took occasion to walk up town to buy a few lemons and ask Mother to make a pitcher of lemonade which he invited everyone to sit on the porch to drink.

The Fourth of July was always a thorn in Grandpa's flesh. He was an Englishman, and a good one to the end of his days.

"What you got to make all this fuss about?" he asked the children with his dander up.

"We're celebrating the day we licked England," they told him whereupon he turned on his heel and shook his cane in their faces.

"You little villains, you don't know what you're talking about. England is the Mother of this country."

Abruptly he turned his back on the whole gang of little villains, walked out into the yard and settled himself under the big cherry tree and was soon sound asleep. This indifference to

the Glorious Fourth was too much for young Bill who slipped
out and put a fire cracker under Grandpa's chair. When it ex-
ploded Grandpa didn't say a word, just picked up his cane and
his hat, stomped into the basement and would not put in his
appearance again the entire day. The absence of Grandpa was
punishment enough for the children.

At Orrville the Presbyterian Church and parsonage were right
across the street from us. The Presbyterian minister had a teenage
son just the age of our oldest. It's a hard age to have two boys
such good neighbors; what one doesn't think of the other will,
actually as well as proverbially. One day the boys got both of
their dads into an embarrassing situation. They took their
bicycles, as was their custom, for a ride in the country. This day
being very warm, they stopped in at a farm for a drink. The
farmer, to be very kind, gave them some cider, hard cider in the
bargain. Neither boy knew anything about cider or its effects, so
they enjoyed a relatively large amount, thanked the farmer and
started home. The road led down a very steep hill into the main
street of town. Both boys lost control of their bicycles, careened
across the steep road several times and landed in the ditch, badly
bruised and cut up. Our Bill reached home while the rest of us
were at the supper table. First he went to the back porch to wash
up before facing the family, and while trying to remove the tell-
tale marks of the accident he fell off the porch into the grape-
vines. Hearing the commotion we all dashed to the back porch
and found our son—shall we say slightly inebriated? Perhaps a
bit hasty, I was all ready to give him a good caning when his
mother wisely prevailed against it. Bill recovered but there were
those people in town who liked to remember the time that the
two preachers' sons had drunk too much.

Clara was the little nurse in the family and most of the
children in the neighborhood ran to her if they scraped a knee
or cut a finger while playing. Florence was never happier than
when she had a group of small youngsters to whom to tell stories
or take care of in any way. She was already a fine Sunday School
teacher for beginners.

Bill developed a passion for books, sometimes to my dismay. He would get an idea that the books in the library should be rearranged, and proceed to rearrange them. So when I reached automatically for the concordance which always stood at the right-hand end of the third shelf I came up with Dante's *Inferno*. One week our hundreds of books would be arranged according to color, the next week according to date of publication and perhaps the following week according to subject matter. As a young child he much preferred piling books on the floor to playing with blocks so I should have been prepared for this single-minded attachment, but I wasn't. It was about this time that the catalog of the Methodist Book Concern became his most prized possession. Each fall he wrote for the new catalog and pored over it, holding frequent consultations with his sisters in whispers. Having studied the descriptions of all the calendars offered by the publishing house the children would pool their resources and Mother and I would each receive a beautiful calendar for Christmas.

We were very happy in Orrville and were fortunate in being left there for four years, an unusual length of service for our preachers in those days. So when the fall of 1904 rolled around we were not surprised to have the Presiding Elder call on us to suggest a new location.

"Brother Hyde," he said, "I know you're happy here and so are the people. But I'm going to ask you to leave. I want you to take a church in the northern part of the state; it's a big church and an important church, one with tremendous possibilities. The people in Berea have asked for you and I want you to accept the call."

I will admit my wife and I were pleased. Berea was near Cleveland, an alive and progressive part of the state. Berea was the home of Baldwin and Wallace Colleges, which ranked among our finest Methodist schools. This was a church through whose doors hundreds of young people would pass, and from which many prominent leaders in Methodism had gone. To be the minister of such a church would keep us on our toes, reaching and stretching all the time, and the town would be a fine place in which to raise a family.

After making our decision to accept the call we told the children that we would soon be moving to Berea. To our amazement, by the time school was out that afternoon it was all over town that the Hydes were going to Korea!

9

The Six-Cent Pipe Organ

BEREA was well known across the country. The farmers of America connected it with grindstones, for over half the grindstones in America were made out of Berea grit. Methodists thought of it as the home of Baldwin and Wallace Colleges, appropriately located because it takes grit for many young people to complete their college educations. In 1845 John Baldwin gave the Northern Ohio Conference a plot of five acres on which stood three fine large buildings. Then he added thirty village lots and fifty more acres of land. Baldwin Institute opened its doors, ten years later to become Baldwin College.

On the same campus was German Wallace College, outgrowth of the vision of a group of Germans who came to America in 1817 and settled southeast of Cleveland. There were originally two hundred and twenty-five immigrants in the colony. They bought a fifty-five hundred acre tract and divided it among themselves for farming but hardship and adverse circumstances forced them to pool their efforts and they organized a communal project, a completely self-sufficient community. By the late 1800's the colony was worth about a million and a half dollars. But it was a restless age; greener pastures were ever beyond, and the west beckoned. Also young people have the habit of getting married and moving from the home nest. The colony dissolved in 1898.

The Germans in Ohio were good stock. They believed in education and felt responsible for providing facilities for the German Methodists. First they opened a German Department on the Baldwin campus then later expanded it into German Wallace College. The two institutions always maintained close working relations and supplemented each other in many of their academic offerings. Some years later they united.

The church we were offered was the college church. We were supremely happy to take our family into this stimulating atmosphere. I made a visit to Berea before we moved and on my return home the first question my wife asked me was, "What kind of parsonage?" I didn't blame her for being concerned, remembering some of the dilapidated parsonages we had fallen heir to. Unwittingly I hesitated before answering and she bristled —as much as Mother ever bristled.

"Will, don't tell me it's 'fairly good.' I've heard that so many times and then found out what we really got that I can't endure to hear it again."

"But you'll admit I always went to work on the parsonage as soon as we got into it." That was true. There is no place for shabby church property and I always told a congregation that the condition of their buildings should be an outward sign of an inward glory. One contribution the Hydes made to Methodism was a trail of improved parsonages.

"Just once I would like to move into a house that was in good condition when we went in," said Mother. "Now tell me the truth about Berea."

"The truth is, there is no parsonage."

That situation added spice to our moving; this time we would pick out our house ourselves. Perhaps the house we selected was not exceptional but as one of the children said, "It's like buying a new dress instead of getting a hand-me-down."

The Berea church was a brand new building. Brother Deeds, the former minister, had moved the congregation into it the previous year. It was a fine edifice, brick and stone, beautiful in all its appointments. The sanctuary seated about five hundred people but additional rooms opened onto it so that another two hundred or more could be added. The church had every-thing—Sunday School rooms, kitchen and dining room, ladies' parlor, gymnasium; it was completely equipped to meet the needs of a thriving college community.

But the nice big church had a nice big debt! Forty thousand dollars is not a sum to be taken lightly at any time; in 1904 it was considered a huge amount for a church debt. Obviously, here was my first job; or so I thought. But before I had been in Berea a week I found there was another job to be done before we tackled the debt. I knew it because of two questions repeatedly asked me. As early as my second day in town a fine businessman, a member of the church, said to me, "Are you a fundamentalist or a liberal?"

The cat was out of the bag. No one would ask that question unless there were factions to whom the answer made a difference.

"Fundamentalist or liberal?" I repeated. "Both!" I said with conviction. The man looked at me peculiarly but made no further comment. He was probably feeling sorry for the church that had drawn a preacher who was black and white at the same time. Every time the question was asked me I gave the same answer, "Both!"

Then came the next query and it was really a dandy.

"Are you a lower critic or a higher critic?"

"Now that's a good question," I answered. "How do you define the difference?" Most of them floundered around. But one very positive old lady put me straight.

"It's the difference between being Christian or unchristian," she said.

I pushed her a little. "Which one is the Christian?"

"Now, Brother Hyde, this is no trifling matter. You're a preacher of the Gospel and you ought to know what some of these heretics are doing, trying to make the Bible the work of man."

"Now, Grandma Bates, that's a beautiful flower garden you have. Just look at those marigolds. Are they God's work or yours?"

"Both!" she answered proudly.

"That's just the way I feel about a lot of things," I said. "And the Bible is one of them. God wanted some ideas preserved; God wanted some messages recorded; God wanted to plant some beautiful thoughts in people's minds; God wanted the story of Jesus told the world over; and God had to use men to help carry out this purpose. That is why I say the Bible is the work of both God and man."

There were other people not as easily mollified as Grandma Bates. In the early 1900's the word "higher critic" was a red flag. Most people knew very little about what it meant but many of them used it as a term to send to eternal hell fire any person found tampering with God's holy Word by raising a question as to dates, translations and authorships of the books of the Bible. I realized I was in a church that was split theologically and I knew I would have to close the breach before I tackled the church debt. Our fundamentalist group called themselves Holiness Christians. They formed a clique deeply concerned with sanctification and the second blessing, carrying on its own activities while trying to gain control of other groups in the church. The second Sunday I was in Berea, just as I entered the pulpit one of their members handed me an announcement to read, which I did. "The Holiness Christians will meet this week on Thursday evening." I looked at the congregation innocently.

"I wonder if there is not some mistake in the date. I believe we have our mid-week service on Wednesday evening. Everyone is invited; we all worship one holy God, we read one holy Bible, we form one holy group of worshipers. I am glad to know you stress holiness; nothing is more beautiful."

The Holiness group never again gave me an announcement to read from the pulpit. I found that the regular prayer meeting was being ruined by the competition. Especially the younger married people frankly said, "We've stopped going to the mid-week service; we just can't take the fight between Brother Barnes and Brother Kimball any longer."

Each of these men had a coterie of followers. Mr. Kimball and his Holiness flock sat in a solid group on the right side of the room; Mr. Barnes and the rest sat on the left. Prayer meeting had become a regular Congressional filibuster in which one side sometimes managed to monopolize the entire evening.

I took a drastic step. At a prayer meeting soon after our arrival I warmly complimented the people on their attendance and devotion to the service. Then I suggested that since the group was too large for everyone to participate in prayer or with testimony maybe we could work out a plan so that everyone who felt moved by the Spirit would have a chance to speak. I reminded them that this procedure was the original plan of Methodism, and who could improve over Wesley's plans? So I suggested that each person limit himself to three minutes and that we alternate sides of the room for speakers. Because I hesitated to be a timekeeper I further suggested that each person call time on himself. (I knew that a few of the younger un-Holiness Christians had a plan up their sleeve if this design failed.) Brother Holiness Kimball rose to his feet and began his usual long-drawn-out testimony. Several watches came out. Two minutes. Two and a half minutes. Three minutes. The good brother made the mistake of pausing for breath and the other side guilelessly took advantage of the pause to come out with a fervent old-time Methodist, "Amen, Amen." Before Brother Kimball could recover from his surprise one of the Amen-ers said, "May we sing a verse of number two hundred and seventy-nine?" We found the place in the hymnal; the song was, "I am Resolved No Longer to Linger."

I am sure there was much discussing, and maybe some plain cussing, of preacher Hyde in many homes that night. But the plan worked and I have since heard of other churches who used the "singing down" practice in their testimony meetings.

Another phase of the Holiness theology that bothered me was reflected in one of their favorite hymns:

> It is a point I long to know;
> It oft times costs me anxious thought;
> Do I love my Lord or no?
> Am I His or am I not?

One evening I was a little hot under the collar and chided them. Didn't they know if they loved God? I suggested that each

man go home and take a good look at his wife—think of all the
things she did for him and the many things she sacrificed for the
benefit of the family, then he should say fervently to her,
"Darling, there is a thing I long to know:

> It oft times gives me anxious thought.
> Do I love you, dear, or no?
> Am I yours or am I not?

Rubbish and nonsense! If you love your wife you know it. And
if you love God you know it. You may not love Him enough,
that's a different thing. But if you love God there is a peace in
your heart and a song on your lips and you *know* you love Him.
You don't have to ask Him; you have His abiding presence with
you. The great hymns of the church have been built on reassur-
ance, not doubt. Charles Wesley sang,

> Jesus, Lover of my soul,
> Let me to Thy bosom fly.

He knew he loved God and that God loved him.
    Toplady cried out,

> Rock of Ages! Cleft for me,
> Let me hide myself in Thee.

He was singing from the certainty of his need and the certainty
of God's promises.
    The matter of a "second blessing" on which the Holiness
Christians laid such stress also bothered me. Their idea was
nothing to argue against, it was a matter of showing them how
narrow they were when they boasted of blessings not accorded
the ordinary Christian. Second blessing? Why, each one of us
has received a second hundred and a second thousand blessings.
I asked them to sing:

> Count your many blessings,
> Name them one by one.
> Count your many blessings,
> See what God has done!

"Blessings Unlimited." That's the name of God's factory. Why credit Him with only a paltry second blessing?

In the late fall I held a revival meeting in the Berea church and it served as a cementing element for the divergent points of view. The Holiness people found I had something of their emotional fervor and that took some suspicion off my theology. It was a spine-tingling experience when our whole church full of people stood up and sang together:

> Revive us again!
> Fill our hearts with Thy love.
> May each soul be rekindled
> With fire from above.
>
> Hallelujah! Thine the glory.
> Hallelujah! Amen.
> Hallelujah! Thine the glory.
> Revive us again.

Emotion? Certainly. But much more. I never believed in making a revival an emotional jag, but I do believe it can open the floodgates and wash out much of the selfish interest which has plugged the channel to God.

It took only a few months to make us feel that we were all working together. Now we were ready to tackle our financial problem. Of course considerable groundwork has been laid before we opened what we called the Church Building Campaign. The Berea church had a wonderful official board; night after night they met in the church study to prepare lists of names to be canvassed, to enlist members to work on canvassing committees, to divide among themselves the business firms they wanted interviewed. Work, work, work. But who cared? We are going to be free of debt by one o'clock on a not-too-distant Sunday.

Not only the official board, but everyone else in the church got to work. The Epworth League took responsibility for raising a specific sum; the Aid Society took a big lump, and how the pies, cakes, bread, doughnuts, embroidery work and chicken dinners spun around! We appealed to the community, for a church is not merely a soul-saving institution, it is also a great force in making the community a better place in which those saved souls may live and grow. We followed the same approach we had used in Groton; simply saying to the people of the town, "You need the church; the young people in the college need the church; no one would want to live in Berea if there were not churches to help make it a better place. And the church needs you, so let's get together and clear our church of debt."

The canvassers went out, and the money came in. There is great excitement in raising money for a good cause. With each dollar enthusiasm mounted, and the next dollar came easier. Also there is a by-product to raising money that we did not overlook. Every gift or pledge meant someone was interested in the work of the church, so whenever a gift came from an individual who had not shown previous interest we tried to bring the person into our working fellowship.

Five thousand dollars left to go—four thousand—three thousand—we watched the figure run lower and lower while our jubilation ran higher and higher. By the time the day arrived for burning the mortgage, our spirits neared the boiling point. This was to be no ordinary bonfire. The church was packed with interested participants, a special altar was ready, and the Presiding Elder himself came down from Cleveland to bless the conflagration. That day we walked out of the church with pride.

A preacher leads a peculiar life; he usually has more projects on foot than Ringling Brothers circus and while he keeps one eye trained on all the acts in progress the other eye is peering into the future as he maps out the next act to be added. One might think that a preacher would be satisfied with a debt-free church, at least for a while. But that isn't the way preachers work. Give them one task completed and they are champing at the bit to be at the next one. Preachers are definitely hard on congregations!

This Berea church, for example. I ought to go back and apologize for not letting them rest on their laurels for a while.

But I was plagued with the conviction that a fine big church should have a pipe organ. At the same time I was reminding the people that they had sold their parsonage to get cash to put up the church, so morally they were not out of debt until they rebuilt the parsonage. I let the official board mull over the parsonage idea while I went to work on the organ.

Mr. Andrew Carnegie had recently established a fund to be used for building organs in churches across the country—somewhat on the order of the libraries he had underwritten. There were certain stipulations—a church had to be free from debt, it had to be a community-serving church, it had to have an adequate building and it had to be a church recognized in its own denomination. If all these conditions were met then the Carnegie Fund paid half the cost of the organ. I could see no reason why the Berea church would not qualify for a Carnegie organ, but I didn't want to raise undue hopes. So I decided to write the Foundation on my own initiative, asking for application forms and enclosing a stamp to cover reply. I could invest four cents! In ten days I received the official forms to be filled out. The financial condition of the church appeared to be of greatest concern to the Foundation; evidently they were not going to invest in an organ which the church might later sell to pay off a debt.

I let only two other local men in on my secret project, figuring we had better continue to play safe until we saw what would happen. I asked the president of the college and the president of one of our local banks to write the Carnegie Foundation. Then I wrote to Bishop McDowell and asked him to send a letter of recommendation to New York. Later I found the Bishop had written a most enthusiastic letter and I wondered if the fact that he had married a girl from our congregation might have influenced him. These three men, Mrs. Hyde and myself were the five people who knew what was in the air.

Then I prepared the official report for the Carnegie office—a financial statement emphasizing that the entire debt on the building had been cleared within four years, explaining that the church was a social center, a recreational center, an educational center for the community as well as a worship center, detailing the relation of the church to the college. I thought the report made right good reading!

I became impatient with the mails. A week went by with no answer. Then ten days—the time it had taken to get a reply when I wrote for information—but not even an acknowledgment of our application. Two weeks faded into three weeks. Why this delay? What had I omitted? I was more than glad I had not mentioned a Carnegie organ to the general public!

Then came Saturday afternoon of the third week. I was in my study thinking through the next morning's service when the doorbell rang and a special delivery boy handed me a letter. It was from Mr. Carnegie's office in New York. Surely it would not come special delivery unless it had some news that would be encouraging. Were they taking the matter under consideration? Would they send a representative to look into the situation? All these thoughts raced through my mind in the second or two it took to tear open the envelope. The letter was signed by James Bartram, Mr. Carnegie's secretary, and it read: "Your application has been received and fully credited. I am authorized by Mr. Carnegie to grant a new organ for your church. You are at liberty to purchase an organ from any company your official church organization may deem wise. You will not need to pay for any of it. Enclosed is a form which your trustees will please sign when the organ is completely installed. When this form is countersigned by the organ company that makes the installation they will receive the amount in full."

In full! My best dreams had never contemplated *that*. If this was true we would not have to go before the church to ask for any money. And that meant the parsonage could be built much sooner. What a glorious day! How beautiful was life! And how good was God!—with Mr. Carnegie's help, I had to add in all honesty.

After the Estey organ was completely installed I gave myself the honor of buying the stamp that mailed back the final form to

the Carnegie Foundation. Three stamps, six cents, and the Berea
Methodist Church had a pipe organ.

Winter and spring had torn several sheets off our calendar
since coming to Berea; summer arrived with its slower pace, then
vacation and camp meeting took off three more pages and we
found ourselves facing September. Fall meant that we took up
a stiff pace again. School began for our children; college brought
back hundreds of young folks to the campus and the church.
Before the upswing of the fall leveled off perhaps we ought to
get at the new parsonage.

"We don't really own the church," I told the membership,
"until we have repaid the parsonage fund." They knew that was
true and were almost as eager as I to own a parsonage again; it
was both more convenient and better business. We decided to
make this money-raising compaign short and intensive. After
selecting a site about four blocks from the church, we drew up
plans and submitted them to the denominational Building
Society for approval. Then we got bids and we knew to a penny,
with a few left over for emergencies, what the house would cost.
The project was given wide publicity among the church members and all the money was to be raised at one special occasion.
We set aside an hour after church on a particular Sunday when
again the Presiding Elder could be with us. About thirty-five
hundred dollars was needed but to play safe we decided to raise
four thousand dollars—about sixty-six dollars a minute.

Sunday morning arrived and the church was packed with a
tremendous crowd. Every person there knew he would be
expected to contribute and he came prepared; but also every
person wanted to see what every other person contributed.
Instead of a benediction at the close of the regular preaching
service we offered a prayer of dedication and began the service
of money raising. Using a method popular in those days, we
began with the highest amount expected from anyone and then
worked down. As each amount was specified everyone who
wanted to give in that category raised his hand and his name
was recorded by the clerk. When the pledges came in fast from

all parts of the auditorium it was a little hard on the craning necks. One thousand-dollar gift had already been promised and since the donor was not present we announced the gift and proceeded. Five hundred dollars? Two hands went up. This was fine! Two hundred dollars? Hands popped up all over the room. One hundred? We gave the clerk an assistant to record the names more rapidly. Fifty dollars? Hands by the score. Ten dollars? Five dollars? We were almost exhausted with joy. Finally collection plates were passed for all those who wanted to contribute smaller amounts and while the congregation sang, "Take my life and let it be consecrated, Lord, to Thee," the clerk totaled the pledges and the cash. The whole amount was taken care of! We had faith it would be but it was good to see the assurance in black and white. Now we could put our minds to something else.

The building activities at Berea were only one phase of our work. There were at least two sermons a Sunday; a three-week revival at our own church each year, and usually I served as evangelist for one or two revivals at other churches; then camp meetings in the summer, the student activities, and that most precious part of a pastor's work, personal counseling. All of these professional duties along with a little family life made up our days. Is it any wonder a preacher finds life exciting?

No one knows how many times a preacher's doorbell or telephone rings and a voice at the other end says, "I have to see you right away. I need help. May I come right over?" These calls are given first place, no matter what time of day or night. People carry such burdens!

One morning a woman in our congregation called at the study; she was still under middle age, attractive, capable and a person of some wealth. Although she was not a member she came to church quite regularly but I had never met her husband. This morning she opened the conversation right to the point.

"I want to talk to you confidentially, Brother Hyde. It is about my husband."

"Yes?"

"Bob is a wonderful man. He is good to me and wonderful to our four-year-old son, Tommy. But his business frequently takes him on the road and sometimes he drinks too much. He doesn't drink regularly, but when he does he may be drunk for three or four days; then he goes quite a long time before it gets ahold of him again. I can see that he is beginning to break under the strain and I know it's making a difference in his business record. I'm worried he might lose his job and that would really be the end of him. I don't think he could take that."

"There should be some way to work with him," I began, but she interrupted me before I got any further.

"I have a plan I think would work if you could possibly try it."

"I can surely try. What is it?"

"Bob loves to drive in the country. You know that beautiful horse I drive? It's really his and he loves that horse. We've often heard you mention that you loved horses too. So I wondered if once in a while you might be willing to take a drive out in the country with Bob, then maybe you could find a chance to talk to him."

"Wonderful," I told her. "That's a fine idea and I'd like a chance to get out and relax once in a while. You suggest it to your husband some time soon."

It was not long before Bob called me to know if I could run out in the country with him, he had an errand, and it was a beautiful afternoon.

"Sure thing," I replied. "Could you pick me up at the church about four o'clock?"

That was the first of several short excursions. Bob talked easily on many subjects. He wasn't sure we ought to elect Taft, but Teddy Roosevelt, now, there was a great President; he thought we ought to organize one of those new Rotary Clubs in our town. Bob was good company and I found myself anticipating these drives, and even wondering if his wife might have been mistaken about his weakness for drink. Then one afternoon he slowed down the horse and sat holding the reins meditatively.

He looked out across the fields and spoke in a voice much more tense than his pose indicated.

"Brother Hyde, there is something I want to speak to you about confidentially."

"Yes?"

"I have one terrible habit. I don't like it, but when it gets ahold of me I seem completely helpless to withstand it. I get an awful urge to drink, and when that urge comes I just make a fool of myself and get dead drunk. In a few days it all passes away and I'm fine for weeks. But sometimes I think it's beginning to get the best of me. And this week—I don't want my wife to know—but this week the company hinted I'd have to stop drinking if I wanted to hold my job."

"I don't have to tell you that you're in a serious situation, Bob. The question is, how badly do you want to get out of it?"

"I'd do anything—honestly anything, Brother Hyde, to break this awful curse. I've got to do it for my job, and I'd do anything for Millie's sake. She's a wonderful wife! Yes, I'd do anything." This big, strong businessman sat there and let the tears run down his face like a helpless child.

"If you really mean that, Bob, the way is clear for you."

"Mean it? God, man!"

"You've already mentioned the beginning point—God. He has laid down a few rules and if you will follow them He can bring you through."

All the way home we talked about taking God as a companion —right in the buggy wherever a man drives; about asking God for strength for each minute as it comes when one is in the face of temptation; we reviewed God's promises to "everyone that asketh."

"I'll try," were the last words Bob said when he left me at the church just before suppertime.

I was surprised that I heard no more from Bob. His wife continued to come to church but made no mention of our talk. The invitations to ride in the country stopped. I kept track of

Bob's job and knew that he held it but beyond that fact I knew nothing about him.

Then one Sunday morning Bob and Millie came to church together. As we were singing the closing hymn this man with his wife beside him walked to the front of the church. There were deep lines in Bob's face, but they were lines of strength, not of weakness.

"May I say a word?" he asked as he took my hand.

I nodded. He turned toward the congregation.

"You all know me, but many of you do not know that two months ago I was a slave to drink. I kept it covered, mostly. But with God's help I am now a free man; the shackles are broken and I am no longer a slave. I want you to know this because it may help someone else, and it gives glory to God to tell you it was with His help that I did it."

He said it just as simply as that. This testimony was good old-time Methodism which was becoming a thing of the past, and in my heart I thanked God for Wesley and his fostering of the soul purging relief of testimony.

Not long after this experience Mother and I were in Millie and Bob's home for Sunday dinner. Both of them had been at church and Tommy with them. I had preached that morning on "Flowers for the Living." I'd said that I would rather have one lovely flower, or one appreciative word during my lifetime than a floral shop of wreathes dropped on my grave and an eloquent oration over my casket. During the course of the dinner Tommy reached into the center of the table and picked a flower from the centerpiece. Millie tried to smooth over his behavior but he did it a second and a third time. With each daisy he mumbled a few indistinct words as he dropped the petals on the floor. Millie became more embarrassed but obviously hated to make a scene before guests. During a lull in the adult conversation we heard Tommy saying as he dropped each petal, "Take that, Hyde, take that." His words became another family slogan, along with the "Basket of peaches for Dad."

There was a third remark the family liked to use to put me in my place. Many people talk about grasping the "golden opportunity." But in our home the family always wanted to "silverplate the occasion," especially if it seemed to offer financial reward. Every once in a while a preacher gets an idea that ought to work out better than it does. One year our expenses were pushing our salary pretty hard so that summer I decided to set up a small silver-plating outfit in our basement. Plating is a simple process and I was sure that a few spare evenings (which seldom arrive) could be given to plating old silver and the boys and I could work up a good little business on the side. An advertisement made the whole procedure very clear. I figured Bill could do the actual work with me and one or two of the younger children could collect old silver to be replated on order.

We set up the simple equipment and collected a few orders. But I found the silver didn't replate as easily as the ad had said it would. The first several pieces came out rough and unsightly. One set of silver was so unco-operative that I never could get a good finish on it and had to replace it with a new set. Then someone was always spilling part of the mixture and the acid burned holes in several pairs of trousers and one new sweater. We gave up the project.

"Throw it out the window," said Mother, which was the nearest equivalent to swearing that ever passed her lips.

During our years at Berea I often felt that if I had ten lives to live I would want to spend them all working with college people. Of course, I'd felt the same way about working on the prairies of Dakota; I actually think I've been blessed with liking any job I've had, but college students gave a new kind of satisfaction.

Since Baldwin-Wallace was a Methodist institution and since we were the college church, students and faculty made up a large part of our Sunday audiences. If at first I was occasionally tempted to be a little erudite before such an august group I tried to remember that these professors came to church for the same reason any other man comes, to worship, not to impress others with their professional standings; that students came to church to worship, not to be awed with sesquipedalian words; this realization helped me preach the same old, but ever new gospel of Jesus, "who went about doing good."

The students and I exchanged courtesies—they came to church and I joined them frequently in the classroom. I had to know what they were thinking before I could enter into their problems. So I sat through many class sessions in science and philosophy, in history and religion. The entire faculty were very co-operative but I came to rely most on Professor Hoyt. He was a wonderful man to work with for he had the respect of the students and was very active in the work of the church. At a recent General Conference he had missed election to the bishopric by only three votes. What the bishopric lost, Baldwin-Wallace and Berea gained. Often Professor Hoyt would tell some of his students, "Go over and talk to Brother Hyde; he'll help you with your problems."

I think the students liked the fact that I never read a sermon. What's more, I never even used notes. I always prepared notes carefully but I have a very photographic mind and once I have organized my thinking on paper I can discard the notes and carry them in my mind. This method of speaking gives a preacher a chance to talk more directly to his people. As one of the students commented, "Jimminy Christmas, you look right into us when you preach!"

Scores and scores of people have asked me how I could prepare so many sermons year after year. In the course of any year I suppose I prepared a hundred and twenty-five regular sermons not counting the patriotic talks, and addresses for community, club, conference, and other special occasions. I give my memory credit for part of the accomplishment. Writing out sermons is a time-consuming occupation. The only sermons I ever wrote were the ones I had to prepare when I was ordained as Deacon and then as Elder. Of course a preacher uses some of the same material more than once but it is always in a new setting. Because I never wrote out a sermon I never had—thank fortune—the proverbial barrel of sermons to dig down into.

The morning hours I reserved for study and thought were my salvation. How often I entered my study feeling completely empty and blank only to come out refreshed and refilled with ideas and enthusiasm. The habit of reading at least one book a week was also a source of stimulation. In my early days of preaching I heard a bishop make the statement, "Gather your wheat from every field; put it through your grinding mill; then the flour is yours."

Home, in Berea, was a gay place. We made quite a houseful with Bill in college, Florence, Clara and Ethel in their teens and Leonard tagging along not yet ten years old. One summer Bill worked in a factory that made the little caps for torpedo canes which, when hit on the sidewalk, emitted a resounding "Bang!" There were always a good many imperfect torpedoes which the factory workers could buy very reasonably, so that on the Fourth of July our family was well supplied with noise. At the end of one hot and weary day of celebration the children were finally in bed and noise-aching ears were recovering when at midnight there was a series of explosions that wakened the entire town. Every hour the electric train from Cleveland arrived at Berea, and some time after eleven o'clock that night someone had placed dozens of torpedoes on the tracks. The midnight train set them off. The town turned out en masse, remembering that two years previous some older boys in the community had done this same trick and had been arrested after a good tussle with the police.

This time there was a wide search for the culprits but no gang was found. It was the next summer before I found out that my oldest son and his three sisters, along with a couple of neighbor girls who were spending the night at our house, had tiptoed out shortly after eleven o'clock and as quietly tiptoed back just in time to watch the whole celebration from their upstairs windows. The one excuse I can think of is that their mother, with little Leonard, was visiting in Canada.

Our own youngsters were only the beginning of the young things in our home. We were overrun with high school pals and almost swamped with college students. But there were never too many! I never could figure out whether it was because Mother was such a good cook—the smell of those apple pies as I came into the house!—or because there were three girls in the family, or because Mother and I had the philosophy that the more fun your children can have at home the better off they are; but something in the combination made the parsonage a hilarious place.

We had a phonograph and we purposely did not tack down the rug in the living room. It is sometimes hard for a preacher to know where he stops being a hired hand of the church and starts being a father in his own right. In the gymnasium of the church the young people did not dance—that regulation was the desire of the church members. In our home the young people could dance. Frequently it was the old-time Virginia Reel or other folk dances but they also practiced a few modern steps. It was gay, energy-using fun and we accepted it as such.

Old Grandma Bates used to click her false teeth and say in a squeaky voice, "Tck, tck, Brother Hyde, I hear the devil was at your house last night. He swung a mighty fast tune."

"Well, Grandma, I have to have someone to fight to keep from getting fat."

"It wouldn't hurt you, Brother Hyde, to put a little meat on those bones. With such a good cook as Mrs. Hyde I don't see how you stay so thin."

By the time we had exchanged comments she had forgotten that the devil had lured the young people in the preacher's house.

The Methodists frowned on card playing, that is, with euchre cards, but Flinch and Rook were perfectly harmless. Around the campus Rook was called the "Methodist Five Hundred" and I suppose we wore out several sets of the cards at our house.

But the evenings of music were my favorites. We had a great deal of music. Mother had been singing since she was a child so it came natural for our children to grow up with music. The violin was my favorite instrument. I would have loved to sing if I could, but I early got the idea of listening rather than participating. Oh, sometimes at home I would "lend a voice" but I learned my lesson at a camp meeting one summer. The song leader called out, "Now sing! Everybody on the chorus! SING!" So I sang. The man standing next to me nudged me, "Sing on key, brother." All those wasted hours in Groton when Bessie had tried to help me! I can still remember the do, do, do, etc., which formed the bass of "There Shall Be Showers of Blessing," but finally Minnie told me gently that I never did start on pitch nor stay on key. So I gave up.

Students did not always come to the house for the fun they had there. Many were the hours I sat with a group of them discussing some of the deeply perplexing problems of their student generation. Perhaps the worst problem was commonly referred to as "the fight between science and religion." In reality a person might as well talk about the fight between truth and beauty for there should never have been any cleavage between science and religion. The professors at the college were Christian teachers, but the whole era was tinctured with the conflict that arose with the advent of the "scientific method" and many students were confused.

I often told them that science and religion are the two greatest words in any language; they are different interpretations of the same truth. Science works with the materials and energies God created. Theories of science may change, but science is truth and truth is eternal. Theories of religion change, but the search for God, this Creator of the world's forces, is eternal; and God is eternal Truth. The test of the truth of either science or religion is, Does it work? When a scientific theory works, it is true. When religion works, it is true.

By 1908 we had been in Berea four years, an unusual length of time for a Methodist preacher. Although a minister was occasionally left in a pulpit an extra year Mother and I were seriously asking ourselves what our attitude toward a move should be. We loved every minute of our Berea ministry. But were there some opportunities our children were missing by remainnig here? Would a larger city give them more advantages? Of recent months tempting bait had been cast our way to see if we would nibble on the idea of moving to Chicago.

Dr. Traveller, my first friend in the United States, now well along in his years, was living in Chicago and still active in Methodist work. Also McDowell, an Ohio boy whose parents had been members of my Centerburg church, was now Bishop of the Chicago area. Together we had served in the North Ohio Conference for four years and were very close friends before he went from Tiffin to Denver to become Chancellor of the University. Nine years later he became Corresponding Secretary of the Methodist Board of Education and again we had close contacts. Now he was Bishop in Chicago and soon to become my boss! For after months of weighing the pros and cons, and after most earnestly asking God to guide our decision, we made up our minds to accept the invitation to transfer to the Rock River Conference of Illinois as soon as there was a vacancy.

Thirteen years we had spent in Ohio—Belleville, Centerburg, Orrville—happy years in each church and happy reunions when we were invited back for festivals or revivals. Now we had completed in many ways the busiest four years of our lives at Berea. We knew we would never find greater joy in any location. But there seemed to be pressing work to do done in Chicago, no doubt against greater obstacles than we had ever faced before, so we sharpened the edge of our spiritual shovels and prepared to dig in Illinois soil.

10

Before the Judge

IN 1895 the Hydes with four little children had come out of the West. In 1908 the seven-member family backtracked to take up residence in Chicago.

Chicago. On the train from Berea to Illinois I had a good laugh with Minnie over my first night in Chicago. The older I got the younger my youth seemed to me! Imagine being so "scared" of this city, as I was in 1886, that I hotfooted it (via horse car) straight from the railway station to the Y.M.C.A. because the city was too evil for me to risk its streets at night. As I look back at that not too prepossessing country boy on his way to Dakota Territory I think he probably would have been safe in any part of Chicago.

Although we had passed through Chicago several times on our visits to Canada we usually had small children with us so that sightseeing was not an easy proposition. To be sure we had also been there for an occasional church conference and had occasionally taken a conducted tour, but being good conference delegates we spent most of our time in the convention halls. We might be said to have had a speaking acquaintance with Chicago. Another twenty-five years and there would hardly be a block of her Gold Coast or a street in Little Hell that we did not know, while the Loop would be as familiar as the center square at Centerburg.

Our first church in Chicago was not to be a large one for we were in somewhat the same position as when we went to Ohio— we were making a last-minute request to enter an already filled Conference. When we requested membership in the Rock River Conference there was no vacancy but there was one change

which the Conference thought desirable. The previous year a
minister had been transferred from a country parish to a city
church but the transfer had not worked out happily for either
the church or the minister. This man was interested in the
church I was vacating in Ohio so we exchanged pulpits and Conference memberships and I took the Hermosa Methodist
Church for a short time. Within a few months there was an
opening in the Wheadon Methodist Church in Evanston, the
first suburban community north of the Chicago city limits. My
membership in the Rock River Conference has been continuous
since 1908.

It is difficult to appraise churches. If judged by size, then we
made a backward move, for the Wheadon church was not as
large as the Berea church. If judged by budget we had not
progressed because this church raised no larger budget than our
former church. If judged by the importance of being "a big toad
in a small puddle" we had definitely taken a jump back. The
Berea church had been *the* big church of the community; the
Wheadon church was one of more than a hundred Methodist
churches in the Chicago area, and far from the most pretentious
of them.

But it was not by any of these standards that we appraised
our new location. This church was an important factor in our
lives because through it we began a quarter of a century of work
in the Chicago area and while working in it we found one of the
most rewarding experiences of our many years of ministry, the
opportunity to work with the students of Northwestern University, and especially the theological students of Garrett Biblical
Institute, the Methodist seminary connected with the University.

Northwestern University is a Methodist school in no narrow
sense. A majority of its board must be Methodists, but otherwise
it is nonsectarian. Garrett Biblical Institute is located on the
Northwestern campus and works in close affiliation with Northwestern but it is not a department of the University. It is a
beautiful memorial to a woman whose wealth was put into the

service of humanity. Under the guidance of two of her ministers, Mrs. Eliza Garrett, wife of a former mayor of Chicago, gave a sum of three hundred thousand dollars to establish a Methodist seminary. The doors of the school opened in 1858 and since its first days it has served a much wider student body than the Methodist Church alone provides. This same statement could be made about most of the leading theological seminaries in the country. One of the strong forces making for interdenominational co-operation in America is the undenominational character of the basic training young ministers receive. To be sure, preachers are well founded in the history and practices of the denomination of their choice, but we now educate our preachers to understand and appreciate the points of divergence and the areas of agreement among various denominations, and we emphasize the fact that the Church Universal is more universal than any particular denomination.

In the Wheadon church we found that reviving the practice of a Sunday evening service opened an easy and unexpected approach to the seminary students, commonly called "Bibs." Soon after our arrival in Evanston we sent out a few tenuous feelers among the members of the congregation relative to some changes in the church program, among them the suggestion for a Sunday evening service because it seemed to us that we were wasting half of the day that was in a special way the church's own time. When I made the proposal to the official board they were somewhat skeptical; the church "hadn't been doing it that way" and they doubted if the congregation would be agreeable but if I wanted to try there was nothing to prevent me. I was tempted to tell them that their apathy was one thing that might prevent success, but instead I thanked them for giving me a free hand.

It was to this evening service that the "Bibs" began to come in increasing numbers. I felt complimented to see each man taking notes on my sermons, until I began to suspect what was happening—these young preachers studied hard all week and then had to preach every Sunday morning at some outlying church; back in town in time to attend the evening service, they found me a source of material for their next week's sermon! I was sure I had diagnosed the situation correctly when in a single week I heard comments from the members of three small churches on recent sermons by their student pastors on the topic, "Tried in the Balance"—my text two weeks earlier.

It became common practice for a half dozen of the most inquiring minds to wait around after church until the other members of the congregation had left and then raise some question in theology suggested by the sermon. Usually we adjourned to our home and the discussions sometimes lasted long into the night. Students such as George McDonald and Merrill Holmes raised problems which bother every thinking Christian at some time. For instance, "What about eternal punishment?"

"No!" was my first answer. Then after the initial blast we thought through a more tenable position. "Eternal," I commented, "eternal is a man-made word applicable to our concept of time. God does not have the same sense of time as we have so the eternity of punishment is not for us to worry about. However, any idea of continual punishment is not part of Jesus' teaching. Jesus was always ready to help every person who showed the slightest indication of wanting to be helped. Picture Him on the hillside overlooking Jerusalem, the city which He loved and yearned with His whole heart to save; but Jerusalem refused His help and Jesus could only weep at her plight as He said in great tenderness, 'O Jerusalem, Jerusalem . . . how often would I have gathered thy children together, as a hen doth gather her brood under her wings, and ye would not!' Jesus had an outgoing love that tried to encircle the world; He was not interested in condemning to eternal punishment."

"Do you think there is no punishment, then, for sin?"

"Of course there is punishment for sin. But it begins when the sin is committed. The realization of sin, the knowledge of the harm it does, the guilty feeling that accompanies transgression, these are the beginnings of the punishment."

"Then where does it end?"

"No one knows. But this we surmise. The life after our sojourn on this earth is a life of continued growth. We live with Him who is the Source of all life and love; therefore our next life is opportunity for greater growth into the nature of life and love."

Good students have inquiring minds and I was happy when these theological men asked questions that showed they were hunting answers. No man can be a good minister who is not honest in his thinking. The man who closes a door on any avenue of thought closes one avenue to God. Even honest doubt may be the beginning of wisdom.

During that winter one young "Bib" became much discouraged with his Greek which was a required subject and if he flunked it he was out of school, unless he took the course over. One Sunday evening, so he told me later, he threw down his Greek book and started to walk out of his room but was stopped by his roommate who asked where he was going.

"I'm going to quit school, if that's what you want to know. I'm quitting tomorrow. Tonight I'm going over to hear Hyde."

That night in our discussion after church he asked me, "What would you do if you were flunking a course even after you'd put your best efforts into it?"

"I'd pray and then try some more," I answered.

"What has prayer to do with a passing grade in your subjects?" he pushed me. "Do you actually think God has nothing to do but help pull a dull student through with a passing grade?"

"My kind of God isn't interested in passing grades," I answered; "He is interested in passing men. He wants every man to be as big a success as possible."

"Where does the prayer come in?"

"That's a good question. Prayer is a form of co-operation. Real prayer is an expression of your faith in God's power and your dedication to co-operate with Him."

"Why can't His power work without man's puny prayers?"

"I'll answer that with another question," I told this discouraged student. "Would you expect God to grow potatoes without the help of a farmer? Would you expect God to provide you with a wool suit without the help of a weaver and a tailor? In the physical world men work with God to produce food, clothing, houses—everything that does not exist in a natural state."

"And you really think, Mr. Hyde, that in the spiritual world the same co-operation is needed?"

"Why not? Prayer is the voice of faith. Faith makes a man work for the thing he believes in. The sinner who *wants* to be better prays for help to be better; then he works for that result. The student—to get back to our original idea—who wants to do better work prays for help. That prayer is an expression of his faith that he can do better; then he goes to work and God has a chance to work with him. Maybe the student needs to learn to concentrate; maybe he needs courage to talk to his professor; maybe he needs friendship from some of the other students. His prayer not only opens a way for God to come into his life but it expresses his desire to work with God."

In this group of young theologians there was one especially brilliant young man, Gene Wadham, who was inclined to be cynical. He doubted every axiom of the faith, not for the sake of wisdom but for the sake of doubting—or as I really thought, for the sake of seeing if he could shock some of the professors or older preachers. I used to enjoy giving him a lot of rope in an argument in order to watch him hang himself. He was a fine-appearing man, tall and commanding in his bearing, with a vibrant voice and a piercing eye. It seemed to me he could become a great man if he could be persuaded he was not God's greatest gift to the Methodist Church.

One evening Gene brushed aside a few preliminary remarks made by the other men with the not too original statement, "You know, Mr. Hyde, I have a peculiarly constructive mind."

"Oh yes, we all have," I admitted airily.

"But mine is different from many. I have been studying

philosophy and I want to tell you right now that I do not believe in anything that cannot be perceived through the senses."

Of course he wanted to get me into a discussion of the relative merits of the philosophical theories of Kant, Locke and others. I decided he could engage in this go-round with his professors; I would meet him on a different level.

"All right, Gene, I'll accept your statement and I'll prove to you in less than ten minutes that you are not a human being."

A look of surprise came over his face, and the other students settled down for an enjoyable session.

"I'd be glad to hear your line of reasoning, of course, Mr. Hyde."

"Let's begin with the characteristics of human beings. For example, the understanding. Do you admit that understanding *is* a characteristic of a human being?"

"Yes," replied Gene.

"But did you ever taste understanding, or see it or smell it?"

"That's a little absurd, isn't it, Mr. Hyde?"

"We'll answer that question a little later," I told him. "You admit you never tasted or felt understanding. All right then, what about the process of reasoning? Did you ever feel reason? Or can you describe its physical proportions as seen by the eye or felt by the hand? If not, then you have no process of reasoning, a deficiency to add to your lack of understanding."

Gene started to interrupt me.

"Hold on, Gene. I have six minutes of my ten left and then you can take over the argument. You doubtless would admit that will is a function of the human mind and therefore an attribute of a human being. I would be glad to have a sensory description of will—not of its results, we all can see that, but of the nature of will itself."

There was a slight discomfort in Gene's face and a growing delight on the part of the other students whom he frequently heckled with his dogmatic opinions.

"Now just two other questions." I said, "Love is an affection, and affections are usually ascribed to human beings. What is the size, shape, sound or color of love? But if you do not want to pause for that question I will present the last one. A human being has a conscience, I believe. As to the exact nature of it men have differed, but they generally agree to the reality of something by that name. Now did you ever have a dish of conscience served to you for breakfast, or a bouquet of it set on your desk, or a transcription of it played for your ears?"

There was a general laugh at this comment but I was aiming at something more serious than these surface reactions.

"Gene, by your own statement you have no understanding, no power of reason, no will, no affections, no conscience. These elements are all characteristics of personality. If you do not possess them you are not a human being."

Gene bristled up and an angry flush showed on his face.

"Reverend Hyde," he said rather stiffly, "you have reduced philosophy to an absurdity."

"No, Gene, I have only tried to show you that your peculiarly constructive mind is trying to posit truths on very inadequate opinions gleaned from superficial study. A preacher needs a much more constructive mind than you have yet developed."

"Am I not, as a preacher, entitled to my own opinions?" he flared up.

"Yes, indeed, you're entitled to them. But you must always remember that opinion does not make anything true. You go to facts for truth, and even then you find that people who deal in truth are the most modest in making dogmatic assertions. A man needs to be so sure of what he knows that he can back his knowledge with his life, if need be. When you go home tonight take your Bible and read the verse from Job, 'I know that my Redeemer liveth,' and then go back and read the first eighteen chapters of Job and see upon what Job based his assertion. Such knowledge is hard come by."

Those were grand mental bouts that we had, but it was from such sharpening of the wits that ideas were brought to their fine points for me as well as for the students.

From the contacts I had with the Garrett "Bibs" came a

request to teach Homiletics in the Evangelistic Institute, an interdenominational seminary in Chicago. So for ten years, in addition to any other duties I might be carrying, I tried to teach young preachers how to preach. Memories of my first sermon at Groton helped me realize the struggle some of these men were going through, although students in a seminary were getting practice under supervision that those of us who started our ministry in the earlier days never had.

Many times during my own life and especially during my work with theological students I tried to evaluate the place of education in the development of Methodism. The circuit riders in America, those stalwart early Methodist itinerants, carried their books and magazines into the wilderness, not only for their own study but to loan to their converts in order that they might be better founded in the faith. As early as 1816 the General Conference had ruled that courses of reading and study should be organized in the various states, that preachers should pursue these studies and pass an acceptable examination before being ordained as Elders, meaning fully qualified ministers. Methodists, along with Baptists and Disciples, never required their ministers to be college graduates. Congregationalists and Presbyterians laid much more store by seminary training. In 1910 we might laugh at the statement of an early American church leader that higher education provided only "learned dunces and third-rate preachers," but we agreed that his basic premise that the "call" to the ministry and the dedication of a life to the Master's service were substantially the first requirements; a man could start to preach and let his education follow. The Methodists could be proud of their record of establishing colleges across the country; emphasis on education was part of their genius as a pioneering religion.

Perhaps Mother and I understood the problems of students because we had young folks growing up in our own home, facing the problems of all young people—what to study, which business or profession to enter, how to stretch a meager allowance or salary, what sort of amusements, clubs, sports to go into, who to "date," what to believe about religion, politics, social problems. Within our own four walls we had daily exercises in the art of living. A family is the best educational institution ever evolved—especially for the parents.

Our house never lacked activity. Bill and his books! He was now employed at the Methodist Book Concern and so busy with his own work that occasionally I could safely leave a book out of place in my own library. I found it was not long until he could tell his Dad a few things about books and very occasionally he made the discovery that his Dad already knew something about books. Youngsters are funny that way—the older they get the more their parents seem to know.

Florence had gone into training for kindergarten teaching. Sometimes I thought our children had one-track minds as I watched their childhood interests develop into professional careers. All those youngsters Florence had tended in Centerburg or Orrville or Berea, all those classes of little tots she had taught in Sunday Schools were part of her passion for children which grew stronger as she went through high school and decided to enter the National Kindergarten Training School in Evanston.

Clara and Ethel were average scatterbrained high school girls. Maybe "scatterbrained" is too strong a word because each had her moments of seriousness. Clara was dedicated to her future as another Florence Nightingale and Ethel—well, Ethel was dedicated to the joy of living with plenty of time to settle the fate of the universe. Later Clara and Ethel attended Lakeview High School and one fall developed unusual knowledge of roller coasters, which seemed strange to me because we did not often go to amusement parks. Then I discovered a certain strain of financial genius in the girls. They had to transfer on the streetcar at a point close to Riverview Amusement Park; outside the Park limits there was one roller coaster on which there was just time for a ride in the few minutes allowed on their transfers. So the girls saved part of their lunch money each day to use for a roller coaster ride on the way home. Since neither of them suffered from malnutrition it proved a good experience in learning that one cannot buy two things with the same money—either you eat and do not make merry, or you play at the expense of your hunger pangs.

Leonard was still in the grades. Ethel alternated between being little sister to the older children and big sister to her small brother. Between them they had one standing joke. Each had a scar on the forehead which dated back to their life in Ohio. One day in the woodshed Leonard had accidentally whacked Ethel on the head with the hatchet and a few days later Ethel had pushed Leonard off the curb; each had had to have stitches taken to close the wounds. So for years when they had a little difficulty—real or in fun—one would say, "Do you know where I got this scar?" and the other would answer dramatically, "And do you know where I got *this* scar?"

With three high school or college age girls in the house we were well aware of the fact that our own two sons were not the only male members of the community. We had always had young men in and out of the house and as the girls grew older they were still in and out of the house, but with a difference!

The church work moved along at good speed. It seemed our lot to fall heir to churches which were ripe for some kind of building program. The Wheadon church, with a membership around four hundred, was outgrowing its plant. During our first year we built an addition and laid plans for an entirely new sanctuary two years later.

In the Wheadon church I found one of the most appreciative congregations with whom I ever worked. Our men's club met on Thursday evenings, with a large membership including some of the leading men in Evanston. We always had a short religious service, then a fine program dealing with one of the pertinent problems of the church or community, and finally a social hour. In the early spring of our first year I was presiding at one of the meetings and was about to adjourn the group when the president of the board of trustees indicated that he had something to say. I gave him the floor.

"Wait just a minute," he said in a very unbusinesslike way.

Within the minute another of the men appeared from a side room rolling a fine bicycle beside him. The president made a brief speech about this gift's being a mark of their appreciation for our ministry and expressing the hope that it would lighten my work; whereupon he presented me with this shiny and very new-fangled bicycle. As soon as the meeting was dismissed the men crowded round to see the ultra-ultra tires with inner tubes!

This bicycle would be a great help in making calls. My horse-and-buggy days were left behind in Orrville and automobiles were not yet common enough for the average preacher to own, while distances were great in Chicago where congregations were beginning to spread out. It was quite the vogue for ministers to make their professional calls by bicycle. But first I had to learn to ride one!

That night when I got home the family expressed all the proper joy at this new arrival. I think their father gained a new appreciation in the eyes of his two sons. Before retiring I told the family not to wait breakfast for me, that I would be up early and gone from the house. I had a busy morning's work laid out. I kept my word and took the new bicycle out very early hoping to be able to ride it reasonably well before any of the neighbors were on the street.

In front of our house it happened that for a length of two blocks the street was torn up. We all thought it a nuisance to have bicyclists mingling with the pedestrians on the sidewalk but it was about the only way a cyclist could get down the avenue. I was out so early in the morning that I knew I would not interfere with anybody's walking if I practiced close to home. About seven o'clock, just as I was making headway at balancing myself, a couple of exceedingly burly policemen came down the two-block stretch. I was having a pretty bad time to stay on the two-wheeler, but with the greatest dexterity I steered between them and to my joy knocked down neither officer. As I wheeled reelingly past I called out a cheerful, "Good morning." But immediately I felt someone clutch the seat of my bicycle.

"Where are you going?" demanded one of the policemen.

"I don't know," I replied. "I'm not really going anyplace," I added truthfully.

"Why are you riding on the sidewalk?" They were gruff with this question.

"It's about the only place there is to ride around here. And since it is too early for anyone to be on the street I thought it would be a good chance to learn to ride this new contraption."

"Don't you know the ordinances of your city? 'No riding on the sidewalk.' "

"I suppose I have heard of such a thing," I had to admit, "but with the street torn up it's been common practice for everyone to use the sidewalk on this block. And, of course, I never had a bicycle before so I suppose some of the bicycle ordinances haven't registered with me."

"They will now," announced one of my captors. "You're under arrest. We're out with orders to arrest anyone riding on the sidewalk."

"Yes sir," I said, "I see, I'm arrested."

"You sure are. What's your name?"

"W. J. Hyde." I left off any identifying title.

The information was entered on a ticket.

"Where do you live?"

I gave my address.

"Where's your place of business?"

It would be out now, so I might as well make a clean breast of it.

"Gentlemen, you see that church up there on Ridge Avenue?" They looked in the direction I pointed. "I am the pastor of that church."

The two policemen looked at each other.

"You see," I continued in my own defense, "I am the minister of that church and this new bicycle was given to me last night by the men of the church. I am just trying it out this morning."

"This isn't so good," said one of the policemen and they both laughed.

"No? Why not?" I queried.

"Well, we were sent out this morning with orders to arrest anybody, *anybody* found riding on the sidewalk. The police force is all fed up with the violations of the city ordinances."

"All right, do your duty," I said amiably. "You're paid to enforce the law. You promised to do just that when you were put on the police force. So do it."

"That's pretty straight talk," said one of the men. "I don't know what else we can do either, but it really bothers me."

The other officer shook his head. "Now see here," he offered, "there's no reason for running you in. I guess you could be put on your honor." Both men thought that a good joke for some reason. "You meet us at the entrance to the police station at five minutes to nine. The judge'll be on hand at nine."

I thanked the officers, turned my offending bicycle around and pushed it the two blocks home, arriving while the family were at the breakfast table.

I solemnly told them my plight, but the solemnity didn't last long. The boys would have given anything to go to the police station with their Dad, but we decided it would not be entirely proper since I probably would not need anyone to bail me out. The girls made up headlines such as might appear in the daily papers. "Local Preacher Reels Down the Sidewalk." Shades of the temperance movement, with its headquarters just a few blocks from our home!

At exactly five minutes before nine I met the two police officers at the entrance to the police station and they rather uncomfortably led me into the judge's presence. Behind two husky, broad-shouldered policemen my not-too-tall and not-too-wide figure was not too visible. As we entered, the judge barely glanced up from the docket he was reading.

"Your Honor," said one of my friends, "we have a man here arrested for riding a bicycle on the sidewalk."

"H'm," said the judge absent-mindedly and did not look up for several seconds. He was a handsome man and I had a good look at his strong profile. Then his reading finished, he raised his eyes and when he saw me standing behind the two officers I thought his eyes would pop right out of their sockets.

"Officers," he said in a dignified voice, "you have done your proper duty. I can only commend you." His voice had a difficult time remaining serious and finally lost the battle and he gave himself a good laugh. Then he spoke to the men more seriously. "This man you have arrested is my pastor and the worst of the situation is"—again he had a good laugh—"I presented him with the bicycle myself last night. I happen to be president of the Men's Club."

The two officers relaxed enough to enjoy broad grins.

"Now there is only one thing I request," continued the judge looking at the two policemen. "Don't say a word about this episode to anyone. You have done your duty properly, but keep the action quiet. No use letting the newpapers have a big spread at our expense. Leave the culprit with me. I'll take care of my friend."

The officers shook hands with me before they left me in the tender care of the judge.

I used this experience as the basis of my sermon the next Sunday, employing the text, "We shall all stand before the judgment seat of Christ." I told the congregation the story of my arrest and tried to show them what it would mean if when we stand before the Judge of all the earth, Christ Himself, we could hear Him say, "This is my friend, I'll care for him."

11

Plows Provide a Preacher

THE routine of life was well established in Evanston; the
Wheadon Church with its new addition was growing at an
encouraging rate and we were about to settle down to a more
normal pace when a letter came that disrupted my plans to relax.
The letter was from Bishop McDowell asking me to leave my
regular pastorate and go into a new type of work. I read the
letter with keen interest, not only because it pertained to my
services but because the idea it presented was so basically sound.
Bishop McDowell explained that Mr. William Deering, a manufacturer of plows and other farm implements (they fitted well
into my life picture along with the grindstones of Berea), had
approached him with a plan of underwriting the work of some
minister who would be known as an "evangelist pastor" and
whose services would be free for any Methodist Church in the
Chicago area which wanted a series of revival meetings. The
evangelist would receive a salary of twenty-five hundred dollars
a year plus rent for a house. I had been selected to fill the position. Would I accept?

Here was a poser. I had never decided which phase of the
ministry I really liked best. When faced with a job of money
raising for a new building I felt like the fire engine horse when
he hears the bell. Still, that phase of the work did not give me
the glow which came from evangelistic work. For the past
several years I had found myself looking forward to our vacation
periods because I could use part of that time to hold evangelistic
services in other churches or to be one of the preachers at some
established camp ground—a regular "postman's holiday." I
think I was a Methodist preacher, rather than a preacher in

some other denomination, because the Methodist emphasis on soul-saving found a natural home in my heart. If I were to count my happiest moments in life most of them, outside the family circle, would be connected with people whom I had brought into the church and whose lives God had changed. There was a tug at my heart for the work of evangelism.

But now that this letter brought me face to face with a decision, I knew after several days of contemplation that my deepest joy came from the all-round work of a regular pastorate. Added to the always-present need to raise money and the always-present need to save souls there was the satisfaction of living in close harmony with a congregation, helping families with their problems, guiding the education of the youth—all these activities combining to form that beautiful relationship called friendship. Mother and I talked and prayed over the request from the Bishop and then I answered that I would prefer to stay in a pastorate.

However, it was not for long that I enjoyed the emotional release which follows making a decision. A second letter from the Bishop asked me to come to his office. It was during this visit that I learned the whole story behind this new work.

"A few months ago, Mr. Deering walked into this office," began Bishop McDowell, "and told me about this idea yeasting in his mind. Deering doesn't like high-pressure evangelists who tour the country, preach in the largest city auditoriums, are covered by elaborate news stories, wear out the sawdust trail with converts and then move on for a repeat performance."

"He has a point," I agreed, "yet, evangelism is certainly part of the work of the church."

"That's just Deering's point," enthusiastically continued the Bishop. "Deering wants to put evangelism on the same basis as educational supervision—a continuous service for the churches wherever and whenever needed. He wants the kind of evangelism that is geared to the needs of each church and he wants it carried out by a man who lives in this district. Particularly, he does not want fly-by-night evangelism; that's why he calls this service 'pastoral evangelism.' "

"His idea is sound," I had to admit, and with a little interest, too.

"And to make it more sound"—the Bishop opened the desk drawer and took out a check—"here is his personal check for five thousand dollars to start the project. Other money will be forthcoming as needed."

"No wonder you want to get the work under way immediately," I said.

McDowell smiled warmly. "You may have guessed that I have invited you down here to ask you to reconsider. But you ought to know how we happened to select you."

"That would be interesting, of course."

"Deering was willing to finance the project but he said to me, 'You select the man. That's your business.' I knew that the choice was not a one-man job so I called into conference the three Chicago District Superintendents, thinking we could dispense our business rather quickly."

The Methodists had recently changed the title "Presiding Elder" to "District Superintendent" and it still sounded strange to my ears, but we were all trying to get accustomed to its use.

"There are several thousand Methodist preachers," I commented, "and sometimes a wide choice only complicates a selection."

"I thought I had a pretty smart idea," continued McDowell. "I gave paper and pencil to the Superintendents and asked each to be thinking of the man of his choice while I explained the whole idea. After they had written their choices, we read the names—three different men had been selected. So we discussed the work a little further and took another vote. No unanimity yet; we repeated the process and still came up with different individuals.

" 'We give up,' one Superintendent said. 'You're the Bishop, you make the selection.' You're the man I named, Hyde. I told them that they probably did not know you because you had been in the Rock River Conference only a short time but I gave them something of your background and work."

The serious tone in his voice changed to a much lighter note as he added, "Of course, I had to cull all the best out of our years of association but I finally found enough in your record to make you sound acceptable." The Bishop never bogged down; he had a sense of humor which ran the gamut from wit to gentle personal ribbing.

"I told the men to go out to the Wheadon Church and look over your record there," continued McDowell, "but you know how District Superintendents are—they'd rather take the Bishop's word than the extra work." A laugh took the sting out of the criticism. "So, Hyde, you were unanimously selected."

"That's one way of getting unanimity," I conceded.

"Seriously, Hyde, will you reconsider?"

"Seriously, Bishop, I have."

"What's your decision?"

"What would you expect a Methodist preacher's decision to be? It's not in the tradition to pick and choose. Besides, I'll enjoy the job."

The Bishop put out his friendly hand whose clasp was like a pontifical blessing, and almost immediately the work was under way.

I wanted to meet William Deering, benefactor of Methodism. I found him a tall gentleman, erect and dignified in his bearing, a delightful person to know. His long beard added distinction and his high silk hat—"plug hat" to the common man—indicated a certain aristocracy which his genial friendliness reduced to the same level as those of us with whom he worked.

Although this evangelistic project was entirely financed by Mr. Deering he made no attempt to dictate how the work should be done. We met frequently in the course of the next three years and usually he would greet me with the question, "How are things going?"

"I'm a poor one to ask," was my reply; "go to the District Superintendent's office where the records are kept; they tell the unbiased story. But I can say it is a marvelous work to be connected with."

And it was. There were no financial problems to worry over. I went into a church only on invitation so there was always the heartiest co-operation. Usually I spent three weeks in a given church preaching every night excepting Saturday, then often twice on Sunday. As I became identified with the network of Methodist churches in Chicago the setup took on the pulsating vitality of a human being—its brain the university campus, its arms reaching out to the immigrants, its feet following families moving into the suburban areas and its great heart throbbing for the men and women in sin and degradation in the red-light districts and the flophouses on Maxwell Street.

Methodism has a proud history in Chicago. The first church was established in 1838, just five years after the town was incorporated, the building being bought for six hundred dollars and then brought across the North Branch of the Chicago River on an old scow and placed on the site of the present towering Methodist Temple. Three Methodist ministers were working in the town before there was a resident minister representing any other denomination.

By 1910 Chicago had almost two and a quarter million people whom the Methodists served with more than a hundred churches. My services took me into churches of every financial and social level, with great divergence in their theological liberalism or fundamentalism. A three-week meeting in the Union Avenue Church of which the Swift family were prominent members was followed by a revival in an outlying church served by one of the Garrett "Bibs," a church so poor that it could hardly afford to heat the building for the three weeks of service. Then from the Western Avenue Church on the west side of the city I jumped to Grace Church on the near north side. The variety of the churches was balanced by the uniformity of the needs of the people everywhere—Jesus and His boundless love.

In the Hyde household there was no slackening of activity with the years. Each of the children was getting deeper into his own field of interest. There were lively discussions around the dinner table. We all shared the enthusiasms of each member of the family and we rejoiced together when rejoicing was in order —good grades, election to an office at school or church, a raise in salary or a promotion.

And then came the first break in the family circle. Florence Mae, nineteen, a student in the National Kindergarten School at Evanston, contracted pneumonia and died. Mother and I faced the experience through which we had helped so many other parents and we found the eternal truth upon which our faith was built to be sufficient for our need. We learned for ourselves that underneath *are* the everlasting arms; that God *is* closer than our very breathing, and that Jesus conquered the horror of the grave and remains the Life and constant companion of all who travel along the Way. He traveled with us day and night and led us into joyous new faith in the eternal goodness of God.

Along about 1913 we found that our hours with the Garrett "Bibs"—not only hours but gallons of coffee and mountains of sandwiches—were about to pay big dividends. One of the students, Homer Waltmire, liked the Hyde family so well that he asked permission to join it via marriage to our daughter Ethel. They gave us the first rich experience of a wedding in the family and the even richer experience of watching one of the children found her own home. Homer became a Methodist minister and Ethel—I am sure I am unbiased in my judgment—an excellent minister's wife. But she should have been good at the job because she had lived with a perfect specimen for all her young life.

The death of Mr. Deering three years after he started the evangelistic program cut off the funds and the work had to be discontinued. So in 1914 we found ourselves ready and eager to go back into a regular pastorate. For a third time in our lives we took the only available vacancy in the Conference and for the third time we found that any church can use all the energy a minister and his wife can put into the work. We accepted the call to the Sawyer Avenue Church on the west side of Chicago. Our service to this church was temporary and the next year found us located at the South Chicago Church, a church with a large membership composed to quite an extent of members connected with the iron and steel industry.

The South Chicago Church brought us face to face with problems we had never met before in any of our congregations. Chicago, like all industrial cities, was in the grip of the conflict between the rights of capital and labor. The strife engendered terrific heat which warmed the discussions of many church gatherings from local congregations to national and international conclaves. Being set down in an area whose major interests were industrial we had to give some concentrated study to the whole new and controversial topic of the church and the social order.

Around the years 1912 to 1914 the most hotly discussed books were those written by Walter Rauschenbusch such as *Christianizing the Social Order*, and Harry Ward's *The Social Creed of the Churches*. From many pulpits and from many more industries rose an ear-splitting howl over the church's "poking her nose" into the practices of industry and business. On the other hand, the heartbreaking wail of child laborers, the sighs of women broken by long working hours, and cries of lives ruined physically and morally by improper working conditions sounded in the ears of Christians, ministers and laymen, and would not be quieted.

Children were then universally employed in textile mills, mines, canning industries and truck gardening. There were probably close to two million children in industry and in thirty states in the Union they could work at night while in thirty-three states their accepted working day exceeded eight hours. Here was a waste of precious life that the church could not condone. The Bishops' Report at the Quadrennial Conference contained the words, "Neither Milton nor Goethe's devil could have devised a plot more demonical than this outrage upon helpless childhood by commercial greed. A Christian Congress would stop it before daring to adjourn. Only a pagan Church could be silent."

This pronouncement by the bishops was in line with Methodism's general practice of taking a stand on social questions. As early as 1892 the General Conference had passed a resolution concerning the attitude of the church toward social injustice and every General Conference since that time had given attention to this topic. The first forthright and challenging declaration in any national assembly of a Protestant body came from the Methodist Church in 1908 when its Committee on Church and State drew up a Bill of Rights, specifically listing fourteen planks in a social platform for the church, including such aims as the abolition of sweatshops and child labor; protection of the working man against industrial hazards; old age pensions, minimum wage, and the acceptance of the principle of arbitration.

Some of the great denominations in America stood appalled at this tendency to meddle in business and industry, but the Lord be eternally praised, the sentiment in favor of such social action by the churches was growing fast. Within a few months after the Methodists adopted their Bill of Rights the Federal Council of the Churches of Christ in America was organized with thirty-three participating denominations. The most creative session of their entire series of deliberations was the one devoted to The Church and Social Service whose outcome was the adoption of the Methodist Bill of Rights, with but few minor changes, as the Social Creed of the Protestant Churches co-operating in the Federal Council.

During the decade 1920 to 1930, the Methodists comprised nearly one third of the total Protestant church membership, and they were mostly the plain people, the group who as a whole had little to lose in the struggle for industrial democracy and much to gain by the application of the principles of Christianity to the working world. So the denomination kept hammering away on those social problems that needed the speediest rectification—for improvement of conditions for women in industry at a time when only three states had an eight-hour workday and when women often worked from seventy to seventy-six hours a week; for workmen's compensation when less than half the states offered any protection through accident compensation; for the release of the workingman one day in seven; and for other social improvements listed in the Bill of Rights.

The opportunity to work among people whose hourly interests are industrial rather than agricultural or educational is an experience from which every minister could profit. Our two years in South Chicago gave us a new appreciation of the problems of people who fight a long and wearisome battle against society and a new understanding of Jesus' concern over the laborer who is worthy of his hire.

And then we moved into a different environment. We accepted service with the Julia Gay Memorial Church, located in a good residential neighborhood on Garfield Boulevard in southwest Chicago. The larger portion of this membership was made up of business and professional people who worked in other parts of the city, but we were near enough to the Chicago stockyards to have a few members who were employed there. Our parish was not a wealthy neighborhood, just good average American citizens whose splendid church had been made possible by a substantial gift from Mrs. Julia Gay. It was a beautiful church, both inside and out, but as was frequently our lot on coming into a fine church we fell heir to a fine debt also.

I sometimes wondered why I found it so easy to raise money for the church but was so unsuccessful in personal financial projects. No preacher goes into the ministry because it is an easy profession in which to accumulate a fortune; on the other hand, few ministers ever actually starve to death. But between those two extremes lies that great group of "average preachers" who are completely dedicated to the cause to which they are giving their lives but who at the same time find themselves with professional, social and educational obligations beyond their pocketbooks. So I think nearly every preacher has tried to augment his salary with an occasional adventure into business. Some ministers succeed better than others. Our Berea silver-plating experiment should have been a lesson to me, but at times I felt I had acquired sufficient business acumen to sally forth on a new venture.

There was the pecan grove, for instance. Through one of my parishioners, an honest and well-meaning individual, I became interested in the possibilities of a pecan grove in Georgia, a grove that was sure to pay fine dividends. So I invested, not too heavily, through my friend. During the next year the backs of a large number of old envelopes were consumed figuring our possible income at the end of two years, five years, and so on. It was wonderful to think of the day when our investment would be an asset to Mother and me after the children were grown and gone and we were old. Time went on—but no returns from the investment. Then the great day arrived! We received a letter stating that our first dividends would be paid—wait a minute—not in cash but in produce. Cash would have been preferred although it would be good to have a supply of nuts off our own "vine and fig tree."

We waited anxiously for the arrival of the expressman and in the meantime planned how we would divide our nuts with our friends. This would be a good way of showing our appreciation to some of the families who had been gracious to us. Even the waiting was exciting and not the least part of our satisfaction was having a business venture that paid off.

The box of nuts arrived. We apportioned them out, all right. One nut to each member of the assembled family. Just put a period there!

As usual, I was more successful with the finances of the church and the financial burden of the Julia Gay Memorial Church was lifted when we paid off the mortgage. Whenever a church was working on improvements for itself I always insisted that it work equally hard to increase its giving for the larger work of the church in its world outreach. Self and others must always go together. So I put some pressure on the members of the church to increase their benevolent giving while paying off their debt. That idea was hard for some of the members to

take. "We can't raise two funds at once! Wait till we take care
of our church debt and then we will discuss increasing our
missionary giving."

"On the other hand," I argued, "if we grow in both directions
at the same time it will keep us from becoming lopsided." I
think I can safely say that every church in which we paid off a
debt developed a wide interest in world evangelism.

The years at Julia Gay, 1917 to 1919, were years filled with
world tragedy. The First World War engendered hatreds that
tested many a Christian's faith; it strained the financial resources
and drained the human resources of America. The churches
made their service flags, filled them with blue stars and watched
many of the stars turn to gold. The superb hope of a people who
fought a war to end all wars was mingled with the despair of
seeing family circles broken as sons, husbands and fathers paid
the price of securing democracy for the rest of the world.

Three service stars represented the Hyde family. William Clifford, our oldest son, served overseas, but before he left he made
the family happy by adding a daughter to the household. William and Edythe Sandahl were married in a quiet ceremony at
the parsonage in January, 1918. Then our daughter Clara, serving as a nurse with the armed forces, met Roy A. Walther,
serving as a doctor with the armed forces. They combined forces
and the next wedding in the family took place at Travis Field,
in Texas. Leonard, our second son, joined the Marines.

November 11, 1918—Armistice Day—and what a day in Chicago! People were delirious with joy, as well as deafened by
noise from the bells, whistles and sirens. Paper snow showered
down on wildly milling crowds all pushing down State Street,
Michigan Boulevard, Maxwell in the Ghetto and Twenty-Second
Street in China Town just to push back up the same streets
again.

When "the shouting and the tumult ceased" American citizens became more serious and countless thousands of them were
ready to kneel before the altar of God. The Sunday after
Armistice Day most churches, Julia Gay along with the others,

were filled with people uniting in services of thanksgiving that the war was ended and in dedication of themselves to the "unfinished task before us."

Added to the horror of the war was the tragedy of the influenza epidemic. In many homes the days were dark with anxiety and for doctors, nurses, parents and ministers the nights brought no rest. Not infrequently I would have two funerals in a day. It is in such times that the Christian hope shines with intense light.

I was often asked how I explained the fact that I did not contract influenza when I spent so much time in places where the germs were prevalent. Of course, I have no complete scientific explanation excepting that a strong and healthy body can resist many strains made upon it. But the experience of that epidemic and a long association with people, both well and ill, have given me a certain philosophy concerning health. I would be the bane of the medical profession and most certainly the despair of psychiatrists for I have never had a day's illness in the ninety years of my life and I have never had a worry. Problems? Yes. But not a worry. Worry is a frame of mind, a hopeless attitude which I have never allowed myself; worry is a dulling, discouraging outlook on life which is neither Christian nor conducive to long life. On the other hand, the habit of looking for the good in every situation, of enjoying the beautiful and the bright, even if they are sometimes infinitesimal spots in a very black background—this habit makes for health of mind and body.

Hard work is the second ingredient in the potion for healthy living. People in every church where Mother and I have worked told us we shouldn't work so hard. But how can a man preach a good sermon without working hard? A preacher puts everything he has into a sermon and comes out of a service limp and exhausted, albeit exhilarated. Exhaustion is the price of a good sermon, but who would be willing to deliver a poor one just to conserve his energy? No, give all you have and then retank through study, meditation and prayer, a never-failing source of

spiritual and physical rebuilding. Most of the people who cautioned me not to work too hard have died and their advice has
died with them.

The third ingredient in the elixir of life is a sense of humor.
To be able to laugh at the world—and at yourself! Real humor is
chiefly a matter of perspective. I know I have laughed a lot in
life; ninety years provide a good deal of laughter. I didn't realize
quite how much I indulged until I met a former friend, Dr. John
Versteeg, at a summer conference at Lakeside. I had slipped into
the back of the room where he was lecturing to a large group of
young people, perhaps two or three hundred. To my embarrassment Dr. Versteeg paused in the middle of the lecture and said,
"There's my old friend, W. J. Hyde. He's just come into the
room and I want to introduce him to you young folks." I walked
to the front of the room and he took my arm.

"I don't know how old Dr. Hyde is, but I know one thing—
he will never be really old because he has too fine a sense of
humor. He laughs so much that there is no room left in his face
for wrinkles."

To be perfectly truthful, I was proud of that introduction because it meant that I had succeeded in one of my life's aims, to
let the joy of the Christian faith take hold of my life and help me
interpret all of life's perplexities.

The final component in my recipe for long and healthy living
is religion. The Christian religion offers all the positive suggestions and approaches to life which make for peace of mind. A
Christian has no right to lie awake at night because he is discouraged. He has only to talk with God, to cast his burden on
the Lord—and do it actually—and the Lord will give him the
ideas he needs and with them the peace conducive to rest and
physical rebuilding. The Christian religion is based upon faith—
faith in the eternal goodness of God and in His continued presence in the universe. This faith releases a man's energies to make
his strength ten times greater than it could otherwise be. Faith
keeps a man close to God and also helps him see the best in
his fellow men, and this attitude leads to love, greatest of the

Christian virtues. And the greatest reward. No wonder the Christian breaks out at times with spontaneous joy.

> I sing because I'm happy!
> I sing because I'm free!
> His eye is on the sparrow,
> And I know he cares for me.

By the time the fall of 1919 rolled around I had seen church history repeat itself so often that when I looked over the situation at the Julia Gay Church—debt paid off, missionary giving increased, organizations working well—I had no doubt but that I would soon find myself the shepherd of another flock. Bishop McDowell, my good friend and for the past years my Bishop, had been replaced by Bishop Thomas Nicholson; but the shift made no difference in the nature of my appointments; every Bishop I've ever worked under seems to have had the same proclivity to fit together the words "church building" and "Hyde." Bishop Nicholson asked me to take the Mayfair Church which faced an immediate and heavy building program.

So the Hydes moved again, and this time I had the distinction of taking Mother into the worst parsonage to date. Any run-down dwelling is unattractive, but a dirty, sagging house in a rat-infested city is about as bad a combination as one could ask even a cheerful minister's wife to accept. We did something about that parsonage with the greatest possible speed.

The Mayfair situation was one of contrasts. The church was located in northwest Chicago on Kilpatrick Avenue, a rapidly expanding area of average American people who were finding themselves pushed into the "upper classes" simply by the influx of immigrants and "lower class" workingmen who were taking over the older sections of the city. The Mayfair community was composed of families who were building fine new homes at a tremendous rate. And right in the center of this mushrooming, new-paint residential district stood the Mayfair Methodist Church, a shabby frame building which would have been an eyesore anyplace.

It was this glaring discrepancy between the church and the new homes in the area that made money raising for a new church somewhat easier than might have been expected. After very careful thought I laid before the trustees the proposition of building a one hundred thousand dollar edifice which would include a gymnasium; and then (reminiscent of both Groton and Berea) I reminded them that a pipe organ would have to be installed before we could consider the job done. Some gasped feebly, "One hundred thousand dollars!" Others were firm in their negative reactions. Still other members did not know what to say and it was to these that I addressed my first appeal.

"There are two things I always put together when I am considering a new project," I told them. "One is the need and the other is the opportunity. Your need is an adequate place in which a fast-growing membership of five hundred may worship, educate its young people, and serve its community. Your opportunity is to accept the privilege of ministering to this section of the city."

Most of the trustees and many of the church members could see the logic of the argument, but there were still those who said, "It can't be done." Maybe I spoke a little plainly to this group, but I told them frankly that I was not interested in people who hid behind the word "can't." There were plenty of Christians, and not a few among the Mayfair Methodists, who believed that with Christ as a partner all things are possible. This group of people would accomplish the task.

The cost of the gymnasium was the biggest stumbling block. "Why do we need a gymnasium?" they asked. "We have done all right for years without one; other churches don't sink money into a gym; why is it so essential for us to add the several extra thousand it will cost?"

"Each church builds for the task of its day and for the future," I told them. "Do you want to build for your parents and grandparents or for your children and grandchildren?"

Then I suggested that the members of the church read the report of the Chicago Vice Commission. It didn't make good reading—page after page of case studies covering young people from fourteen to twenty years of age who had no place to go at night except to the pool halls, or more disreputable "joints." The report pointed out that even the ice cream parlors with their curtained back booths were feeders for the juvenile courts. For those church members who could not stomach the Vice Commission report I suggested they stand for an hour every night for a week on any street corner of the city and watch the gangs of youngsters rushing—where?

Then one night I took some of the church officials with me to the Salvation Army Hall where I preached to the down-and-outs. The church people were surprised at the youthfulness of some of the drunks and prostitutes who were trying to win back a place for themselves in normal life; they listened to the testimony of these young folks who had hit the lowest levels and were taken back by the frequent repetition of such phrases as "just wanting some fun," "looking for excitement," "no place to go at night."

I kept reminding our people that the young have to have fun and that we had the opportunity to provide it for all the youth of the community. So the gymnasium was accepted as part of the building program.

I was never afraid to present facts to a congregation, but I was always wary of scolding them. An appeal to the best in people is a much better policy. Perhaps I was inclined at times to over-estimate the good in people; the family used to think I was a bit gullible, believing all the hard-luck stories of those who came to the parsonage for help. They reminded me that tramps had a way of marking houses that are generous with sandwiches or pie and I would not be surprised if the Hyde households were fairly well marked up. The children remember one woman who came to our home in Chicago late one night with the story that she had come in from the country, was out of money and could not get home. Naturally, I helped her. I think she came once more—if I were pushed I might admit twice more—but the children insist it was three or four times. They may be right, but

I learned of several other Methodist preachers who were taken in by the same woman so she must have been good at her job. I never helped beggars on the streets but when someone came to the home the appeal seemed more personal.

So now with the Mayfair Church, when the people had the facts, and the facts appealed to their best judgment they responded marvelously. As soon as the church accepted its responsibility I got to work to ease the load for them. From the Chicago Church Extension Society, headed by John Thompson, a warm personal friend, I was able to secure ten thousand dollars. Also at this time the Methodists were engaged in their Centenary Movement and from that fund we got the promise of forty thousand dollars. Half the amount we needed was in these two pledges. The other half was not too difficult to raise, for after all these Mayfair people were devoted to their church and I found again that if a community realizes how invaluable the church is to their lives they respond joyfully in enlarging the services of the church.

As the gym began to take shape certain of the church members were concerned over the use to which it would be put. Some of the newer churches in Chicago were using their gymnasiums for church and community dances. I told the church members they could decide that question but that I would favor omitting dancing from our program. I thought we had better leave out anything that would offend any of the members. As Paul said, "Wherefore, if meat make my brother to offend, I will eat no flesh while the world standeth." If we would provide the young people with a place, a little supervision and a fairly free hand they would develop tremendous resources of their own.

By the end of five years the Mayfair congregation had an edifice of real beauty; thousands of people each year were going through the doors, some for prayer and worship, some for social service, some for study, some for recreation, some to bring personal problems into the minister's study, some to go into the uttermost parts of the world as ambassadors of Christ, some to be dedicated in their early days to a Christian life, and some to be laid to rest with the tender solicitude of friends who had worked with them through the years. A church is a beautiful community of kindred minds.

The Bishops should have learned a new way of saying it— but they used the same old words again in 1924. "Brother Hyde, there is a ticklish building job to be done and we want you to take over the church." I sometimes wonder if when I reach the pearly gates there will not be at least a little remodeling on which St. Peter would like me to lend a hand.

12

To the Glory of St. John

THE story of St. John's Church is the story of one of the happiest wedding ceremonies I ever performed; it records the marriage of two churches. Perhaps it would be more accurate to say that I led the bride to the altar and that Bishop Hughes performed the ceremony—but at least it was a happy and a lasting union and I am grateful to have had a part in the matchmaking.

I was introduced to the prospective bride on the last day of the 1924 Conference which met in the Methodist Church in Sterling. The Bishop and other officials had conference offices in the hotel just across the street. During one of the convention addresses I felt a tap on my shoulder and Dr. Fred Stone, one of the District Superintendents, whispered to me that I was wanted in the Bishop's office, so I slipped out of the session and went across the street where I found Bishop Hughes in deep discussion with five Superintendents.

"I'm glad you were located, Hyde," said the Bishop. "We're trying to complete our list of assignments for the coming year and you are giving us some trouble."

"That's unfortunate," I said as sympathetically as I could.

"The trouble is," went on the Bishop, "the Mayfair Church has presented us with a unanimous request for your return—"

"That's fine," I said.

"But the Superintendents want to move you. That leaves the final decision to me, and I don't like to make it, so—" the Bishop laughed and relaxed into a little slang—"so I decided to pass the buck to you."

"Perhaps you better give me a little of the dope on the situation." If the Bishop could use slang, so could I!

"We have a big building job on our hands." The Bishop raised one eyebrow as if to judge the effect of his first thrust.

"But I have just finished a building job," I parried.

"Perhaps that is why we are pushing you into deeper water. To be frank, we need someone we are sure can swim and not sink." I took this statement to be a nautical version of Dr. Traveller's "dig or die."

I still had not been told the location of the church to which they were contemplating sending me when Bishop Hughes turned directly to me and said very seriously, "I don't want to be arbitrary in this appointment, so we are asking you first if you are willing to accept it."

"Bishop," I replied, "I am a Methodist minister."

That was all I needed to say because the Bishop knew that when I was ordained I covenanted to go any place I was sent.

"Thank you." That was all the Bishop needed to say because I knew that we were into the job together and that I could rely on him for help.

I returned to the Conference session and within an hour we were listening to the reading of the list of churches and their ministers for the coming year. I followed them all with interest and my curiosity was satisfied when I heard the clerk read out,

"Seventy-seventh Street Church. W. J. Hyde."

This church, later known as the South Shore Church, was to be the bride at our wedding. It had an interesting history, having been organized as the result of a peculiar coincidence about the time I went to Parker, South Dakota. In 1890 the Weightmans, a Methodist family with one small daughter, moved into the South Shore district and found no Methodist Church near their home, so the little girl attended the Sunday School of another denomination and didn't like it. Approximately at the same time the Reverend Mr. Shawcross, an Englishman living temporarily in America, fell ill and was cared for in the Weightman home. With the return of health, the minister and his host canvassed the community and were surprised to find a decided interest in starting a Methodist Church. Mr. Weightman rented a hall, bearing all the expense himself the first winter, and Pastor Shawcross took over responsibility for preaching. In the spring a church was duly formed and brought into the Conference.

The congregation met variously at Leach's Hall, the old Enterprise Hotel, and the Odd Fellows' Hall until a building was completed on Seventy-seventh Street at Coles Avenue. Over a period of thirty years this church had a fine record of service to its denomination and its community. With pride the members pointed to Louise Raven (later to be the wife of the Reverend Robert Shields), who served first alone and then with her husband at Vivi and Loanda, Africa; and to Ray Bond, one of their own South Shore boys who won a place of honor as a District Superintendent.

It was with this church, as the last in a line of eighteen ministers, that we took up work in 1924. We found that the church building in the course of the years had been slowly deteriorating while the congregation had been growing larger and wealthier. A majority of the families in the neighborhood, some of them members of this church, were paying two or three hundred dollars a month for their apartments. On a Sunday morning many chauffeur-driven cars could be seen rolling out of the neighborhood taking their owners to the more beautiful church buildings in other parts of the city. Here was definitely a church which was not keeping pace with its parish. Moreover, the congregation was aware of its plight and had started a building fund under my predecessor, R. E. Bethards, but there were no immediate plans for building.

Such is the life story of one of the parties to the church marriage. The other party, the groom perhaps, was the Parkside Methodist Church whose history began with a Presbyterian mission bought by the Methodists about the same time that Mr. Weightman and the Reverend Mr. Shawcross started the work which resulted in the South Shore Church. A steady growth in membership brought the Parkside roll to about one hundred in

1907 when they dedicated a new building on Cornell Avenue and Seventy-second Street. This congregation had the distinction of having had as a minister the Reverend H. Clifford Northcott who twenty-five years later was to become a bishop to serve the churches of the mid-west.

When the Parkside and the South Shore Churches turned their eyes toward each other and began to talk union the Parkside Church was served by J. W. George who, perhaps understandably but nevertheless unfortunately, was not in favor of the marriage. The courting was done under his eye but without his approval which threw upon the shoulders of the South Shore minister some of the details that it would have been a joy to share.

About ten days after taking up the work with the South Shore Church we had the first meeting of the official board and almost immediately the discussion centered around the prospects for increasing the building fund. From reports I knew this same discussion had been conducted repeatedly with little progress. Sometimes, of course, the best progress is made slowly, but there comes a time when discussion is only procrastination.

I have been told that sometimes I open up a problem somewhat abruptly. Maybe I had better plead guilty. But repeatedly I ask myself, "When you know a job must be done, why skirt around its unpleasant fringes? Why not get into it?" As a youngster, if I were slated for an unpleasant interview with my father I wanted to get it over as soon as possible so that we could get onto more pleasant relationships again. So in dealing with churches I preferred to face every problem at once rather than evade the touchy ones until they were forced upon us by an ill savor. That was the only way I could work. However, in my own defense I will say that I never forced a decision beyond the wishes of the group who had to make it. I honestly enjoyed listening to everyone talk as long as he wanted to, and I knew it was profitable to get as many points of view as possible; then I always tried to help a group arrive at a conclusion that was really their own so that they could be enthusiastic about carrying it out.

As the men sat around the room in this first board meeting, they made an interesting study for a new minister. Predominantly they were prosperous business and professional men; they talked in terms of their Buicks and their Hudsons; their minds handled figures with dexterity; but—and I say it in all kindness—they were a typical church board meeting with a new minister for the first time. They were going to proceed cautiously. The chairman explained to me that there was a small nest egg toward a building fund and that overtures had been made to the Parkside Church looking toward union.

"That's wonderful," I said. "The Bishop gave me about the same story and during the past week I have gone over countless building plans with the Church Extension Society and have brought a set with me this evening which you men may want to look at—just to get all our imaginations going."

"Do you think we are ready for plans?" asked a retail merchant.

"Plans add a lot of fun," I offered, "and money comes easier when everyone in the church knows exactly what they are aiming at."

"But it would cost a considerable sum to have blueprints drawn up and circulated," objected a real estate agent.

"Only about three thousand dollars," I said.

"That seems a bit out of proportion to our total estimated cost," the chairman commented.

"What sum are you figuring on?" I asked.

"About seventy-five thousand dollars."

"That complicates things," I said. And I said it seriously.

"Why?" asked several of the men at once.

"Because that means I have apparently taken the wrong appointment, and you have the wrong preacher."

There was absolute silence in the room.

"Exactly what do you mean by that statement?" This question was the first real interest shown by a manufacturer of some financial status.

"I mean just that." Now I talked directly to this man. "Bishop

Hughes and his cabinet asked me to take the South Shore Church because they wanted a good building, adequately equipped to serve this community. We estimated that it would take at least two hundred thousand dollars."

"Such a sum was mentioned by them," the manufacturer volunteered, "but we have not accepted it, and in our own minds I think we never intend to. We feel it is beyond our resources."

"Your resources or your faith?" I questioned; but it was only a rhetorical question that was its own answer. I moved right ahead with the discussion.

"Two hundred thousand sounds like a lot of money. But you already have a start. We can sell the present property—"

"We'll realize only about fifteen thousand dollars on it," broke in the real estate man.

"I think your estimate's too low. Double it, I'd say. Then the Parkside Church will be sold for a reasonable sum, too, but I don't have any estimate on that yet."

"Even with that substantial sum we will be left with a big debt and this church has hardly known anything but debts since it was started. New people in the community won't want to join a church carrying such a financial burden."

"There isn't going to be any debt," I told them cheerfully. "You still haven't figured all your resources."

The air cleared a little.

"The Building Society is interested in ventures like this one. But more important, I don't think you are giving your congregation enough credit for what they can do."

The retail merchant spoke up. "Evidently Dr. Hyde isn't a novice with figures. I move, Mr. Chairman, that we authorize the Building Committee to proceed with plans and estimates."

The chairman made a wise move. I think he realized that even if this official group sanctioned pushing the building program the church as a whole was not sufficiently convinced that the right time had arrived. So he suggested the action wait until another meeting of the board.

I gave a great deal of thought to my sermon for the next Sunday. This could be no ordinary sermon that would send people home secure in the assurance of their own salvation; this sermon had to be charged with enough dynamite to shake the congregation out of its timidity. I recalled an experience Ezekiel had recorded, how the Lord had led him into a valley strewn with dry bones. There were very many bones and they were very dry bones. (There is something frightful in the very sound of "dry bones!") The Lord told Ezekiel, "Prophesy unto these bones, and say unto them, O ye dry bones, hear the word of the Lord." Ezekiel prophesied to the bones, and God breathed into them the breath of life so that they stood upon their feet and became a great army. And the Lord says, "I shall put my spirit in you and ye shall live . . . then shall ye know that I the Lord have spoken it." The revived dry bones proceeded according to God's commands, inherited their land, and were blessed with God's abiding presence. "I will make a covenant of peace with them" said the Lord; "it shall be an everlasting covenant . . . yea, I will be their God, and they shall be my people."

The story is dramatic, and the story was written for the South Shore Church just as surely as it was written for the children of Israel. The next week the board and the trustees met together and the motion to authorize the building committee to proceed with plans was the main item of business. Discussion continued for some time, then the vote was taken. There was noticeable variation in the enthusiasm with which the "Aye's" were voiced but the vote was unanimous.

And then the fun began. I use the word "fun" advisedly for I know of no sport in the world as exciting as tackling the seemingly impossible and then watching the barriers vanish under the impact of work.

The committee purchased a lot with a 125-foot frontage on Jeffrey Avenue at Seventy-fourth Street. We sold the South Shore property, which had originally cost three thousand dollars for the lot and thirty-five hundred dollars for the building, for a total of thirty-five thousand dollars. The official board began to believe it could work miracles!

By June, 1927, the Parkside and South Shore Methodist Church plants had both been sold and temporary arrangements made for carrying on their separate services until the merger could be completed. The laying of the cornerstone for the new church was set for September, but as yet the new church had no name. Its selection was reminiscent of the naming of John the Baptist whose father was asked, "What will be the child's name?" and who responded, "His name is John." Likewise when the question of a fitting name was placed before Bishop Hughes, he responded, "It shall be called St. John's Methodist Episcopal Church." And so it was.

The final cost of the plant, with the later addition of a pipe organ, was a little over two hundred and twenty-five thousand dollars. The lovely structure, almost free of debt, was dedicated by Bishop Hughes on Sunday, April 22, 1928.

By this time I had given the bride in marriage and had withdrawn from the family scene. In church life, as in family life, it is frequently good sense for all the in-laws to withdraw and leave the young couple on their own. Mother and I felt this attitude to be the right one in this case. The members of the South Shore Church requested that we continue as the minister, but the Parkside congregation was divided. The majority of the members had worked wholeheartedly during the entire process of merging the two congregations but a few were lacking in enthusiasm for the project, so it was only natural that they would be lacking in enthusiasm for the preacher who had headed the project. When the Bishop asked me about continuing as pastor of the new church I told him that my work with St. John's was finished, that the congregation should select a new minister who had had no previous connection with either of the former churches.

St. John's Church was the last in a series of church building projects begun forty years earlier in the little town of Groton, Dakota Territory. Many times I have been asked which of all our building enterprises brought the greatest satisfaction but I have never been able to give a satisfactory reply. I can only answer with the further question, "Which of your children do you love most? The first one, or the last one, the biggest baby or the frailest child? You love each one for his own sake. There are no comparative values in parent love. And a preacher feels the same way toward his churches."

Our last pastorate in Chicago was the Garfield Park Methodist Church. Each winter as we approached the holiday season Mother and I wondered if our good fortune would last and we could have all the family together again for Christmas dinner. We knew that a family with diversified interests and shifting residences couldn't always hold together, so each year we prized our Christmas Day more than any that had gone before.

Christmas dinner was a tradition in the Hyde establishment. Mother, the best cook in the world, excelled herself for this dinner. We used to laugh over the way one of the girls would try to fool the family into thinking that something she had cooked had really been cooked by her mother. On one occasion the girls served a beautiful apple pie which looked exactly like Mother's—it was fluted around the edges in her way and had the air holes in the top crust made with her particular trade mark. We were all elated over Mother's having made apple pie for us because it was no longer as easy for her to bake as it once had been. Then Bill took a bite of his pie and looked up with an expression that clearly said, "There is a traitor among us." He looked around. "That pie looks like Mother's, but it certainly doesn't taste like hers!" With such appreciation for Mother's cooking is it any wonder that we looked forward to Christmas dinner for at least eleven and a half months?

Our turkey always came from Brother Jim who lived out in Lisbon, North Dakota. It was the center around which the meal was built. Mother stuffed it with a bread dressing special as to flavor; then she made scalloped oysters to serve at the side of the dressing. Mashed potatoes, mashed rutabagas, sometimes called yellow turnips, gravy, and all the trimmings such as pickles and jelly in assortments. The one dish that kept our English ancestry before us was the suet pudding—not a dessert with hard sauce in usual American style, but a steamed suet pudding

served with its own white gravy as part of the main course of the
dinner. Mother also made nut bread for this dinner, and we
topped the meal off with apple and mince pies.

Sitting around the table was the family. Always Mother at
her end of the table but otherwise each year brought innova-
tions with a new son-in-law or a daughter-in-law, or an added
high chair. Our children were watching their children (and later
their children's children) and teaching them their "manners" in
the customary way. Nothing in the world is quite like a family!
After Christmas dinner was over the youngsters went back to
their toys under the tree in the living room until time for naps.
The oldsters talked, napped, walked, washed dishes and rather
aimlessly tidied up the house—but there wasn't much use in that
operation until later in the day when the families left for their
own homes again and Mother and I slipped a new pearl of
memory onto our chain.

Mother and I had a good laugh over some of the perversities
of fate. In accepting the ministry of the Garfield Park Church
we found ourselves in possession of the best parsonage it had
ever been our lot to live in just when we didn't need it—our
children were grown and gone from home; and just when we
couldn't use it—the grinding and jangling of the streetcars past
the house day and night made it impossible for Mother to rest.
So we moved into a near-by apartment, but we soon found that
even this move did not entirely solve our problem. It was more
than the noise of the streetcars that was irritating us; it was the
frantic rush and constant clamor of the big city wearing on
our nerves. Could it be we were actually getting old? To be
sure we were past the age of retirement. The people of Garfield
Park did everything they could to prolong our pastorate with
them and we were grateful but we knew our wisest move was
to leave Chicago where we had put in a quarter of a century
of service.

So in 1932 the beautiful little town of Oregon, Illinois, not far
from Rockford, became our home. The Methodists had a church
to match the beauty of the town, a friendly church made up of

such fine people as I have never seen equaled. In Oregon we found all the relaxation we were looking for: spreading trees filtering the sunshine gave composure to our souls and the leisurely schedule was suited to two people near their seventies. But the quiet! I thought I would go mad. The medicine proved almost worse than the disease. I felt that life was passing us by while we sat secure in a calm little haven—even though a beautiful and a friendly one. And lonely? Not for lack of friends but for lack of people. The hundreds of folks whom I passed daily on the streets of Chicago had come to be part of my inspiration for living, a constant reminder that there was much for the church to do. Now in our peaceful retreat I could cover the entire town in a few short walks. We were bountifully blessed with the very blessings we had come to obtain and I just could not take them. The boisterous city was still in our blood. Mother might have been satisfied to settle down but she certainly did not raise any objections to our trying a new location.

So we compromised. No great city but no quiet town either. Apparently we found the right middle ground in Joliet, Illinois. We were the butt of the usual jokes leveled at people who move to Joliet where the state penitentiary is located, but in spite of our friends' apprehensions that I might land in the wrong institution I was happy to have some contacts with the men "inside the walls" and I welcomed every opportunity to meet them as preacher, counselor and friend.

The Grace Church at Joliet was almost an ideal church. We took up the work there feeling like people who are about to enjoy a final "fling." I was now sixty-nine years old, four years past usual retirement, but according to Methodist practice retirement may be postponed year by year at a man's option until he reaches seventy-two when it becomes mandatory for everyone from the highest ranking bishop to the lowliest local preacher. We had three years to go and we wanted to fill them as full as the other forty-seven years of our ministry. Here we had no lagging membership, no building program, no debt to pay off, no pipe organ to install. The situation scarcely seemed natural. We stepped into a church where all we had to do was to work with people, and how we loved it! People! People! They have been the passion of our lives. We found them about the same everywhere whether on Prairie Avenue in Chicago or on the prairies of Dakota; we found they had their sorrows, their joys, their jealousies, their moments of selfishness and their hours of generous living. It is people who make life rich and from this point of view ours had certainly been the multi-millionaires' existence. There is a simple poem Mother and I have liked for many years because it expresses in ordinary language the creed of our ordinary lives.

> I live for those who love me,
> For those who know me true;
> For the heaven that smiles above me,
> And awaits my spirit too;
> For the cause that lacks assistance,
> For the wrong that needs resistance,
> For the future in the distance,
> And the good that I can do.

In ninety years of living I have been fascinated with the study of science, of history, of religion. I respect the great minds which can whittle theological questions to fine points and then polish them off with their mental carborundums. But my greatest help in living has come from a verse tucked lovingly by Peter into the story he told Cornelius, "God anointed Jesus of Nazareth . . . who went about doing good . . . for God was with him." What a perfect summing up of the life of Jesus, who talked with the lonely, healed the sick, gave the cup of cold water to the thirsty, comforted the mourning and encouraged the downhearted. That was the Jesus who said to his disciples, "Those things which ye . . . have seen in me, do."

At Joliet I had the opportunity of doing all the things I liked best to do, except raise money. There were countless calls for addresses before women's clubs and men's clubs; there were young people's groups to work with; there were close interdenominational associations; and we had a revival service each of the three winters we were there.

The three years rolled quickly by and with their passing came the end of our active ministry. To some people there is a sad note in completing a phase of life—they hate to see their youth go, they hate to pass beyond middle age, they hate to feel old age creeping up. How foolish! Life is all a great venture and when the poet sang,

> Grow old along with me!
> The best is yet to be,
> The last of life, for which the first was made:

he was expressing a joyous philosophy. On closing our last regular pastorate Mother and I felt that a new and exciting period in life was opening up for us when we could live without a daily schedule geared to the demands of pastoral work. Now we could do all those things that the busy life of the parsonage had not permitted.

"Let's get going!" Mother and I said to each other.

13

Retired into Activity

BY THE time I had been a preacher for fifty years I discovered that I had one thing in common with the drunkard or other addict—a lifetime habit so firmly fixed that it seemed impossible to break it. Here I was, retired from active duty, as free as a schoolboy when the bell has rung for the last time on a hot June day, and all I could think of was finding a nice little church to preach in!

Life seemed off center without a Sunday sermon around which to pivot its activities. What was the point in reading, in studying, in thinking, if they didn't result in a sermon? For fifty years I had lived with the ever-present companionship of Scripture texts, illustrations, points one, two and three, and I found my mind out of focus when I realized that my reading no longer needed to "head in" to a sermon. So we decided I had better ease myself out of the pulpit by taking a temporary appointment for a few months. The Highland Park Church in a Chicago suburb helped turn the trick. There Mother and I, in a few months, eased ourselves into the idea of retirement.

I guess the Lord knows when it is about time for His children to change their manner of living because He had us well adjusted to the idea of slowing down before Mother's break in health made it absolutely necessary. Then we found an apartment in Chicago not far from Bill and Edythe. At this point we began to live life in reverse. After all the years of taking care of that unpredictable, energetic son, William Clifford, we now found him taking care of us—and maybe we were as unpredictable and incorrigible in his eyes as we had once thought him. That knowledge is something parents can only guess at. But Bill and Edythe made it possible for Mother and me to attend everything we wanted to go to; church every Sunday, Conference every year, so that I rounded out sixty-six years in the ministry with never an Annual Conference missed. The days in Chicago were filled with church meetings, anniversaries, outstanding speakers—in fact, the days were so filled with eating the frosting of life that we forgot to be sorry that we no longer had to help mix the dough.

These were years in which we relived, reflected, re-evaluated and revisited. One day I was down at the Evangelistic Institute where I had once taught homiletics to young preachers, and I found that young preachers still had the ability to ask questions that were pretty hard to answer. One of the men posed this one: "If you could preach just one more sermon what would it be about?"

"That's a tough one," I said. "Not as tough though as it would have been twenty-five years ago when I stood at the halfway point in my ministry. But before I tell you the sermon I would preach, may I have the privilege of selecting the audience to which I would preach it?"

"That's fair enough," said my young interrogator.

"All right, then, I would want my one sermon to be to young people, maybe along in the middle and late teens. And the sermon would be on memories. I would like to tell them that there are two things in life no person can get away from—himself and his memories. He can run away from home, from school, from a community he doesn't like, from responsibility he doesn't want to accept; in fact, he can escape from almost everything. But a man can never run away from himself or his memories. A store of good memories is the finest treasure a man can lay up on earth, while bad memories make hell out of this present life. 'Live so that your memories are good companions to the end of your days.' I think that is the one sermon I would preach as my last."

In the fall of 1936 the Rock River Conference met at the Austin Methodist Church and it was a meeting of peculiar interest to Mother and me. For the first time since 1886 I would not wait to hear my name read on the last day when the appointments were made! This year we didn't face a single one of the customary uncertainties. It was a new and a peculiar feeling, but because of our detachment from the immediate problems we could watch the whole panorama of the Conference without having our emotions as involved as usual. Merely interested spectators. Or so we thought. Then Saturday afternoon arrived. We were walking down the street when we met Bishop Waldorf.

"Glad to see you, Hyde," said the Bishop. "Where you been keeping yourself, you old reprobate? I've been looking all over the church for you. Why aren't you in there getting some religion?"

"Bishop, your religion these days is so watered down that I can take a little stroll and not miss much while I'm gone. Now in the 'good old days'—"

We both laughed. Then the Bishop said, "Hyde, I want you to do something for me. I want you to make the talk tomorrow afternoon where the Bishop's Address is scheduled."

Bishop Waldorf was quite a joker and I took this statement to be the introduction to some ludicrous situation he was going to recount. "I always liked your sense of humor, Bishop; go on with the rest of the joke."

"I'm serious this time, Hyde. You are just completing fifty years in the ministry—a half century of the romance of America and the march of the Methodist Church. You have preached in everything from the sod house to the great tabernacles and I want you to take my place tomorrow afternoon."

"Even if the request made sense," I said to the Bishop, "I would have no time to prepare for such an occasion."

"That's just what I don't want you to do!" he said quickly. "Tomorrow is the high hour of dedication for the young men entering the Methodist ministry. As the Bishop it is my responsibility to give the charge to these young ministers. I have never before asked anyone else to do it, but this year I want you to tell them the story of your ministry—if you could see it as I do it is

the saga of religion in America—and I want you to let these
young men see what you saw and feel what you felt. I don't
want any fancy trimmings or high-falutin' oratory—I could give
them that!"

Bishop Waldorf seemed so in earnest that I decided he really
meant me to take the request seriously.

"It hardly makes sense to me," I told him, "but if you will
take the responsibility, I'll try."

I attended all the intervening sessions of the Conference, the
Saturday night lecture, the worship service Sunday morning,
determined to do just what the Bishop had asked me to do,
prepare nothing formal but simply review the high points of fifty
years. Sunday afternoon came. This service is always a deeply
moving experience. The young men ready to be ordained had all
been examined and were there in a group for the final Charge.
On the platform were to be the Bishop and his five District
Superintendents, very dignified in their robes. They even asked
me to wear one! But I knew I would feel out of place—which is
the beginning of looking out of place—so I begged off.

The beauty of the music, the solemnity of the worship service,
the eagerness of the young men sitting in front of me—there was
a certain emotional throb that came from being part of it all.
Within an instant after I rose to speak I was back on the Dakota
prairie and a wave of fervor for those early days swept over me.
I found myself repeating the poem which expressed my feeling
toward the west—and toward life:

> My task accomplished and the long day done,
> My wages taken, and in my heart
> Some late lark singing,
>
> .   .   .   .

So I told these young men about Dr. Traveller and my first
letter from him, the terms which he laid down for any young
fellow who would join him in the work in the Territory, of his
"dig or die" admonition. Then I told them the story of the lives
of people on the prairie and the church ministering to them, of

my return to Canada to get "the girl I left behind me," of the church in rural Ohio, the church among college students, the church working with the dregs of a crowded city, the church developing with the changing life of a great industrial center.

"And, if I had my life to live over again I would want to live it the same way."

As I sat down Bishop Waldorf turned to me and said, "Brother Hyde, is that girl you left behind in eighty-six here today?"

"She's been with me for forty-eight years, Bishop, and she's here this afternoon."

"Where is she?"

Someone in the audience stood up to attract the Bishop's attention to the pew where Mother was sitting.

"Mrs. Hyde, we want you up here with your husband," said the Bishop as he walked down the steps from the pulpit to meet Mother and bring her up to sit beside the Bishop and the five District Superintendents. Really, that is where Mother belonged for I sometimes thought it would take a Bishop and five assistants to accomplish all the things Mother accomplished!

With Mother seated on the platform the Bishop turned to the young men who were presenting themselves for ordination. "There still remain seven of the thirty minutes allotted for the Bishop's address," he began, "and I shall use them myself to say something that Brother Hyde could not say. That is, in fifty years of service he never asked for a good location, nor for a preferential appointment. The life of a District Superintendent or a Bishop is harried by preachers bringing special requests for appointments on the plea that their talents are not appreciated where they are serving, that they need a wider field in which to exercise their ability. But if any of you young men will accept the terms of appointment, or of life, in the spirit that Brother Hyde has accepted them, there is a chance that your life will pay off at the end of fifty years with the same rich reward he is reaping, the love and respect of the whole denomination."

In proportion to the multitude of little things that had made up my life those were big words to have the Bishop say. Sometimes I think it is good for a person to hear a word of commendation about himself; words are more precious in the file of memories than are silver dollars—or a fine obituary. I felt that all the dust storms, the blizzards, the relentless heat, the misunderstandings, the mistakes and the sorrows of fifty years were rewarded by the experience of this Sunday afternoon.

There were just two brief years between the recognition of fifty years in the ministry and the celebration of our fifty years of marriage. A Golden Wedding Anniversary! The day fell, of course, on the Fourth of July. The Queen whose birthday we had once observed on that date in Canada had long since passed away and her rule had descended to her son, then to his son and to a second son. The United States, thirty-eight states old when we were married, had long since acquired her forty-eighth member and was on the way to becoming "safer and saner" as far as Fourth of July celebrations went.

That anniversary was truly a golden day. Bill and Edythe held open house in their home which was turned into a veritable bower of yellow roses; the lovely yard stretching back of their home was in storybook perfection so that the two hundred guests could wander around and visit in small groups without any feeling of being in a congested city.

Mother always loved things "properly done" and I know her heart was glad with the beautiful appointments of the tea table, its yellow roses and its tradition silver service (Mother had been a little provoked when Bill gave it to Edythe as a Christmas gift many, many years ago when there were so many things a young couple needed more! Now I think she looked with favor on the seeming extravagance). There was iced punch, inexhaustible infinitesimal homemade cookies, and a tremendous wedding cake.

Family? Almost the entire Hyde clan was there—the American branch in toto and the Canadian family by a good representation. Perhaps it wasn't a quiet day—it would be impossible to get sixteen members of the immediate family together at one time and keep the air quiet; there was too much to remember, too much taking one another down a peg, too much laughter. The fun of a family is the best fun in the world. And we really had family that day: Bill and Edythe with their Jane; Clara and Roy Walther with their two sons, Roy, Jr. and Leonard; Leonard and Madeleine Hyde with young Richard; Ethel Waltmire and her three girls, Dorothy, Martha and Mary. Ethel's husband had already stepped on ahead into that city where family ties are never broken, to await the coming of the other Hydes. Among the relatives from Canada, the most important was my brother Dan who fifty years earlier had driven Minnie and me from the Grills home into Belleville to the train that important July 4, 1888. Yes, Dan made the trip all the way to Chicago to link our lives again with the days of our youth.

Friends? Mother and I could only say again that it is people who make life rich and meaningful. They came from Ohio, even from Orrville which we had left in 1904. The many churches we had served in Chicago passed in review before us as we greeted friends from every one of them. We tried to live to the full every minute of the day, but we also lived in a realm that was not shared by any of the others, for under the greetings of the friends to "Brother and Mrs. Hyde," under the good wishes of the children to "Mother and Dad," under the "Best of everything, Grandma and Grandpa"—under all of these affectionate names there were moments when we were again, fleetingly, just Minnie and Will. That day Mother and I experienced the "late lark, singing in our hearts."

During these years life continually paid off on the investments of our early years. Some investments pay off in money—those were the investments in which I had little success. But some investments pay off in a warm glow around the heart, and from this variety I received many dividends. For the next few years we lived near our son in Chicago or shared the home of our daughter Clara and her doctor husband. Roy was a fine doctor who understood both medicine and people and this combination made him almost the ideal man for a suburban community such as he lived in outside St. Louis at Overland, Missouri. Mother's health was failing over a period of several years so it was always good to be in the hands of these children who could give her every professional care as well as every loving ministration. With Ethel living in Champaign, we could always have a good visit with her when we shuttled between St. Louis and Chicago.

So the summer of 1944 arrived and we were in Chicago and Mother was definitely losing ground. We decided it would be wise to get to Clara's where Roy could keep a constant eye on her. Ethel drove up from Champaign in her car to take us to her home for a brief halfway stop but by the time we reached there we knew it would be the better part of wisdom to put Mother into the hospital for a while.

Mother had one little vanity—she never liked to tell her age. It is true that in her seventies she was very erect and carried herself with the same beautiful bearing that had characterized her all her life. Her hair had been snow white since her early thirties so that there were no increasing gray hairs to show advancing age, and Mother really fooled people, quite to her delight. Moreover, she never refused to do anything because she was too old—she either did what the others did or had some very plausible excuse for not doing it, but that excuse was never her age. She never wore purple or black—they were old folks' colors! She preferred shades of blue, navy for her more tailored things and softer shades for "dress up." I don't know how Mother managed it, but from our earliest meager salaries, through the days of raising five children, and on into our years of retirement on a Methodist preacher's pension, Mother always dressed well and I think this fine care for her appearance helped keep her looking young.

Well, we arrived in Champaign and put Mother into the hospital, a very sick woman. Nurses and doctors were at her bedside and Ethel and I were waiting in her room when the doctor in charge began to ask her a few questions. I am sure it was just to feel out her condition because he had most of the answers already filed. Finally he said in a somewhat routine way, "How old are you, Mrs. Hyde?"

Ethel and I both looked at Mother and saw her raise one hand and motion the doctor closer; she made him lean over the bed and then she whispered something in his ear, which no one else in the room heard. I thought this was a good sign that Mother's spunk was still up and she was fighting along with the rest of us for her recovery. Later when we were out in the hall the doctor laughed as he said, "Do you know what your wife whispered to me? She said, 'I'm eighty, young man, but all these nurses standing around here don't need to know it.'"

What love and care Ethel gave us during the next two months! As owner of a ladies' furnishing establishment she had a busy schedule but she never missed a day of visiting the hospital three times. She was a source of strength for Mother and a tonic for her Dad. I wonder how many times during those weeks she said to me, "Remember, Dad, blue skies ahead!" quoting back to me the philosophy I had tried to instill into the children from their earliest childhood.

Finally it seemed wise to leave the hospital in Champaign and move Mother to Clara's, so Clara came with an ambulance and again Mother and I relaxed as best we could under the circumstances in the capable care of one of our children. Now Mother had the constant medical attention of the best of doctors and the love of the best of children during those days when she was preparing to move into her final manse in that "city four square." There would be no more sagging doors or chipping paint for her to struggle with but all would be burnished gold, softened with the patina of pearl—and maybe Mother would get a little delight from the fact that "they count not time by years!" Who could ask Mother to delay her trip? The Master called her home on the thirtieth of November, just a few days after Thanksgiving.

The love of family and friends—the most beautiful possession on earth—I am sure it is a token of that greater love which our mortal lives cannot comprehend, that love of God which we will realize only when we see Him face to face. Every hour of the following days and nights was filled with thoughtful consideration. The Reverend H. Clifford Northcott came to conduct Mother's services. Clifford and our Bill had been pals together when they were young and I suppose Clifford had eaten as many pieces of Mother's famous apple pie as any young man of our acquaintance, and how like him now to take time from the crowded life of a minister of a large church to come to pay tribute to Mother and speak words of comfort to the members of the family. This service was another cord that bound him tightly into our affections.

And so Mother rested from her labors.

But for the rest of us life had to go on. We all knew it. I knew it. But how? The day after the service I was sitting alone in the bedroom at Clara's—just thinking. Mother had walked with me for nearly sixty years and I knew now how much I had leaned on her even when I hoped I was helping her carry her burdens. I could not evaluate the contribution Minnie had made to my life. I could only think, "She was wonderful, wonderful, wonderful." The door opened softly and Ethel came into the room. I had often thought Ethel had one of my characteristics, and one for which I was sometimes criticized; Ethel said what she had to say without too many preliminaries. I am glad she was like that because this day she was just what I needed.

Ethel said, "Dad, what do people live for?"

I couldn't help but smile a little; she was putting me through the catechism that I had used on the children many times.

"They live to help others, Ethel."

"That's what you've often told me, Dad. Do you remember the next question? What things are impossible?"

"Only those things which are never attempted," I answered as I had led her to answer countless times.

"Well, Dad, what is your favorite motto?"

"There are blue skies ahead."

"That's right, Dad. I wonder if you would like to ride down to the market with me while I do a little shopping for Clara?"

After Mother's death I made my home with Clara and Roy but I tried to give them breathing spells by themselves. Each year I made a visit of a month or two to Chicago when Bill and Edythe saw to it that I revisited all the old scenes and met all the old friends, attended the Rock River Conference and generally kept my finger in the Methodist pie that I had helped make for so many years. Part of the time Leonard and his family lived in Chicago, but for several years they were in New York and our visits during those years were scarce. Then for Christmas I usually found myself at Ethel's and soon after that I would head for Florida.

My first trip to Florida I made at Ethel's invitation and from it I learned a lesson about judging from appearances. I had the misfortune of having an infection in my nose so that it swelled up to twice its normal size and had a thoroughly red color. I think I missed a lot of sympathy because my friends could only laugh at my appearance and congratulate me on the fact that I carried my liquor without staggering. I was sitting on the train bemoaning my pain and appearance, when a big, loud-talking, somewhat staggering and extremely red-nosed man walked through our car. His eye landed on me and at the sight of my nose his face lighted up. He stopped at my seat, gave me a burly whack on the shoulder and began to spill a tale of woe about the inconvenience of travel during wartime when priorities take the planes and all the other comforts away from civilians. I did not need to say much, but sat there hoping he would not again dislocate my shoulder and start the pain throbbing in my nose, when my new friend leaned over and said confidentially, "Mister, I got a flask of it in my pocket. When we get well under way you come down to the men's lounge and I'll give you some if you don't have enough of your own."

"I don't have any," I said truthfully.

"Well, you just follow me," and he began to get quite pally.

"Thank you, brother, that's very generous of you," I replied.

"Birds of a feather, I always say." And he progressed down the aisle with a few more lurches than the motion of the train necessitated.

Back from Florida each spring for a visit in Chicago and then on to Lakeside for July and August. Lakeside was almost a tradition in our family. It was the location of countless camp meetings during our years in Ohio, then as the children were married they carried on the habit of frequent vacations at Lakeside which as the years went by had become one of the great centers in the United States for summer conferences. There was never a week during the summer months when some denomination was not holding a conference, or some youth group in session. Outstanding speakers in America and from the Continent came to Lakeside. A summer there was a course in religion plus the finest fellowship to be found in the land. It was here that I regularly spent two summer months.

I suppose one of the things I enjoyed most about Lakeside was the fact that I kept running into former friends. As a person gets older he has much joy in small events, many of them insignificant in themselves but important because they start a train of reminiscences. One day I was eating lunch with another old-timer in a restaurant when I felt a hand on my shoulder and a voice said, "Well, hello, Hyde!" I turned around and faced a minister from Cleveland whom I had know perhaps thirty years earlier. "How did you know me from behind?" I asked in surprise. "I'd know your voice if I heard it in perdition." Then he joined us for lunch which extended into the early afternoon as we recalled the days when we were co-workers in Ohio.

Another day I was sitting in the hotel lobby with a group who were talking about preachers from "back home." Finally I slipped over to a writing table to write a few cards and soon my ears pricked up with the mention of my own name as I heard a man ask, "Did you ever know W. J. Hyde? He was my pastor in Centerburg when I was a boy. He took a big interest in the kids of his church. I remember he was in Chicago for many years but I've lost track of him." The group of men began to laugh as one of them said, "Your W. J. Hyde is sitting right over there." And the man who headed toward me was a genial Congressman from Ohio.

Small incidents but to a preacher they are part of the dividends that life pays. One's years of work are well invested if any good from them remains in the lives of people. This residue is a kind of immortality. There are several kinds of immortality. The immortality of the soul makes human personality part of the indissoluble eternal. Then there is the immortality of name. A preacher likes to know that his name lives in the records of a church. It is a natural satisfaction. In the cornerstones of the Mayfair and St. John's Churches I know my name is preserved, and I am glad.

One fall I went back to Sioux Falls, South Dakota, for a conference and while there I met the minister of the Groton Church. Fifty years fell away and I found myself asking about the friends of my day. How many of them he had never known! But enough of them were still in the vicinity that he insisted I should return home with him to visit the church. It didn't seem possible for me to take the time but finally I decided to give myself the joy of returning to my first field and spending one night there.

There was a new church at Groton, much larger, much more dignified, much more modern than the little frame church we had built in 1888. The minister took me into the new church as the sun was shining brilliantly through one of the stained-glass windows, as lovely a window as I have ever seen. Warm tones of rose combined with the blue of an April sky, highlights of gold tucked into the corners. We stood in the back of the church some minutes while the beauty of the stained-glass art flowed through us. Then the minister spoke.

"What do you think of it?"

"I think it has the most beautiful colors I have even seen in a leaded window."

"I'm glad you like it. Do you notice anything else?"

I looked at other parts of the room.

"No, I mean about the window. Come up a little closer."

We walked toward that glory of color and as we neared it my eye caught the letters at the bottom and I saw, "W. J. Hyde."

This window was dedicated to that kid preacher who had come from Canada on Dr. Traveller's terms, and it made "old man Hyde" very happy. But as rewarding as is the perpetuation of name in stone and glass there is a more meaningful immortality of name when it is carried generation to generation by one's sons, grandsons and great-grandsons.

A third immortality is the immortality of influence. No preacher knows what words he has spoken that may have encouraged some faltering person, or comforted someone in sorrow, or cleared up the doubts for some struggling believer. A preacher works like the sower—he throws the seed and some falls on stony ground, or weedy ground, or good ground, or barren ground, and frequently he never knows what the yield is. But there are always enough returns made known to him to keep him encouraged, and sometimes they come when and where they are least expected.

One of my most cherished moments came years ago at a camp meeting where I was giving a series of sermons. There was a fine group of men working as leaders. I recall that the District Superintendent prominent at that camp was a very tall, very thin and very dark individual whose height was accentuated by the build of his song leader, a blond Englishman who had the appearance of being sawed off at the bottom and pressed down at the top. But the Englishman could lead singing! His choir of a hundred voices was worth attending the camp meeting just to hear. It became a habit for quite a group of us to meet in one of the tents after the night service to compare notes. One Sunday night I preached on the topic, "The Significance of the Cross." The next night a number of us were in the tent next to mine when along about one o'clock the Superintendent picked up a penciled sheet of paper off the table and said to the man who lived in that tent, "This looks like a poem. What is it?"

The author took the scrap of paper and commented, "Last night after Hyde's sermon I couldn't sleep. The place of the

Cross in Christianity has always troubled me, but I saw things differently last night and I jotted down a few lines. They are just my own musings."

He read them to us.

> On a hill far away
> Stood an old rugged cross,
> The emblem of suffering and shame.
> But I love that old cross
> Where the dearest and best
> Of the world for lost sinners was slain.
>
> So I'll cling to the old rugged cross
> Till my trophies at last I lay down.
> So I'll cling to the old rugged cross
> And exchange it some day for a crown.

That was forty years ago! But as I have said, memories are good companions.

Easter, 1953, and I was in Chicago again having just returned from Florida with a good sun tan and my best shuffleboard stick to pack away until next winter. There were two new great-grandchildren to baptize on Easter Sunday so I had to be on hand. Then after a short visit I would go on to St. Louis, put away my winter things and get ready for another summer at Lakeside.

The world was beautiful that Easter Day with all the promise of life and new vitality that Jesus gave to the world that first Easter. After the Sunday morning service a good number of the Hydes—four generations in two branches of the family—gathered at Jane's home. Jane is the daughter of Bill and Edythe and the mother of three fine children; the newest one born on Christmas was one of the babies to be baptized that day. In the car, between the church and Jane's house, one of the other great-granddaughters about four years old who had recently started Sunday School said to her mother, "Mommy, which of the children is Grandpa going to crucify today?"

During dinner that Sunday the conversation got onto statistics.

Someone had recently computed how many times the height of
the Empire State Building would be equaled if all the Bibles
published in a year were stacked on top of each other; or if all
the books printed by the Methodist Publishing House were laid
end to end they would reach from New York to ——? The
family began making wild guesses on all kinds of statistical measurements.

Finally someone said, "Grandpa, you were always good at
figures. How many babies would you estimate you had
baptized?"

Gracious! How could I even guess? In sixty-five years, fifty of
them actively in a pastorate, there are a lot of babies dedicated
by Christian parents.

The best I could answer was, "I never had time to lay all the
babies end to end so I can't be too accurate, but I would guess
maybe five thousand."

"Oh, boy!" gasped a little great-grandson, "if there are that
many babies in the world maybe we could get a little sister!" I
encouraged him that maybe he could eventually.

Among these children I had baptized were five of our own,
and seven grandchildren and twelve of our fifteen great-grand-
children. We are a close-knit family. I can never go to Florida
until after Christmas and I have to be back north by Easter;
birthdays and anniversaries—what big occasions we make of
them. Home is still the center of the Hyde household as it has
been since the early days when Mother and I tried to make
it the happiest place on earth for our children and their
friends.

There is a little poem that I last used at the dinner after the
rehearsal for Jane's wedding. The club dining room, full of
families and guests, was gay with anticipation of the big event
only a few hours away. There were speeches and toasting of the
bride, when Jane turned to me and said—and she looked very
much like my Minnie at that moment—"I want a word from the
greatest grandfather in the world." Even in her own great joy
she tried to make others happy with words of appreciation. I

looked at radiant Jane—what could be said to a person so supremely happy? The words of an old poem came to me.

> Home's not merely four square walls,
> Though with pictures hung and gilded;
> Home is where Affection calls,
> Filled with shrines the Heart hath builded!
> Home!—go watch the faithful dove,
> Sailing 'neath the heaven above us;
> Home is where there's one to love!
> Home is where there's one to love us!
>
> Home's not merely roof and room—
> It needs something to endear it;
> Home is where the heart can bloom,
> Where there's some kind lip to cheer it!
> What is home with none to meet,
> None to welcome, none to greet us?
> Home is sweet—and only sweet—
> Where there's one we love to meet us!

The bloom of Easter was still in our hearts when along came another marvelous celebration, warm with the renewal of old friendships. St. John's Methodist Church was having its twenty-fifth anniversary the week of April 19 to 26. On Tuesday night was held the big Homecoming Anniversary Banquet with Bishop H. Clifford Northcott making the main address. It was the same church that Bishop Edwin H. Hughes had dedicated in 1928, and it was still adequate for a membership of seventeen hundred. I was glad we had built for the future. After all, that's the best way to build, whether it is a life or a church.

The speakers' table was arranged on the rostrum and seated at it were the Bishop, the church officials, several of the former pastors, and myself. It seemed good to be sitting near Carl F. Bledsoe again; he and I had sweated through many tough hours together when he was chairman of the official board of the South Shore Church and I was its pastor; and now for twenty-five years he had guided the official board of St. John's Church. A mighty record!

Each person at the speakers' table was called upon for a greeting. Of course, I had never been a pastor of the church, but I was the pastor under whom the church was built, so I started my greeting with the lines,

> He that planteth a tree erecteth to himself
> A monument more lasting than granite.

"It fell to my lot," I continued, "to plant a tree that has grown to be one of the great sources of strength in the city of Chicago. As long as the tree—this church—keeps alive it will be full of the promise of continued service to humanity. The service of the Church built into the hearts of its people is a monument more lasting than granite.

"I am ninety years old—I have seen a lot of life—and I know it is the person, or the church, that keeps his heart turned to the future that finds the trek into the sunset 'beautiful and serene.'"

Mr. Bledsoe had a broad smile on his face when he rose again —he was evidently recalling something too good to keep to himself, so he shared it with the crowd.

"More than twenty-five years ago," he said, "this man preached a sermon that put dynamite under everyone in the church. The title of that famous sermon was 'The Valley of Dry Bones.' Dr. Hyde read the story from Ezekiel and I can still feel the shiver down my spine as he came out with the words, 'O ye dry bones, hear the word of the Lord.' When the congregation left the church that morning everyone knew who the dry bones were— and from that day the membership of the church began to 'shake their bones' to get the new building project under way. Here is the man responsible for the church built to the glory of St. John—no, to the glory of God, the Father, eternal and everlasting."

I went home that night wondering if ever there could be a more beautiful relationship in the world than that of a minister and his flocks. My life had been blessed with working with the finest people in God's big world.

Epilogue: "Late Lark Singing"

Harriet Harmon Dexter

THE Tuesday morning after Easter spring was in the air. The April sun was having its way with the murky skies of winter and had dissipated much of the ever-present smoky gloom. It had lured the lilac leaves out to play and had enticed the box hedges to lay a soft green cushion over their brown stubble. Even the tall maples and elms were feeling young again as they began to unfold the millions of leaves that would soon trace shady designs on the Chicago sidewalks. The joy of living was in the air and even the fact that I arrived at the Bill Hyde home at the unjoyful hour of 7:00 A.M. did not quell the air of happiness that scampered out to greet me when the door of their apartment was opened.

Here were Bill and Edythe. I knew them through some of Mr. Hyde's reminiscences which I had read—but I had never seen them, just as I had never seen W. J. Hyde, whom I felt I knew rather intimately. A few minutes later while I was carrying water glasses to the table in the sunny breakfast porch I heard Edythe say, "Good morning, Grandpa," and I turned and met Mr. Hyde! He included me in the family greeting just as if we had known each other since early Dakota days. He was like that; time, distance, age—nothing was a barrier to friendship. His firm handclasp was accompanied by a sparkle of blue eyes, a sparkle that never dimmed as we sat together for the next three days and relived most of the ninety years of his life.

For hours at a stretch, morning and afternoon, Mr. Hyde and

I sat in the living room with a table between us on which we spread notes, pictures, books or whatever we needed to use together. He was fascinating when he talked. Sometimes his eyes looked straight at me with piercing intensity as he expounded some problem in theology, emphasizing the main points with an energetic motion of the index finger; or again, his eyes raised to the big window, he traveled with the speed of memory to the windswept prairie of Dakota.

While my imagination followed on these breathless excursions my eyes studied the man himself. He could not be ninety! Such energy, such eagerness, such zest for living, such immaculate appearance, such plans for the future—these things did not tally with almost a century of living.

Sometimes I would ask Mr. Hyde a question about some experience or concerning his point of view on a controversial question and invariably he would reply with great enthusiasm, ".Yes, yes, that is a good question." Then would follow a little chuckle as if his mind were enjoying the prospect of recollecting through the years while his body settled a bit more comfortably into the chair. Then we would be off for another hour or two of uninterrupted reminiscing. When completely lost in his story, he unconsciously took his white handkerchief from his pocket, wrapped it carefully around three fingers of his right hand, smoothed out the wrinkles, then in a moment of emotional emphasis pulled the poor handkerchief off to give it a vigorous flip, inserting it again in his pocket. One morning while telling me about Minnie he commented that she was always fearful lest he go into the pulpit with a handkerchief with a hole in it. "She frequently told me that I had a habit of using my handkerchief most peculiarly while I was preaching." I laughed right out. Then so did Mr. Hyde, for there he sat, carefully wrapping it around his hand, completely unaware of what he was doing. His memories were well punctuated with discussions of modern methods of church financing, social problems, international entanglements or new theories of psychology. Here was no man living in the mist of the past!

The days went by too fast. I had to return to college teaching; and Mr. Hyde, who was enroute from a winter in Florida to his permanent home at Clara's, planned to leave Chicago in the near future, too. His plans for another summer at Lakeside were vivid in his mind. For days after reaching home I found myself living under the spell of Dakota, Ohio, Chicago, the Hyde household and the personality of this man whose life had been a blessing to every person it had touched during the many, many years of his ministry.

Mr. Hyde reached Clara's on the last Monday in April. It was certainly more than time to pack away winter clothes in the St. Louis area, so these and the various mementoes of his Florida trip were sorted and stored until another season. There were friends to be greeted and stories and incidents to be related, many of them dealing with the grandchildren and great-grand-children in Chicago. A week passed almost before it had begun and Saturday night arrived. Mr. Hyde, following the practice of a lifetime, carefully laid out everything he would need for Sunday morning—his white shirt, necktie, snowy handkerchief, shoes and suit.

But during the night he called Clara because he didn't feel quite right. His doctor son-in-law, quickly diagnosing the case, rushed him to the hospital; and on Sunday, the day always reserved for special service to his Master, Mr. Hyde stepped into His presence.

When I received the message from Bill the first picture that came to my mind was of Mr. Hyde standing in the kitchen with his hand on the back of a chair while we completed some discussion. With great exultation and finality he said, "The form of our immortality is not important; however, this much we know, 'It does not yet appear what we shall be: but we know that, when he shall appear, we shall be like him; for we shall see him as he is.' That's the Father's promise. Wonderful isn't it?"

From this scene my memory followed him into the living room where many times during our days together he had looked a long look out the window as he repeated some line from a poem he loved:

> *My task accomplished and the long day done,*
> *My wages taken, and in my heart*
> *Some late lark singing,*
> *Let me be gathered to the quiet west,*
> *The sundown beautiful and serene.*

The family gathered at Clara's, at Overland, Missouri, where a few years earlier Mother had been laid to rest. Bishop Northcott, beloved by the Hyde family for so many years, joined them for the final service, leading their thoughts through prayer and meditation to the Source of all comfort and life. Fellow ministers served as pallbearers and walked with Mr. Hyde as far as man is privileged to walk with a fellow sojourner.

In Mr. Hyde's Bible was found a clipping across the top of which he had written, "To this I subscribe. January 1, 1953." Bishop Northcott read the lines as his final tribute to Mr. Hyde.

I am still at work, with my hand to the plow, and my face to the future. The shadows of evening lengthen about me, but morning is in my heart. . . . I have had varied fields of labor, and full contact with men and things, and have warmed both hands before the fire of life.

The testimony I bear is this: that the Castle of Enchantment is not yet behind me. It is before me still, and daily I catch glimpses of its battlements and towers. The rich spoils of memory are mine. Mine, too, are the precious things of today—books, flowers, pictures, nature and sport. The first of May is still an enchanted day to me. The best thing of all is friends. The best of life is always further on. Its real lure is hidden from our eyes, somewhere behind the hills of time.

Set in Linotype Electra
Format by Edwin H. Kaplin
Manufactured by The Haddon Craftsmen, Inc.
Published by Harper & Brothers, New York